Colin Wilson, a Celebration:

Essays and Recollections

Colin Wilson in 1982

Colin Wilson,

a Celebration:

Essays and Recollections

Edited by Colin Stanley

Introduction by Angus Wilson

CECIL WOOLF · LONDON

First published 1988
© 1988 Cecil Woolf Publishers

Cecil Woolf Publishers, 1 Mornington Place, London NW1 7RP
Tel: 01-387 2394

British Library Cataloguing in Publication Data
Colin Wilson, a celebration: essays and recollections
1. Fiction in English. Wilson, Colin, 1931- -Critical studies
I. Stanley, Colin
823′.914
ISBN 0-900821-91-4

Contents

6　*Contents*

Acknowledgements

This book owes much to suggestions made by Bill Hopkins in particular but also by Howard Dossor, Jonathan Guinness, Robert De Maria, Joy Wilson, Laura Del Rivo and Gail Stanley. I am grateful to Hilary Smith for retyping some of the manuscripts. My thanks are also due to:

The Editor of *The Leicester Mercury*, for permission to reprint the interview with Pete Barraclough first published in *The Leicester Chronicle* on 29 May 1970.

The Editor of *The Hollins Critic*, for permission to reprint R.H.W. Dillard's essay, *Toward an Existential Realism: the Novels of Colin Wilson*, first published in *The Hollins Critic*, vol. 4, no. 4, October 1967.

The Editor, *The Sunday Telegraph Magazine*, for permission to reprint Daniel Farson's article first published in issue no. 219, 7 December 1980.

The Editor of *Books and Bookmen*, for permission to reprint the reviews by Alan Hull Walton which appeared in the issues for December 1971 and March 1979.

Frederick Muller Ltd, for permission to reprint the chapter from Sidney Campion's book, *The World of Colin Wilson*.

The Editor of *The New Statesman*, for permission to reprint J.B. Priestley's review of *The Outsider* which appeared in the issue dated 7 July 1956.

Times Newspapers Ltd, for permission to reprint Cyril Connolly's review of *The Outsider* which appeared in *The Sunday Times* on 27 May 1956.

The Editor of *The Observer*, for permission to reprint Philip Toynbee's review of *The Outsider* which appeared in the issue dated 27 May 1956.

The Countess of Cork and Orrery for permission to reprint Kenneth Walker's review of *The Outsider* which appeared in *The Listener*, vol. 55, for 7 June 1956.

Joyce Carol Oates and Colin Wilson, for permission to reprint the former's Introduction to *The Philosopher's Stone* published by Warner Books, 1973.

Gale Research Company, Detroit, U.S.A., for permission to reprint the article by John A. Weigel which appeared in *The Dictionary of Literary Biography: British Novelists Since 1960*, vol. 14, edited by Jay L. Halio (Copyright © 1983 Gale Research Company), Gale Research, 1983, pp. 780-87, and to Jerry Drost of the State University of New York at

Buffalo for drawing my attention to that article.

In addition, I should like to thank Viola Owen (Marilyn Ferguson's Secretary/Assistant), David Bolt and Tom Greenwell.

Colin Stanley

Introduction

ANGUS WILSON

Colin was someone very special in my life. Apart from his immense
energy, sensational sense of youth, amazingly wide reading and total
commitment to his message, he was a very pleasant and likeable
companion, though he was always different from, and more impressive than the other members of his circle.

He was very natural in all he did, for example there was no sense of
commitment to the image then so popular with the new old-fashioned
revolutionaries. I belonged to the then dead left, and was always very
puzzled by this new right-wing progress. But he accepted everything
that happened and adapted himself to it. For example, when I lent him
my cottage in which to write for one whole winter,* (he had nowhere
in London), nothing in the least degree bourgeois was stirred in him.
Although there were beds, he slept in a sleeping bag on the floor. The
postman, a Cockney from London, recognised him as 'an intellectual',
but found no evidence of intellectualism as he understood it. When
Colin's name and photos deluged the English Press, the postman expressed his amazement to me, 'He's not a clever man,' he said, 'Can't be.
He doesn't even take a daily newspaper.'

The esoteric nature and the enormous breadth of his reading, knocked
over the average intellectual like myself. He was at his happiest, I think,
providing his disciples with abstruse teaching and a knowledge of
foreign literature. This when he was very poor, but when success over-
whelmed him, he treated all his many friends with incredible generosity.
To have known him then was to have been treated to the story of success
at a high speed.

He went West and I remained in the East. We only met once there-
after, at a John Cowper Powys occasion in Cambridge. His speech was,
as always, with believers an enormous shock to the fervent JCP
disciples, but a very good shock. It was this mixture of brilliance,
journalism, and the guru that I sought to put over in my story 'A Bit
Off the Map'.†

---

*According to Sidney Campion, this was the winter of 1955-6 when Colin Wilson was working on rewriting *Ritual in the Dark* (*World of Colin Wilson*, page 123). — Ed.

†First published by Secker and Warburg in 1957. For further details, see my introduction. — Ed.

Editor's Preface

COLIN STANLEY

A great deal has been written about Colin Wilson over the last thirty years—most of it immediately following the publication of *The Outsider* in 1956—concentrating mainly on his personal life. Little, however, has been written about his work, which is a great pity for Colin Wilson is essentially a writer of ideas and as such deserves to be treated more seriously. This has become increasingly clear to me, particularly over the past five years, when I have read my way through all his seventy-odd books and pamphlets, plus a fair proportion of his papers, in order to construct a bibliography and guide.* My aim was naturally to stimulate further interest in Colin Wilson's work but more particularly to try and 'break the ice' among the academic fraternity which, it seemed to me, had largely ignored his work for too long. During the course of my research I made contact with a few of the 'pioneers' of Colin Wilson criticism and it soon became apparent to me that I was in the ideal position to compile and edit a volume of critical essays and recollections. This fascinating and varied book is the result.

But before I go on to provide some background to the individual contributions I should, perhaps, acquaint the reader with the little that has, to date, been published about Colin Wilson's work and although a bibliography has been included as an appendix to this volume, I think it would be useful to complete the picture with a few details.

In 1962 the Leicester writer Sidney Campion published *The World of Colin Wilson*, a curious book in some ways and one not wholly approved of by its subject, but none the less fascinating and useful for the interesting extracts from early journals (quoted verbatim) and the author's obvious enthusiasm for his subject's early work. Regrettably Sidney Campion died in 1978 and the book, long out-of-print, now fetches vastly inflated prices on the second-hand market.

The next landmark in Colin Wilson criticism did not come until October 1967 when an American scholar R.H.W. Dillard published an article in *The Hollins Critic* entitled 'Toward an Existential Realism: the Novels of Colin Wilson'. This was no doubt inspired by the subject having been writer-in-residence at Hollins College during the previous year. This important essay covers the novels up to and including *The

*To be published in the United States by Borgo Press, San Bernardino, 1988.

Mind Parasites and also mentions *The Black Room* which was in the process of being written.

In 1975, Professor John A. Weigel of Miami University, Ohio, wrote the most detailed assessment of Colin Wilson's work that has appeared to date. This was published by Twayne as part of their 'English Authors Series' (no. 181). The book attempts an overall assessment although Professor Weigel, with great insight, singles out for particular attention his subject's contribution to twentieth century thought by dealing with the philosophical 'Outsider Cycle'* books first and foremost and then turning his gaze upon Colin Wilson's development as a novelist and 'critic-of-all-trades'.

Clifford P. Bendau, another American scholar, made a briefer attempt at an overall assessment in 1979 when his *Colin Wilson: the Outsider and Beyond* was published by Borgo Press as part of their 'Milford Series: Popular Writers of Today' (vol. 21). Although only sixty-three pages long, it is more comprehensive than Professor Weigel's effort: the second half of the book assesses Colin Wilson's work chronologically and includes some of the lesser books and pamphlets. It is also, of course, more up-to-date. But being a far slimmer volume, it is naturally not so detailed as its predecessor. Nevertheless it remains an important landmark in Colin Wilson criticism and, used in conjunction with Professor Weigel's book, forms a fairly solid starting point of reference for students.

Two books concentrating on Colin Wilson's novels were the next to appear. The first, published in 1982, by Nicolas Tredell—then a part-time extramural lecturer in literature for the University of Surrey—is based on a thesis completed when he was a student at East Sussex College of Higher Education some years earlier. The second is by a Swedish graduate—K. Gunnar Bergström—entitled *An Odyssey to Freedom: Four Themes in Colin Wilson's Novels* and was written as a doctoral thesis at Uppsala University and published in 1983. Although both books must have been written at about the same time they are entirely different in their approaches. Bergström sees the novels from a philosophical point of view, arguing that to understand them properly one has to study their philosophical background. The relationship between Colin Wilson's non-fiction and his novels is therefore forcefully stressed and the overall

---

*The series of six philosophical books published between 1956 and 1966 as follows: *The Outsider*, *Religion and the Rebel*, *The Age of Defeat* (published in the US as *The Stature of Man*), *The Strength to Dream*, *Origins of the Sexual Impulse* and *Beyond the Outsider*. A summary volume, *Introduction to the New Existentialism*, followed.

result is a book almost as much about the former as the latter. Tredell, on the other hand, dwells more on the literary aspect of his subject's novels: the plots, the style, the development of the characters; and he attempts to place Colin Wilson alongside comparable English writers (chapter 3 is an interesting study of his links with H.G. Wells). Again, as with Bendau and Weigel, the two books should be seen as complementary rather than promoting opposing views.

Two other extended essays deserve a mention: Joyce Carol Oates' introduction to the US Warner paperback edition of *The Philosopher's Stone* and Howard F. Dossor's introductory essay to *The Bicameral Critic* entitled 'Colin Wilson: the Case for Optimism'.

Of course, it should be noted that Colin Wilson *himself* is an excellent 'interpreter' of his own work. This is basically because he writes fluently, in a manner that is clearly understood by the careful reader, regardless of the difficulty of the subject matter. He also presupposes no specialist knowledge on the part of his readers and often goes out of his way to explain his work carefully, using everyday situations to illustrate his points. However, when I learned that he was to select and edit his own 'essential reader' (published by Harrap, London, 1985) I must admit I was somewhat apprehensive, for authors are notoriously bad at looking at their own work objectively. But I need not have worried because the result was an excellent selection of philosophical essays, culled mostly from previously published works, which genuinely is *essential* reading for anyone wishing to come to grips with his ideas.

Ironically it is this great quality of readability that may partially explain why so few academics have attempted critical appraisals. For, on the whole, it must be said that academics prefer to explore the safer ground of obscure or enigmatic writers, preferably long dead, and therefore open to any interpretation. It also explains why some attempts have turned out to be a lot less lucid than the 'raw material' itself.

So Professor Weigel's book, although over ten years old, remains unsurpassed as an overall assessment of Colin Wilson's work. Clearly an update is now well overdue. I sincerely hope that my bibliography and guide, coupled with this volume of essays, will tempt someone to rise to the bait and, indeed, make the task that much easier.

I should now pass to the contents of this volume. It has been a great source of both pleasure and amazement to me watching the manuscript grow during the course of the summer of 1985. 'Amazement' because I had not expected such a response from so many busy scholars and writers around the world, all of whom set aside their own work, without the promise of any financial reward, to write something for this volume.

Brocard Sewell, for instance, stopped work on the translation of a French novel to write his essay, and I received it within one week of having sent out the invitations. Angus Wilson's Foreword followed and Daniel Farson, who was on his way to Turkey, made sure I had his contribution before he went. Tom Greenwell was given scarcely two weeks to produce his piece, but like a true newspaperman he met his deadline.

But the big breakthrough came when I contacted Colin Wilson's good friend, Bill Hopkins, who was able and willing to suggest a number of possible contributors, many of whom, in their turn, recommended others. There suddenly seemed to be no end to the list of possibilities. Colin Wilson, it would appear, is a much-loved and respected member of his profession and so what had started out as a modest idea for a small pamphlet of essays, which I had fully expected to publish myself as a Paupers' Press booklet, mushroomed overnight into something much more substantial.

The essays themselves fall roughly into two categories: firstly, recollections by friends and colleagues and secondly critical appraisals by scholars of Colin Wilson's work. A few attempt to combine the two.

I have tried to cover all aspects of Colin Wilson's work and, indeed, to contact all those scholars mentioned in the first half of this introduction. In the case of Sidney Campion, I have been fortunate to receive permission to reprint a key chapter from his original work, *The World of Colin Wilson*. This deals with the writing of the controversial and important novel *Ritual in the Dark*. R.H.W. Dillard has kindly allowed me to reprint his pioneering essay *Toward an Existential Realism: the Novels of Colin Wilson*, which has never been widely available to UK scholars. Unfortunately, however, I was unable to contact either Professor Weigel or Clifford P. Bendau but have managed to acquire permission to reprint the former's assessment of Colin Wilson's novels up to and including *The Space Vampires*, which appeared in *The Dictionary of Literary Biography* (volume 14). Nicolas Tredell, whose essay forms a major part of this book and is, I think, a substantial step toward an overall assessment of the subject's standing, updates this to include Colin Wilson's latest fiction: namely, *The Personality Surgeon* and the novel which may prove to be his best, certainly his most entertaining, *Spiderworld*. K. Gunnar Bergström succinctly sums up Colin Wilson's essential message and also provides some idea of how his work is viewed in Scandinavia. Howard Dossor more than adequately covers Colin Wilson's contribution to the field of criminology with an excellent piece entitled 'Murder as Existential Act'. Joyce Carol Oates's introduction to *The Philosopher's Stone* (mentioned earlier) is reprinted in this collection.

Also reprinted are Alan Hull Walton's in-depth reviews of *The Occult* and *Mysteries* — Colin Wilson's most significant works on the occult — and Sir Oswald Mosley's intelligent and perceptive appraisal of *The Outsider* in which he managed to grasp the essence of that book in a way that few others writing at the time were able to do. Other important reprints include Marilyn Ferguson's introduction to a recent US edition of *The Outsider* and the four major English reviews by Cyril Connolly, Philip Toynbee, Kenneth Walker and J.B. Priestley which well and truly launched the book and made its author into a household name virtually overnight.

Colin Wilson's own voice is represented by an interview with Pete Barraclough for *The Leicester Chronicle* (then a sister newspaper to *The Leicester Mercury* which has, to its credit, retained an interest in the subject's work despite the fact that he has now lived in Cornwall for the past thirty years).

Among the original contributions special mention should be made of Brocard Sewell, Jonathan Guinness and A.E. van Vogt, all of whom combine critical appraisal and personal recollection with great skill, and Professor Purcell whose essay provides much food for thought.

The personal recollections are all valuable in their own different ways. John Rety, who professes to be Colin Wilson's first publisher, has written not only an interesting social document but also an extremely evocative and witty one. He obviously enjoyed, and got a great deal out of, his association with the so-called angry young men and their circle. Angus Wilson, on the other hand, did not feel quite at ease with them. His short story, *A Bit Off the Map*, mentioned in his foreword, is a satirical portrait, the character Huggett clearly Colin Wilson himself. But it was to Angus that Colin dedicated *The Outsider* in recognition of the assistance he received from the then Deputy Superintendent of the British Museum Reading Room. Tom Greenwell's lively contribution provides even more insight into the period. Stuart Holroyd skilfully completes the picture.

A fascinating cameo by Bill Hopkins brings us into the 1960's whilst the German novelist Renate Rasp takes us into the heart of Cornwall and introduces us to Colin Wilson's social circle of the 1970s. Daniel Farson provides more than a glimpse into the author's family life and daily routine whilst Donald Seaman's essay brings us right up to date. June O'Shea, a Californian bookseller, chronicles her own unique relationship with Colin Wilson in a fascinating piece.

Finally, I was delighted to receive short tributes from Allen Ginsberg and Uri Geller. I wonder if the former recalls trying to bite John Rety's ear thirty years ago in that Parisien café?

My own contribution, unashamedly personal, is an attempt to present a practical example of the 'peak experience', a concept fundamental to an appreciation of Colin Wilson's ideas. For those readers who may be interested in my association with Colin Wilson since I first read him in the early 1970s and met him ten years later (since when we have met and corresponded regularly) I have already written a series of articles which have been published in various journals.* Hopefully, I shall gather them all together in 1988 and publish them as a Paupers' Press pamphlet. As it is, I now submit this collection of essays into the hands of readers, reviewers, scholars and enthusiasts of Colin Wilson's work worldwide, in the hope that it will not only bring pleasure in the reading but also provide good source material for students and literary historians. For there is no doubt in my mind that academic interest is slowly on the increase. At Nottingham University, here in England, three of his major works have appeared on reading lists and the small collection of his books, scattered around the library, are certainly well used by students and staff. It seems that, at last—after all the adverse publicity created in the 1950s had (in the words of Jonathan Guinness) 'relegated him to the status of interesting crank'—a reassessment of his achievement is in the wind as the stoical critics and academics that have held sway for too long are gradually being replaced by younger and perhaps more far-sighted colleagues. The fact that Colin Wilson's early work still reads as well today, is very much in his favour.

Anyway, for my part, I have done as much as I can for now. The rest is left to posterity and, of course, Colin Wilson himself who, I am sure, will continue to produce controversial, important and stimulating work for many years to come.

Nottingham University Library
Autumn 1987

---

*'Voyage to a Beginning: Colin Wilson and Me' *Tentacles* (Journal of the University of Nottingham Library) no. 28, Spring 1982, pp. 10-15; 'Keeping Up With the Outsider', *Cornish Scene*, vol. 2, no. 6, May/June 1987, pp. 32-3; 'The Quest for Colin Wilson', introductory essay to my bibliography and guide, referred to earlier.

1

The Even-Tempered Guide

JONATHAN GUINNESS

Colin Wilson is a Leicester man; and since I have become an inhabitant
of Leicestershire myself, I have come to see this as a clue to his character
as man and as writer. There is a coolness about Leicester men, a distrust
of the highflown. It is not the self-conscious bluntness supposed to be
found further north. A Leicester man does not feel the need to warn you
in a raised voice that he says what he thinks; he just says it, politely but
without equivocation. He says it, to be sure, without any particular
eloquence. A Welshman, say, or an Irishman might accuse him of being
monochrome for the colours in which he depicts the world tend rather
towards the pastel. Or perhaps he is just too self-confident to feel the
need of manipulating emotions through language; his facts, he thinks,
speak for themselves. There is a quiet honesty about this attitude which
we find, too, in a very different Leicester writer: C.P. Snow. But Snow,
who directed his matter-of-fact vision at matter-of-fact subjects,
appears to be headed towards obscurity. This will not be altogether
deserved, for the shifting relationships of the human barnyard, which
are his speciality, have a permanent interest. At any rate Colin Wilson
is very different. His even, unemotional voice recounts wonders. He
surveys the triumphs and miseries precisely of those who have striven
to escape from the condition Snow chronicles with such complacency.
It is true that the contrast between Colin's manner and his matter can
seem a bit comical, as when Emanuel Swedenborg talks of visiting
heaven in tones which would suitably convey a stroll in Kensington
Gardens; but this does not detract from Colin's value, any more than it
does from Swedenborg's. As to his reputation; after a roller-coaster career
at the hands of the critics before they relegated him to the status of
interesting crank, he would seem to be due soon for recognition as one
of the major twentieth-century thinkers. I wonder, though, whether he
really cares much about this either way. He is what he is, 'what he has
written he has written,' and it is up to others what they make of it. It is
a good sound Leicester attitude.

It ties in with his great personal modesty. I mention this because it
is something I have seen myself; also because people have noticed passages in his work where he would appear to be boasting. An example is
in the Prefatory Note to *Poetry and Mysticism* where he claims that in
the six Outsider books 'I had laid the foundations for a new psychology'.

But it is impossible to imagine anyone writing the six Outsider books and not thinking he had done something of this sort. So why should not Colin say so? In any case it becomes clearer all the time that in sober truth Colin has at least contributed to doing exactly this. The remark is not only sincere, it is correct.

Colin's modesty became apparent when, some time ago, my wife Suzanne and I stayed for a weekend with him and Joy in Cornwall. Bill Hopkins was there too. The first evening Colin invited me along to a small regular all-male dinner or *Stammtisch* which took place on Friday nights at a Mevagissey pub. (Bill Hopkins did not come; perhaps he had not arrived.) Colin and I found two other men at the dinner, and we talked pleasantly enough of this and that. I enjoyed it, and as we went home I told Colin so. He pulled me up with an unexpected rebuke.

'You talked too much,' he said.

I was not having this. 'No more than you did,' I returned. 'And everyone had plenty to say.'

'Yes,' he conceded, 'but it was because of you that we all talked more than we usually do. Our enjoyment of these dinners does not depend on talk. We sit eating for minutes at a time, silent and happy.' He may even have said something about my London ways, and added: 'Actually I go to that pub to listen, not to talk.'

Then, next day, the five of us sat long after lunch in a state of collective conversational well-being in which, be it said, Colin fully shared; with friends he will chat for hour upon hour, whatever he does with acquaintances. We gossiped about ideas, and of course about people, in that comfortable elliptical mode where everyone gets all the allusions. Suddenly we were interrupted by a 'messenger from the outside world,' as in a Gerhart Hauptmann play where the arrival of such a person starts off the action. It was a Disciple of Colin's who turned up, quite unexpectedly, complete with hand-luggage. He had hitch-hiked.

Had he been quick on the uptake, the newcomer would have blended in with us all soon enough; we all knew Colin's ideas, and ought to have had a lot in common. But he was not quick on the uptake. What is more, he had a terrible single-mindedness; he was going to sit at the feet of the Master, and he was going to be instructed.

Colin obviously felt sympathy with the Disciple from his own hitch-hiking days, and there is a charm in being admired; nevertheless this particular admirer began to weigh on Colin. We, his friends, could see clearly how much virtue he felt was going out of him as the hem of his garment was thus clutched. Yet Colin's kindness was limitless, luminous. He and Joy made up a bed for the Disciple on the sofa, and Colin lavished on him his time, his attention, his loving kindness. It was touching to watch.

The lack of inflammation in Colin's ego which these two stories illustrate has two implications as regards his work. The less important of these is that Colin will never found a school of thought, let alone a church. Conceivably someone might do it for him, as St Paul did for Jesus or Brigham Young for Joseph Smith; but he will not do it himself. He lacks the censoriousness essential to any organiser; controlling other people bores him. (He has always been a serenely indulgent father, for instance.) Consequently, he avoids politics.

More fundamentally, it was Colin's matter-of-fact modesty that enabled him to write as he does. The men he parades before us in his Outsider series mostly have egos that are outsize and inflammed. That, after all, is why they are Outsiders. Sartre, van Gogh, Nietzsche, Dostoevsky, Gurdjieff, Hemingway, Blake: I mention them in no particular order, but if Colin had been like any of them he would have been incapable of his life's work. (It is also, of course, an advantage that he does not resemble Jack the Ripper.) He can describe these people, and fit them in with one another; often he will enter the strange worlds they create; but none of them ever captures him. When in his later works he deals with the irrational he does so in a strictly rational way. His speciality is that, while himself almost preternaturally balanced, he is so much at home with so many abnormal states of mind. He is like a guide in a museum of the fantastic who shows us around without once raising his voice. Yet the museum is, after all, *his* collection; no one else's. One day a biographer might perhaps succeed in indicating how this might be; might dismantle the 'black box', Colin's internal flight control, which contains the real story of what must have been an extraordinary adolescence. He has described the externals of this here and there, notably in the autobiographical introduction to *Religion and the Rebel*. In his speculations about the youth of Bernard Shaw, he has equally clearly indicated that there is a lot more to be said about it.

Colin has made recognised contributions in psychology, in criminology, and in the study of the occult; and he will no doubt do more in these areas and perhaps in others. He might also be recognised as a philosopher. His aim is to restore the essentials of religion to modern man, though theism is no more necessary to his system than it is to Buddhism. It is possible that he may do this. It will be up to posterity to determine where his contribution was most important, though there is no reason to suppose that posterity will get it right.

But leaving the question of importance aside, there is no question which of his works are the most exciting. The Outsider books, and par-

ticularly *The Outsider* itself, constitute in themselves a one-man university of the humanities. The early, favourable reviews of *The Outsider*
catch something of this; it has since been obscured by the critics' sudden
decision to climb a tree and defecate, as the yahoos did on Gulliver. It
is not that Colin necessarily gets everything right; in fact the more one
knows about any particular one of his subjects, the more one wants to
argue with him. I have space for one example only: Bernard Shaw. I am
an admirer of Shaw's and steeped in his works, but I cannot accept that
he is 'the greatest figure in European literature since Dante' (*Religion
and the Rebel*, Autobiographical Introduction). What is more, Colin in
several places distorts Shaw's message to suit his Outsider thesis. In *Man
and Superman* he says that in the end John Tanner, the Don Juan figure,
'marries Ann who is a very ordinary Insider for whom he is just a talker'.
Surely this is getting it exactly the wrong way round. We are meant to
see Ann as the embodiment of the Life Force who gets her man, recruits
him for her biological purposes. What he says does not affect her, but
the quality of his talk convinces her that he is worth breeding with. In
the ultimate, Shaw wants us to see her as the winner; the man *is* just a
talker, though a good one, and there lies the ultimate twist of the
comedy. But let the reader turn to the play and see for himself whether
he agrees with Colin, or with me.

For the point I am making is that one does not have to agree with all
of what Colin says in these books. A student will rarely agree with his
university tutor on everything. The tutor provides two essential things:
a reading-list, and guidance through it. His summaries and opinions
should stimulate the pupil to explorations which, if the pupil is any good,
will from an early stage take an independent direction. A school-leaver,
instead of bothering with university entrance, might undertake the following programme. He would read the Outsider books, check back
systematically with the sources to see if he agreed with Colin's verdicts,
and go on to read other works that seemed to be relevant. He would end,
I suggest, with more knowledge than most students carry away with them
after their finals. This would certainly be true in the field of modern
literature; French, German and Russian as well as English. There would
be gaps, of course; he would for instance have read almost no lyric
poetry. But let the graduate in whose knowledge there are no gaps cast
the first stone.

Colin's key preoccupation is a concern with the individual's state of
mind; not only whether he is happy or sad, but also whether it can make
him effective. The study of the question of the 'robot', of what actions
we ought to make automatic and what we ought to keep fully conscious,

is extraordinarily acute and fruitful. There is probably nothing Colin
has written (though I can by no means claim to have read it all) which
is not in some way a study of a mental state. To him, the ultimate units
of which our universe consists are not atoms, or mathematical laws, or
even thoughts as Descartes' *'cogito ergo sum'* implies, but *feelings*;
notably, but not only, percepts. That is why he rejects logical positivism
and linguistic analysis except perhaps as subordinate techniques, basing
his viewpoint on Husserl's phenomenology which, following Hume,
starts from the act of perception. Speaking personally, I have come to
find this point of view convincing. We assume that objects exist indep-
endently of our perception, and the assumption is a fair one; but the
evidence on which it depends can only come, itself, through perception.
Logic organises that evidence, language expresses it; but neither supplies
it. This is not just an academic point of view; it has consequences. The
more the *act* of perception is considered, the more it is seen to be, indeed,
an *act*: to be something one does, the result of *will*. We choose what to
perceive and how to perceive it. A baby is biologically programmed to
sort out a selection from the chaos of sense-impressions so that he can
make it mean something; to carve out his perceived universe. That is
only the first step in a process he will carry on all his life. A lot of it
will be done according to assumptions he receives from others, as well
as according to his genetically implanted tendencies. The will is not
wholly or necessarily his will. It is still will, and within the boundaries
it sets there is an area of freedom that is indeed personal, giving him
the possibility of self-transcendence. Colin sees Nietzsche's superman
as the being who will have achieved this.

To be concerned with states of mind means, for Colin, to be concerned especially with unusual states of mind. In the Outsider books we
read of the euphoria and misery of the artist, the mystic's ecstasy, the
cleansed doors of perception that lead to intenser feeling and clearer
inner vision; also of the essential unpredictability in the correlation
between a person's state of mind and his surroundings. This is something
Colin enjoys with a touch of *Schadenfreude*, for it makes nonsense of
'common-sense' materialism. Meursault, the hero of Camus' *Outsider*, is
mentioned several times; after a not particularly unpleasant life he is un-
justly condemned to death, upon which he feels such an excess of joy
that his whole life in its dim ordinariness appears to have been unlived.
Colin would no doubt also be interested in the invalid described by
Borges (*Fictions*) who, bedridden all his life, finds in examining the
cracks on his ceiling enough variety and fascination for a lifetime of
wonder. He is in a sense Meursault's converse. Again, we have probably

all experienced the truth of the saying from Proverbs: 'Better a dinner of herbs where love is, than a stalled ox and hatred therewith'. To be truly ascetic is not to hate enjoyment; that is the mean puritan perversion of asceticism. It is to recognise that luxury is simply an irrelevance. Colin's interest in criminology is another side of his concern with these matters, as is shown by the fact that those criminals which interest him—Jack the Ripper and so on—are always those who commit their crimes to achieve a particular state of mind.

Much of Colin's current preoccupation is to develop disciplines, parallel to those of yogis, dervishes and other religious contemplatives, to achieve self-transcendence as a permanent and communicable state; to develop (I paraphrase him) a teachable technique for flying where Outsiders have crashed or given up, and where those who have perhaps flown have failed to reveal their secret. This, of course, is where his disdain for politics cannot save him from confronting what is essentially a political problem. He is a benevolent man, and does not wish on any élitist grounds to exclude anyone from his insights. There are plenty of passages indicating that he would like man in the mass to transcend himself. But if he is to do so, Colin would certainly say, it will be because each man has found, by his own effort, his own awareness. He would be impatient at suggestions that the 'disadvantaged' might not be able to do this; his own origins entitle him to this impatience. Colin does not believe in the collective motor-coach in which political millenarians aspire to drive us up to the heights, as when Trotsky claimed that after the success of socialism the ordinary man would be a genius on the level of Goethe, and the exceptional man would reach levels now undreamed of. Colin provides no vehicle at all; the most he offers is a map, a rope and a pair of stout boots.

So only those with a particular sort of vigour are likely to accept his message, and they will never be a majority. A self-chosen elite, to be sure, which is always the best sort of elite; but they will still be an elite. Therefore there remains the economic problem. Colin quotes the following passage from Shaw's *Heartbreak House* (in *Religion and the Rebel*) but does not seem to realise the extent to which it challenges his point of view:

ELLIE: A soul is a very expensive thing to keep: much more so than a motor car.

SHOTOVER: Is it? How much does your soul eat?

ELLIE: Oh, a lot. It eats music and pictures and books and mountains and lakes and beautiful things to wear and

nice people to be with. In this country you can't have
them without lots of money: that is why our souls are
so horribly starved.

Colin can quite well say that with the right sort of attitude of mind
Ellie could train her soul to do without these things. But the politician
knows it can be confidently predicted that rather few people will adopt
the right attitude of mind or make the effort to undertake the training.
Like the Grand Inquisitor, he must make what he can of the resulting
situation. The fact that I can be rather disappointed to find in Colin no
solution of the general, collective human predicament shows how easy it
is to think he ought to be actually omniscient. But if a bemused old
friend can approach this state it does point up the fact that his achievement has already been tremendous.

2

Colin: Still an Outsider?

DONALD SEAMAN

Absence on holiday or business excepted, Colin Wilson and I have met six afternoons a week for the past decade to walk with our four dogs across the great headland called The Dodman ('The Dead Man', site of an Iron Age fort) that divides our homes in south Cornwall. Over the years our meetings have turned into a kind of open-air workshop, where we explore any subject that comes to mind—from the major news item of the day to some problem arising from a book that he, or I (separately and on occasion, jointly) happen to be writing at the time.

By coincidence, although it was not this which sparked off the daily discourse, on the day I received my invitation to contribute to this symposium our subject for debate was—coincidence. To savour the point fully you should know that while Colin and I are the best of friends we are also opposites in almost every way. He is a gregarious creature. I am essentially a loner. He begrudges every day spent away from home. Travel has been my life. He sees the dominance factor in every human relationship, I prefer to cross-reference the shades of personality. Colin is an existentialist, I remain an old Doubting Thomas of a reporter at heart in every look at life, especially when treading new ground.

Now you may recall that Colin had this to say on the subject of 'coincidence' in his 1970 best-seller, *The Occult*: 'Probably all that is at work is some "vital sense" of the same order as the eel's homing instinct. The more the mind is absorbed, interested in a subject, the more frequently these useful coincidences seem to occur, as if the healthy mind has a kind of radar system'.

That is a theory I find it difficult to accept. From time to time I have experienced a coincidence so bizarre, so far removed from any current conscious or subconscious train of thought, that I believe there has to be some other explanation for the phenomenon we call 'coincidence'.

Picture then my reaction on the day the invitation from editor Colin Stanley to contribute to the symposium dropped through my letter-box. I read it for the first time *after* my walk in pouring rain with the other Colin (I spent the morning shopping in St Austell). And as I changed into dry clothes I was thinking 'What would make a good subject for my intro to the article?'—when I felt and heard a slip of paper crackling in the hip pocket of my dry slacks. It turned out to be a sixteen-months-

24

old press cutting about Colin Wilson, complete with photograph, under a caption which read 'COLIN STILL AN OUTSIDER'.

How's *that* for coincidence, and an example of the human radar system at work?

As newspaper interviews go (this one had been written by a provincial journalist whose name was unknown to me) it was pretty bitchy. In her third paragraph the lady said 'Colin regards himself as "the greatest writer of the 20th century". His publishers see him as a name to sell books—he has written 55 altogether and is currently in print in 20 languages.' Then in the next paragraph she really socked it to him. 'And the public, *if they remember him at all*' (my itals) 'think only of the banner headlines which told of his future father-in-law threatening to horsewhip him and of his precipitous flight from London and notoriety to the quiet obscurity of a cottage in Cornwall.'

Later she quoted him as saying 'The papers just went on with their lurid stories . . . There seemed to be no escape. Everything we did was magnified and distorted. It was a real demolition job. And I am sure it only went on because I had dared to set foot in the intellectual world.'

Speaking as a reporter who spent a quarter of a century in Fleet Street I reckon I can spot a demolition job when I see one; and I discussed this particular article at some length with Colin Wilson. For a major writer still burdened with that corny old 'horsewhipped Outsider' tag— thirty years and fifty-five books on!—I thought him remarkably chipper. 'You learn to live with it' he said. 'The old pros in Hollywood even argued "There's no such thing as bad publicity", and perhaps they had a point. What *can* hurt, even after all these years, is to find one's work—one's best work possibly on a particular subject—completely ignored.'

One thing's for sure, Colin is not the kind of man to bear his critics a grudge. One of his favourite anecdotes concerns the Irish journalist who savaged him in a review of the film version of Colin's science-fiction novel, *Space Vampires*. The attack was based on a scene in the film which had been dreamed up by the script writers (or whoever)—without Colin's knowledge!

That said, any writer who dares to proclaim his own genius must expect to come under heavy fire from the media. No one who knows Colin Wilson well would describe him as a shrinking violet, but the fact is that the man believes in himself, fiercely and totally. When taxed on this point in the 'Bookmark' television programme (BBC 2, 10 April 1986), Colin's reply was typically forthright. 'The fact is,' he said, 'that I've always considered myself to be the greatest writer of the twentieth century. That's not in any way conceit. It's just that I thought that what I had to say when I started writing was far more important than anything I could see being said around me . . . I still think that's true.'

While not every writer may regard himself as the greatest of the century – or even the decade – all of us recognise that a profound belief in one's own ability is an essential part of every author's makeup. How else to explain the dogged pursuit of a career that will certainly be solitary and totally demanding, all too often poorly paid – even, at the end of the day, wholly disregarded? In my view it takes courage rather than conceit to reiterate this unbending belief in oneself when the flak is coming up. Maybe Emerson – Ralph Waldo Emerson, the 19th century American poet and essayist, got it right when he declared 'To believe your own thoughts, to believe that what is true for you in your private heart is true for all men – that is genius.'

Emerson also said 'Talent alone cannot make a writer. There must be a man behind the book.' In those two quotations you have the essential Colin Wilson; arrogantly, even insufferably boastful to some, but not to those who know the man behind the books. Without any question he genuinely believes that what is true for him in his private heart is true for all of us. 'Genius' is a word I hesitate to use about any writer. What is undeniable in Colin's case is that, thirty years on, there is no sign of any abatement in the man's creative output.

Already that provincial reporter's total is outdated. Colin now has fifty-six books in print, with another four in the pipeline awaiting publication. One of them (a new departure for Colin), a thousand-page fantasy entitled *Spiderworld*, has already landed a handsome paperback sale in America. As with all his books it has a message – in this case, one which will have an oddly familiar ring for all those who acclaimed *The Outsider* in 1956, and have followed his star since. His hero, a youth in search of the important answers which have eluded Man since the beginning of time, is forever called upon to scale fresh peaks in a hostile world (ruled, in *Spiderworld*, by arachnids). Should it be made into another science-fiction film – it has all the ingredients – I can foresee fresh ammunition for that Irish critic, should the script-writers get too carried away.

Colin Wilson is always meeting with some controversy or other, not always of his own making. Our own first meeting was not particularly propitious. We were introduced by our village headmaster at an end-of-term fund-raising party. At the time I had just quit Fleet Street to fulfil another ambition and become a novelist. Colin happened to remark that he too had once worked on *The Daily Express*. I was tactless – and unkind—enough to say I couldn't place the occasion. Colin took his revenge shortly afterwards, when I told him I'd just had my first book published. He asked the title—and promptly said he'd never heard of it. My God, I thought (you know how it is with your first book) horse-whipping's too good for this . . . damned Outsider! When we got home I mentioned the confrontation to my wife, who roared with laughter. 'Greek meeting Greek' she said, and so it turned out. Ours was a tug-of-war that began and ended the same night.

The 'quiet obscurity' to which Colin fled here in Cornwall consists of a rambling sort of house, standing in two acres of garden overlooking beautiful Veryan Bay. A notice at the end of the drive says 'Visitors by appointment only' (a request which he likes to be respected), but that's the only indication of fame you will kind; the natives at 'Tetherdown' are friendly enough. On most nights it's filled with pets and people, all making themselves very much at home. As befits the author of *A Book of Booze* he keeps a splendid cellar and is a generous host. The cocktail 'hour' is a somewhat elastic 5.30 to 7 p.m., always interesting and occasionally an hilarious ninety minutes.

The Outsider's unvarying routine is to take a shower after that walk over the headland and sit by the hearth, drying his hair, as he has his first drink of the day, *circa* 5.40 p.m. That first drink is always a white wine— his favourite is a Chablis—to accompany a plate of locally-smoked salmon. Although he keeps every kind of drink in the house, wine is his tipple. If you remember, he introduced *A Book of Booze* with these words:

> I have been a regular wine drinker ever since I could afford it—that is, since the publication of my first book in 1956. A brief calculation tells me that about 1,500 gallons have gurgled and cascaded down my throat since that time [now much outdated: *Booze* was published in 1974] and that if this wine was poured into the basement room where I am at present sitting, it would flood it to a depth of eighteen inches. It follows that if I live to be ninety and continue at my present rate of consumption (around a bottle a day) I shall have drunk enough to drown in.

All houses reveal something of the character of their owners; the wine lake apart, 'Tetherdown' will tell you a great deal about Colin Wilson. Books and records (he is an authority on music, from jazz to classical) line every wall to fill every available inch of space in the ante-room, lounge, copying room and hallway. Books on every subject under the sun perch on tables, chairs and window-ledges. They invade every bedroom, clutter the passageways, cover the walls of the big basement toom (which is also his study) and march on in their battalions to line the shelves of his extensive, centrally-heated private library outside. Colin *thinks* he has some 30,000 books in all, and roughly the same number of LPs, singles, tapes and discs. As both collections are forever expanding he finds it impossible to be more precise. So, in addition to a wine lake, the man has a book mountain and a record mountain in his home; his video library is growing apace, too.

A first visit to 'Tetherdown' is like opening the pages of a Colin Wilson book—it's full of surprises. Do not imagine you have been invited simply to swap lofty thoughts over a drink or two or three. News time, for instance, is sacrosanct, a no go area in which only THE VOICE ON THE BOX may be heard. Your host likes to listen each night to the early TV news bulletins, and I mean every scrap of the news therein, both local and national, on BBC and ITV. To ensure that nothing is missed he personally controls the news selection by push-button, from his armchair by the hearth; and, since the different broadcasts tend to overlap, this can result in a bewildering change of scene and subject that will frequently leave his guests (particularly first-time visitors) wondering nervously if the wine in their glass is not a great deal stronger than they had imagined.

A side-glance at your host will only tend to confirm this impression, for he will appear to be wearing a tea-cosy on his head. In fact it is a special hair-dryer which leaves his hands free to pour drinks and eat; the hair-drying ceremony (mentioned earlier) just happens to coincide with news time. It is also a time, incidentally, which betrays his switch in political affiliation. Once an ardent Socialist he now veers to the Right, and although he professes 'Really, I'm not political' you will spot a gleam in his eye whenever Mrs Thatcher appears on the screen.

The log fire which burns from autumn to early summer in the lounge is the focal point of the Wilson household; and in the same way that the house itself positively bulges with books and records, so does the lounge always seem to be filled with pets and people each evening. The last time I sat there it held enough animals to grace a zoo: Ben and Rosie, Colin's two burly Golden Labradors (old friends these, from our walks over the headland), George, a handsome, exceptionally big black-and-white tom cat, Sunshine and Sonny Boy, the two Wilson terrapins (complete with water-tank), and two 'emmets'—holiday visitors—a hamster called Toadie, and a young African Groy parrot answering to the unlikely name of Clovis.

Competing with them for a place by the hearth were—Colin's mother, his wife Joy (now an author in her own right, with the publication of her first book and local best-seller, *Around St Austell Bay*), their art student daughter Sally and sons Damon—also a student in London—and Rowan, a pupil at Truro public school. Other members of the Wilson family, on holiday from the Midlands, drifted in and out during the course of the evening. In sharp contrast with that feckless 'Outsider' image, Colin Wilson likes nothing better than to be home in Cornwall surrounded by his books, his family and his friends. The trips to London to fulfil publicity engagements, his lecture tours on the Continent—and, later this year, in Japan—are all seen by him as interruptions of a very special and rewarding domestic routine.

His is a fireside which has welcomed some interesting names during the ten years I have been visiting 'Tetherdown'. To mention a few: composers Alan Bush, the grand old man of English music, Richard Arnell (ballet) and Malcolm Arnold, whose 'Cornish Dancers' formed the background music for the recent Prince Charles television programme; Cornish artist Lionel Miskin, whose vivid painting of the Golitha Falls on Bodmin Moor hangs over the fireplace; the late Poet-Laureate John Betjeman, who was so inspired by one visit that he began to compose a poem in Colin's honour—but completed two lines only, 'When the wind from Gorran Haven / Blows across to Tetherdown', and promptly fell asleep; authors Henry Williamson, Jane Gaskell and Arthur Guirdham (Sally Wilson's godfather); writer and television personality Dan Farson, whose father—the late, great Negley Farson, foreign correspondent and best-selling author in his own right—was also Colin Wilson's friend; actors Alfred Burke and Tony Britton, and psychic Bob Cracknell, for whom Colin wrote the introduction to his book, *Clues to the Unknown*—the list is endless.

One of the more demanding tests for any two writers is to collaborate on a book; friendship as well as professional ability can be at risk. So far Colin Wilson and I have written two books together, *The Encyclopaedia of Modern Murder* and *Scandal! An Encyclopaedia*, the latter published this year. Both were planned in their entirety on our daily walks across the Dodman, and both have done well for us, selling both in Britain and the US in hardback and paperback (*Scandal* has also been sold in Japan). The point I make, however, is that far from proving the prickly Outsider he is still sometimes painted, Colin turned out to be the easiest of writers to work with.

He is, of course, the complete professional. When writing this type of factual book he goes straight to the heart of the subject, mincing no words and wasting none. We had no differences of judgment, neither of us needed to read the other's copy before it left—as the one, bound work—for the publisher, there were no inquests after publication, only mutual satisfaction and pleasure.

Perhaps the sea breezes, whipping across the headland day after day, took their toll. Or maybe the man's mellowing; it is, after all, thirty years since *The Outsider* was first published. Either way, it's the essential Colin Wilson—the man behind the books—I so happily salute today.

3

Shared Experiences

TOM GREENWELL

I'm not going to list the names, because I'd probably forget some very important ones, but it struck me when I was writing this article on Colin Wilson how many of his friends and acquaintances from thirty years ago have gone on to write books and plays, many of them well received by the critics. After the publication of *The Outsider*, when Colin was much sought after by struggling writers from Soho, Notting Hill and Hampstead (the Chelsea lot never seemed to have to struggle) he used to say 'Anybody can be a genius. You've just got to work at it.' And he meant it. For him, single-minded determination and the will to study and work provided an infallible key to success. Well, there might have been a tiny reservation: a bit of luck could help to speed things up.

There were times when I thought he was offering too much encouragement to ambitious scribblers for whom there was no real hope. After all, many of them were clearly in love with the idea of becoming famous novelists or poets without ever having to put pen to paper.

But Colin always thought positively. While he had little time for defeatists and people who refused to see that they were capable of infinite development—I suppose I was one of the few exceptions that he tolerated with affection!—he was a great inspiration to those who already had a spark inside them. He would put himself out to help any old friends or acquaintances who seemed prepared to respond to his optimism.

His own work, from *The Outsider* onwards, has been a sort of Tamino's search for the ultimate in mental and spiritual development, though without any orthodox religious connotation. He has never been shy of picking others' brains. Indeed, his prefaces and postscripts are always full of grateful acknowledgements to sources ancient and modern. He is as generous with his praise as he is brutal in his condemnations. He seems to be constantly asking the question: Does this author or philosopher add to, or subtract from, the sum of positive human experience?

Colin, I remember, would try his ideas out on anybody. Although he quickly got bored or even irritated with people who hadn't a clue what he was getting at, it rarely stopped him from talking if he was already in full swing. Sometimes it was almost as if he were rehearsing his lines in front of a tailor's dummy.

Although we have kept in fairly regular touch over the past thirty years, and I have even reviewed some of his books, the period 1956-60

31

stands out in my not very well-ordered memory. For much of that time I was a Fleet Street gossip writer, which is probably why I remember particularly the 'Angry Young Men' media cult and its sometimes bizarre consequences.

In 1957 the publicity that looked like being Colin's undoing was very likely the making of him. None of his closest friends, such as Bill Hopkins and Stuart Holroyd, thought so at the time. And nor did I. But when media pressures forced Colin and Joy Stewart (they were not married then) to flee to Cornwall it was surely the best thing that could have happened. For despite all his determination and thirst for work I doubt whether he could have avoided being wooed to distraction by London's culture-vultures and socialites, and he would have been pursued by the London and foreign media for as long as the AYM theme looked like providing a rich harvest of literary and gossip stories.

This it seemed set to do for a long time, through the simple device of provoking outrageous assertions from people like Colin (John Osborne was more discreet at that time) and adding virtually any new, vigorous and 'working class' author and playwright to the AYM file. Colin could be very strong-willed when he decided that he must get down to work, and his friends usually, though not always, understood it. But a flat in Notting Hill, within walking distance for barely-remembered hangers-on from the old days and a short taxi ride from Fleet Street would surely have set his work back a year or two.

Although I wrote my share of gossip stories in those days I remember being horrified when the so-called horsewhip story broke. Joy's father — went the embellished story — had barged into their flat in Chepstow Villas, Notting Hill, threatening to horsewhip Colin. Mr Stewart had come across Colin's notes for his novel, *Ritual in the Dark*, and thought that Joy had fallen into the hands of a sex maniac and sadist.

The man who tipped off the Press, and was dining with Colin and Joy that night, was the notorious Gerald Hamilton, Christopher Isherwood's 'Mr Norris'. I could picture his chins wobbling as he panted into the telephone mouthpiece. I had lived in the same house in Oakley Street, Chelsea, at the time when Hamilton was standing in for Churchill's torso for sculptor Oscar Nemon. I can't remember, if I ever knew, how Colin came to know him; but in those days everybody with literary connections and literary or academic pretensions seemed to want to meet the author of *The Outsider*.

Anyway, the Press not unnaturally went wild over the horsewhip story, and there was just as much excitement in Europe and North America. Bill Hopkins was probably right in thinking that it would sell more of Colin's books, but some of us feared that that sort of publicity would overshadow the serious nature of his work. If Colin had not escaped to Cornwall when he did, I think Victor Gollancz would have frog-marched him all the way there.

At that time I lived in a dilapidated house in Chepstow Road, Notting Hill, with Bill Hopkins and Stuart Holroyd. We often wondered if our landlord—a certain Mr Rachman—thought we gave the place the necessary respectable cover for the inoffensive brothel in the basement, for we paid little rent. My room was the best for entertaining in, and especially when Colin came up from Cornwall there would be people there at all hours of the day and much of the night. I used to cover embassy functions, deb. dances, first nights, night clubs and that sort of thing for *The Evening Standard*, and when I got home the worse for wear in the early hours it was rarely to go to bed. Colin would probably have retired earlier to the spare room that John Braine used on his trips to London. But Bill, even when he should have been working on his novel, would like as not be proselytizing or shooting people's arguments down with undiminished vigour. I was a handy foil at that hour.

Of the three authors only Bill seemed to have any instinct for politics. He became involved with the Liberal party's Federal Europe campaign through its magazine, and started the short-lived Spartacan Society with a failed Liberal parliamentary candidate as one of his catches. He roped Colin and Stuart in, but I think they only went along out of friendship.

I always felt that if Colin, with his basic disinterest in politics and his penchant for making outrageous statements, were to become involved with political movements or causes he could only attract bad publicity for himself. There was indeed a plot of sorts once to trap him into a meeting with fascist odd-balls, but a Left-wing poet with a conscience tipped Bill off about it, so if the Press did turn up it was for nothing. I have felt warmly disposed towards that poet ever since, even though later on he played a different sort of role at the Royal Court Theatre and the King's Arms next door.

The publicity from that incident was offensive to the Establishment, and would have been more so but for the fact that people's instincts are generally on the side of fair play for a new playwright, especially if his tormentors are theatre people themselves. Stuart's play, *The Tenth Chance*, was being given a Sunday night performance at the Royal Court —one of George Devine's experiments. During the third act Elaine Dundy, Kenneth Tynan's wife, stalked out of the auditorium making a great deal of noise, and someone whom Colin believed to be Christopher Logue yelled out 'Rubbish'. Stuart had lingered on in the theatre afterwards, but in the pub there was a stand-up row between two factions with Colin, Bill and Michael Hastings (who has since established quite a name for himself in the theatre) on one side and Kenneth Tynan, Christopher Logue and friends on the other. I thought it prudent to usher the ladies into a safe corner and stand guard over them. Anyway, I'd already paid for my whisky and it wasn't safe to leave it around, or try to hang on to it within reach of angrily waving arms.

Sandy Wilson (of *The Boy Friend*) and John Osborne stayed well out of it, too. Osborne just took in the scene and said, loftily 'Terrific. It looks as if the English theatre's waking up at last.'

Fleet Street did quite well out of that little fracas, but it did nothing for Stuart's play. And Stuart, a shy chap even though not lacking in self-confidence, was embarrassed by the scenes and by the publicity, and could hardly wait to get out of town. His first book had been called *Emergence from Chaos*, and the look on his face as he left Sloane Square that night suggested that that was exactly how he was feeling. His next book was *Flight and Pursuit*, which could have been equally appropriate.

I might mention the consequences of another aspect of publicity. I am not an expert on the novel, but I have read Bill Hopkins's *The Divine and the Decay* more than once in recent years, and I am sure that it would have received very good reviews if the critics and the gossip writers hadn't been licking their lips in anticipation of it. Certainly with no discouragement from Bill, who as a former journalist ought to have known the hazards, Colin had hailed him as another genius. While Fleet Street had done very well out of some of the cheeky publicity stunts which had made the new literary scene exciting for some readers and provocative for the rest, the prospect of being able to demolish a declared genius must have sent waves of delight throughout the reviewing and gossip trades. Bill might never have finished that novel at all if he hadn't been pushed by Colin and Tom Maschler (now the boss of Jonathan Cape), and all that sweat deserved better reward.

Some have argued that Colin's work, or at any rate the public reception of it, was bound to suffer because of the lionisation and publicity of the Outsider years. The hostility and the set-backs never deterred him though, and he has outlasted most of the critics who had developed attitudes towards him and his work which were too much influenced by their memories of the rivalries, vendettas, assessments and reassessments of the late 1950s. I have given up counting the number of books he has gone on to produce, but I always did know that there would be no stopping him.

Visiting Colin in Gorran Haven has always been a varied experience. From the very beginning he was strict about his work schedule and almost as strict about organising his relaxations, but somehow there seems to be an aura of spontaneity about everything. Even the most stuffy visitor to the Wilson household is liable to find himself taken off to some tap room in Mevagissey, where Colin unwinds and recharges his batteries by playing darts and supping with a cross-section of the local citizenry. Even when he was still being pursued by reporters and television people, there were some good old days in the back room of the General Wolfe in St Austell, after time, and with a top policeman and other solid Cornishmen wondering what they were going to tell their wives this time. I remember Colin and his pals gently dumping one very large old chap on his doorstep, ringing the bell and scarpering before the missus came out. The last post sounded for the old General Wolfe some years ago, but his soul surely goes marching on.

What I never really got used to was Colin changing long-playing records every couple of minutes and asking: 'What's this one?' But for him music has got to be an experience, something to think about, and not just a listening habit; not just emotion in a vacuum. Actually, although I enjoy taking music the easy way I often found myself getting a kick out of recognising quite esoteric pieces, and it was even nicer when he got it wrong having been the one who had put the record on in the first place.

Joy—who is his wife, cook, secretary, advisor and anchor—seems able to cope with any sudden crisis, and shows no sign of being put out by unexpected and sometimes eccentric visitors. But how she must have often grimaced to herself when bills were mounting up at the same time that Colin, always over-generous, was dispensing wine and whisky to hangers-on, or to visiting media people who might well have been preparing to stab him in the back.

In the Notting Hill days particularly Colin, Bill and Stuart found themselves snowed under with invitations to all sorts of happenings, from art gallery previews to literary soirées; from bottle parties in Earl's Court basements to polite cocktails in Belgravia with the Claus von Bulow set. In public Colin often seemed to be struggling against a natural shyness until it got around to discussing ideas, when he would really take off and, indeed, go out of his way to shock. Bill it was who was the born extrovert. And rather than risk seeming stuffy or impolite his friends felt they had to adopt some of his social habits; such as greeting every woman acquaintance—and sometimes even those newly met—

with a kiss on the cheek, and using forenames on meeting people for the first time. Bill, who was totally classless, was calling the Marquess of Milford Haven 'David' within minutes of their first meeting. They were rivals for the affections of a very lovely and bookish blonde model, and it was Bill who had the advantage.

We all split up when the house in Chepstow Road was sold. Bill arranged to have a blue plaque put up. It was very official-looking, but with the addition of two cherubs blowing their own trumpets. Designed by sculptor Laurence Bradshaw, who years earlier had sculpted the Karl Marx memorial in Highgate cemetery, it was a magnet for the gossip columns. One columnist wrote (it wasn't me!): 'People are normally accepted as being born great, achieving greatness or having it thrust upon them. There is a fourth class: those who get tired of waiting and try to hustle recognition along a bit.' A writer in *Punch* magazine, with no obvious sense of humour, asked angrily: 'Who do these people think they are?'

I moved to a spacious pad in the semi-basement of the New Apostolic Church in Kensington, on which a friend, Robin Turner, had taken a lease. It was great for parties except on choir practice nights, but it wasn't Chepstow Road. John Braine took a room there and Stan Barstow stayed a few times, but we didn't have the intimate discussions and debates which had made the Notting Hill days such an inspiration. Colin stayed only occasionally, though some of his female admirers would suddenly appear in the vague hope that he would be there.

We enjoyed peaceful co-existence with the Church, which was our landlord, although we did have a near miss. One Sunday morning, after a Saturday night party that had gone on a bit, an unexpected visitor spotted a hand-printed notice in the shared hallway which read: 'New Alcoholic Church: Dissolution downstairs, Absolution upstairs'. We got it down minutes before the faithful were due for morning service. I always thought there was a hint of Hopkins about that one.

Colin's ability to write so much, read so much and absorb so much has always amazed me. Journalists who find it hard enough just to keep up with current affairs can only envy his facility. His correspondence files must weigh a ton or two. There is always a new book in his typewriter but when, for example, he is sent something to review he not only meets his deadline but sends in a thoroughly polished job. He has a prodigious memory for facts and ideas which he considers to be important (though I'm not sure what he is like now when Joy gives him a shopping list) and I've often thought that he must have a push-button computerised filing system in his skull which enables him to call up whatever he needs in a matter of seconds.

Thirty years ago Colin was generally regarded as a dedicated womaniser and also the archetypal Male Chauvinist Pig. He respected women who had genius to offer, but seemed to believe that most of the gender had been placed on this earth simply to free their male betters from weary workaday chores, and provide sexual experiences (battery-charging) without making demands on their partners' intellectual and creative energy. He never seemed to approve of the women his closest friends became attached to. That was not out of jealousy, but partly because he believed that such attachments would distract people like Bill and Stuart from their typewriters, and partly because he did not want to have to share the company of his chosen equals with such clinging creatures, however pretty and vivacious, who had nothing in common with him.

Looking back I feel certain that most people who have been associated with Colin more than briefly have profited from the experience — even sceptics, cynics and enemies. While he can be very intense and even irritable, his charm and humour never desert him for long.

As I said in a review a few years ago: 'Colin Wilson does not just write books; he shares experiences with his readers. He uses ideas — good ones and bad ones; new ones and old ones — as a climber uses footholds and handholds to zig-zag his way to the ultimate goal. Sometimes Mr Wilson falters, slips back a bit, and finds new paths around obstacles; but the general progress is upwards and towards the sunlight'.

4

Angry Young Mania and Beyond

STUART HOLROYD

Bliss was it in that literary dawn of 1956-57 to be alive, but to be young and angry was very heaven.

At least it was if you had a taste for being interviewed on television and featured in the Press, hobnobbing with famous older writers, lecturing to student societies and dazzling the girls with the charisma of success, and planning into the small hours frontal attacks on the complacency, obtuseness, philistinism and injustice of British society.

Cyril Connolly and Philip Toynbee paid tribute to *The Outsider*, all London went to the Royal Court to see *Look Back in Anger*. Youth, elevated onto a pedestal, tried to conceal its entirely natural look of surprise and delight behind a mask of grave solemnity, finger raised to admonish or exhort, brow suitably furrowed to convey an impression of deep and responsible concern.

Only anger was *de rigeur*, but that created no particular problem, because even if you didn't feel very angry the Press was adept at making you appear so.

Looking back, perhaps it wasn't all unalloyed bliss, but we had a lot of fun playing doyens and divas. I for one was immensely tickled when I found myself categorised as a 'law giver' in Kenneth Allsop's book, *The Angry Decade*. I wasn't aware that I had done much law-giving at the time, but for the next few months I became a veritable Justinian.

Yes, it was fun, but when we momentarily put aside our tubs and trumpets I imagine many of us felt that it had all been a little too easy. It seemed a damn funny way to run a culture. There was no end of talk about our marriages, divorces and liaisons, what so-and-so thought about Royalty, Shakespeare or Prime Minister Macmillan, about the squalid and dreary jobs in which we'd rubbed along before Dame Fortune and Lord Beaverbrook took us to their hearts, but amid all the hullaballoo there was scarcely a whisper about professional standards. Most of us wanted to be writers and not pundits or prima donnas, and had worked away in healthy obscurity in the years before the media took us up learning the rudiments of our various literary crafts.

The Angry Young Man era, arguably the most successful post-war cultural pseudo-event, died a natural death some time in 1959. Editors must have counted up with satisfaction the thousands of column-inches with which it had enabled them to slake the appetite of their terrible and voracious mistress, the daily blank page. The public turned its attention to bingo or The Bomb, and those of the 'angries' who had it left in them retired to their attics or country houses to lick their wounds and get back to writing.

We talked a good deal about the *malaise* of the twentieth century in those dear dead days, under the comforting illusion that the more words you can spin about a menace the more securely you barricade yourself against its influence. At the same time we mocked the assembled Bishops at the Lambeth Conference when they began to talk solemnly about exorcism: that was medieval superstition. We talked about *angst* and anger, the leap into faith and the definitive choice, challenge and response, hope and despair, genius and mediocrity, the hero and the little man or anti-hero, moral degeneration and cultural apathy, and shaped a view of life and the world in terms of these dramatic simplifications. We were, were we not, the English Existentialists?

We deplored English cultural insularity and looked to contemporary Europe, to Sartre and Camus, Heidegger and Hesse, for our models. We wanted to write philosophy in the manner of a thriller, and novels and plays that were vitalised by philosophy. Mainstream English writers hitherto seemed to us to have eschewed ideas and concerned themselves with trivial subjects of class, personal relationships and troubled but never turbulent consciousnesses, England and English cultural and intellectual life seemed too complacent and cosy. We envied the French writer's and intellectual's status, and if we didn't entirely go along with Camusian stoicism and Sartrian pessimism we fancied that if we enjoyed the cultural centrality that they did we could change the world with our pens; and you can hardly get more optimistic than that.

Thirty years on it certainly is a changed world. We of the 'Angry Decade' are still around, but hardly enjoying the cultural centrality that such beginnings seemed to augur. Are we still the outsiders, patiently and persistently swimming against the tide and biding our time till the world sees sense, our sense? Or did we ride the gravy train of the fifties, but ultimately miss the boat? There was a time, in the seventies, when it seemed that we had been precursors, that our kind of existentialism, with its emphasis on the spiritual, on consciousness expansion and the achievement of a fundamentally optimistic worldview, was becoming more widely influential. Were we the forerunners of what Marilyn Ferguson has called 'the Aquarian Conspiracy', and if so was it to be a conspiracy that would overcome the *status quo*? It is still too early to say. I lack my younger self's confidence to make predictions. Perhaps now is the time to write memoirs. Who knows, before long the fifties may be imbued with a period character and appeal. So speak, memory.

When I arrived in London in the autumn of 1952 I was an out-of-work actor, having worked for the previous year in a repertory company in my home town, Blackpool. As such I drew a dole of some £3 a week, half of which went to pay the rent of an attic room in Pimlico. The room was rather like the room Chatterton had died in according to Henry Wallis's painting: small, with the ceiling sloping in on two sides, and with a little window overlooking the rooftops. I had written a play about Chatterton, titled *The Mad Genius of Bristol*, and when the Blackpool rep had declined to perform it had decamped to seek my literary fortune in the presumably less philistine metropolis.

London was a scarred and dingy city, still with extensive bomb-sites. Rubble, greyness, smog, poverty, whores on the streets in Soho, trams still running along Kingsway, tramps sleeping on the Embankment and under the Arches: it was a run-down city, but for me it was romantic and exciting, and just what I had expected from my reading of Dickens.

I spent my time reading, writing and exploring. My first weeks in London were lonely, but my passion for poetry soon gained me friends. Following up an advertisement in *The New Statesman*, I fell in with a group of young men and women who met every Sunday night in a room above a pub in Westminster to read poetry to each other. They would take it in turns each week to expound a theme illustrated by readings. Then there would be discussion and argument, which for the hard core of the group often continued afterwards in the Strand Corner House.

It was there that I met Alfred Reynolds, one night after I had given a talk and reading on the subject of 'The Poetic Expression of Religious Experience'. I had noticed him in the audience, a man in his mid-forties, heavily built, who spoke with a soft foreign accent. When I mentioned Rilke in my talk, he said in the discussion that followed that it was good to find an Englishman who read foreign poets, even though he himself considered Rilke romantic and mystical to a fault. I took up the argument in the Strand Corner House, protesting that Rilke was a great poet because he was a visionary who had succeeded in communicating his vision by creating a private imagery and mythology. Alfred countered that to retire into a private world was no answer to the problems that confronted modern man. I replied that Rilke hadn't retired into a private world but on the contrary had cultivated the faculty to take the outer world into himself and transform it. Alfred said that was mysticism. We went on at length, and before we parted that night Alfred gave

me his address and invited me to a meeting at his house the following
week.

Alfred was Hungarian, had come to England in the thirties, and had
been employed during the war by British Intelligence to 'de-Nazify'
German prisoners. He had done so very successfully, employing the
Socratic method of leading men by gentle questions and promptings to
contradict or condemn themselves out of their own mouths. As a result,
he had found himself after the war with a following of young German
converts eager to practise his methods and promote his philosophy. The
philosophy was, inevitably in a man of his generation, chiefly political,
and consisted mainly in the rejection of all ideologies and the champion-
ship of the individual. Alfred saw enemies of the individual everywhere.
Politicians, leaders of business, the Churches, people involved in television, in advertising, were all conspiring to produce a world in which
freedom of action or even of thought would be impossible. They must
be resisted by people all over the world meeting together, talking over
problems, freeing each other from illusions and conditioned modes of
thought. Collectively such individuals might be referred to aa 'the
Bridge', for they not only sought to bridge the gap between nationalities,
creeds and ideologies, but also comprised a bridge from the present
pretty deplorable state of the world to a more hopeful future.

I had never been very interested in politics, but the rejection of
authority, the emphasis on the freedom of the individual, and also
perhaps the implied elitism of the 'Bridge' philosophy, appealed to me.
I became a regular at the Tuesday evening meetings in Alfred's house
in Dollis Hill. I think what I chiefly gained from them was an introduction to new literary experiences. The discussions were full of references to Kafka, Mann, Hesse, Koestler, Orwell, Nietzsche, and above all
Dostoevsky, whose *Legend of the Grand Inquisitor* was something of a
scripture for the 'Bridge' devotees. It was all new and exciting, and I read
and thought and talked avidly, until Alfred came to regard me as a
protegé and disciple. I remember he was one of the few guests at my
marriage. Anne, my girl friend since the age of fourteen, had come to
join me in London, and we lived first in a room in Hampstead then in a
small three-room flat in Highgate. She, too, fell under Alfred's spell, and
for about a year we were happy with each other, with our new stimulating life in London, and with the 'Bridge'.

It was at one of the 'Bridge' meetings that I met Colin Wilson. Colin
was critical of what he considered the wishy-washy humanism of the
'Bridge' philosophy, and I found my own reservations about it, which
had been implicit in the initial argument with Alfred about Rilke and

mysticism, made more coherent and focused by Colin's strictures. At that time Colin certainly influenced me, and not only intellectually. Anne later blamed him for the break-up of our marriage. He wasn't in fact to blame, but his influence was catalytic. Before I met Colin I had begun to get dissatisfied both with the 'Bridge' philosophy and with my marriage, because neither seemed to be getting anywhere. I wasn't sure that my work was getting anywhere either. I had sold some stories to magazines, and some articles on poetry to *The Poetry Review*, but my Chatterton play, even though I had rewritten it, had been turned down by theatres and agents, and I felt frustrated and trapped. I even had hire-purchase commitments for furniture. Colin, when we met, had just got out of his marriage. He had left his wife and son in Leicester and cycled down to London with a rucksack full of books and manuscripts. He had got life down to simple essentials. He slept out in the open in a sleeping-bag, worked in the British Museum reading room during the day, and travelled all over London by bicycle, visiting friends, attending meetings, giving talks. Also he had girl friends. To me, with my flat, my furniture, my marriage, Colin's seemed a most enviable life. In the light of it I examined my own, and felt increasingly as months went by that I had settled for too little, made too few demands upon myself. Colin introduced me to Bill Hopkins, who was extrovert, intellectually combative, positive and dynamic. There was heady talk, about genius and mediocrity, the cultivation of the will, the demands and responsibilities of leadership, and I began to abhor my furniture that I hadn't yet paid for, my striped wallpaper that made my sitting-room look like a barred cage, and my cosy, contained life.

Colin had a theory that the major writers of a generation tend to gravitate together before they are published. When we met he was writing and rewriting his novel, *Ritual in the Dark*, and he would come to the flat in Highgate and read long extracts from it. I reciprocated with readings from critical essays I was writing on modern poets. Colin also talked at length about his concept of the Outsider, and about the books and writers that represented aspects of it. It was later said that I urged him to write a book on the subject. I don't know now whether that is truth or legend, but certainly I wouldn't claim, as some critics did, that I contributed anything more than encouragement to the writing of the book, which I remember was accomplished remarkably quickly, as a kind of interlude from the work on *Ritual in the Dark*. It was two years after Colin and I had met that *The Outsider* was published, and my own *Emergence from Chaos* came out the following year. Their reception seemed to vindicate Colin's theory of gravitation, although I'm not sure that Colin did either of his then best friends a favour

when he declared publicly that the only other two literary geniuses in
Britain were Stuart Holroyd and Bill Hopkins.

Colin made enough money from *The Outsider* to buy a house in
Cornwall. He first went to the West Country to get out of the limelight
and reorientate himself. He had no longer been able to work in London.
In three months he had become, to his own and his friends' amazement,
something of a national figure. 'At twenty-four, with his first book, Mr
Wilson steps straight into the front rank of major writers,' one of the
papers had trumpeted. He was inundated with offers from publishers,
newspapers, magazines, theatres, television programmes, hostesses. His
book sold some 50,000 copies in three months, translation rights were
snapped up, and his name became known to millions. The publicity was
not all favourable, for he represented different things to different people.
To his admirers he was the working-class hero who had fought his way
to the top. They made much of the fact that he had left school at sixteen, worked as a laundryman, a hospital porter, a table-clearer in a
Lyons Corner House, had lived rough in Paris and London. To the
academics his success was symptomatic of the erosion of the standards
of sound scholarship. Professor Ayer, reviewing the book, quoted Dr
Johnson's quip about a woman's preaching being like a dog's walking
on its hind legs: 'It is not done well; but you are surprised to find it
done at all'. Literary people were on the whole more generously disposed, and conceded Colin's vitality, breadth of reading and originality of
theme, but some deplored the inelegance of his style, and Arthur
Koestler dismissed *The Outsider* as the work of 'a young man who has
just discovered that genius is prone to *Weltschmerz*'. Both the extraordinary success of the book and the ambivalence of people's reception
of it were probably attributable to the fact that it was the kind of book
that many people felt they could have written if they had thought of
it first. Colin took the acclaim as his due and the criticisms as the
drivel of fools, and went on ploughing his furrow.

In 1957 the other two geniuses of contemporary English literature
were living together in a house in Chepstow Road, Notting Hill. Anne
and I had separated, and after a three-month sojurn in Germany I had
returned to take a room in the house where Bill Hopkins, his girl friend
Greta, and the journalist Tom Greenwell lived. The upper rooms of the
house were cheap, perhaps because they were subsidised by the rents
of the girls who occupied rooms in the basement and on the ground
floor, where they pursued a profession clearly more lucrative than writing, for two of them ran MG sports cars on it. The landlord was a cheery
cockney called Les, aged about forty, who turned up about once a

month to collect the rents. Colin and John Braine shared the rent of one small room, as a *pied à terre* when they came to London. Les followed the careers of his literary tenants in the papers with great interest. Perhaps he thought his leniency over the rents was a form of patronage, or perhaps we served as a cover for the more profitable activities in the lower part of the house.

Whatever Les earned from his property, he ploughed none of it back. On the exterior the stucco was flaking away, and the inside was dingy and shabby.

The social centre of the house was Tom Greenwell's room. Tom was unique among us in that he had no pretentions to genius. He had a genius, however, for friendships, and he would dispense to all comers, at all times of day and night, tea, wine when he could afford it, and conversation, which he regarded as an art. He worked as a gossip-columnist on *The Evening Standard* and was our hot-line to Fleet Street, and he wrote for his own amusement sharp satires in rhymed couplets. The door of his room bore the notice: 'Beware of the Doggerel'.

The house generally, and Tom's room particularly, drew visitors like a magnet. It was not only the association with people and events current-ly in the news — though this was undoubtedly part of its appeal — but also a sense of its being a haven of disorder, a place where there were no set times for anything, where life's normal primary concerns, with eating, sleeping, earning a living, took second place, and primacy was given to conversation, creative work, friendship, and the organization of grand designs. Life began about midday and went on until three, four or even five o'clock in the morning. People called in at all times of the day and night and could be fairly confident of a welcome in one of the rooms. There were fellow writers and journalists, people in pub-lishing and television, and a host of seekers, malcontents and misfits — shall we say 'outsiders'? — who found the conversation and the atmos-phere of the place stimulating.

I suppose the key to the charm of this particular *vie de Bohème* was its spontaneity. If someone suggested going out for a meal, to a party, or to see a particular film or show, or roaming round the junk shops around Portobello Road, or taking advantage of the availability of a car to drive out to see Shaw's house at Ayot St Lawrence, others would fall in with the plan and an enthusiastic little group would be formed for the venture. 'But when do any of you work?' some people asked in awe. My answer was that I liked to write between eleven o'clock at night and four in the morning, though in fact I often spent several of these hours talking in Tom's room, for Tom returned from his even-

ing's gossip-foraging and putting the paper to bed shortly after midnight.
Bill worked more spasmodically, at odd times of the day or night for
an hour or two, or in two- or three-day spurts, when he went off to his
mother's house in Streatham and was incommunicado. He made out
that for him writing was a tremendous travail, a matter of grappling with
his angel, and indeed when he returned from Streatham he often looked
worn out, though he rarely showed anyone what he had written, and I
sometimes wondered about that 'angel'.

Bill was more politically oriented than either Colin or I. He even
tried to launch a new political party, 'the Spartacans'. Bill was an enthusiastic publicist, and he got paragraphs about the new party into the
newspapers. It was the Spartacan publicity that earned us the 'fascist'
tag. Journalists and fellow writers with leanings to the Left regarded
the Spartacans as a sinister symptom, and there was talk of the danger
of the younger generation's disenchantment with democracy. As Bill
predicted, we gained a following. Private and public meetings were
held, discussions and lectures organised, and before long the Spartacan
Society was able to boast a nucleus of some forty or fifty members.
Bill energetically organised, publicised, proseletysed, and sought a
publisher and financial backing for a proposed series of 'Spartacan
Essays'. Colin and I supported him, although I think Colin was as sceptical as I was about the value of action on the political front and did so,
as I did, chiefly out of loyalty.

To consolidate our group, Colin proposed that he, Bill and I should
write a book together. A subject we had often talked about and that
would give our ideas a point of focus but at the same time bring out our
different approaches was the concept of the hero. Why didn't we put
up to Gollancz, he suggested, the idea of a joint book, with essays of
about 25,000 words from each of us, on the theme? We must go on
writing prolifically, Colin urged, force people to take us and our work
seriously. And we must keep each other up to the mark creatively. We
all had our faults, but working side by side, criticising each other's work,
we could iron them out. In a sense he himself was very much a loner.
He often assumed that he'd eventually become a kind of Tolstoy figure,
occasionally uttering gloomy roars from 'Mevapolanya' (he lived near
Mevagissey), and distributing bits of his garments to pilgrims. But really
he hated the idea. He felt that there was too much of the artist in him
to enjoy being a guru. He didn't want followers, because they were
always a trap. But he did need allies, exchange of ideas and criticism,
the sense of working not entirely alone.

I paraphrase a recalled conversation. Characteristically, Colin threw off his 25,000 words while Bill and I were still mulling over the theme, and Gollancz, no doubt pleased to get his literary lion roaring alone and unencumbered by the other two geniuses of the alliance, published his contribution as a separate book (*The Age of Defeat**), saying that he would consider Bill's and my contributions for independent publication when they were completed. Instead I wrote my autobiographical-cum-philosophical book, *Flight and Pursuit*, which Victor Gollancz promoted with great enthusiasm and in which some literary luminaries of the older generation found things to applaud, though the literary critics and the public, no doubt by now sick of the Angry Young Man hype, either savaged or ignored. An even less encouraging reception awaited my play, *The Tenth Chance*, produced at the Royal Court Theatre in 1959. I think Colin has written somewhere that subsequently I retired to the country to lick my wounds. Perhaps he was right. I confess that I was less resilient than he to criticism, and had less conviction of my own genius and less single-mindedness in pursuing its development. Other concerns than to change the world through writing came to preoccupy me, as I related in my 1977 autobiography, *Contraries*.

So there was to be no blue plaque, as the young literary aspirant from Blackpool, who had not seen how life could be supportable without fame, had dreamed. There was one for a short time, though. After our landlord Les was killed in a car crash and his wife sold the house, Bill arranged for a sculptor friend to make a blue plaque similar to the London County Council ones. He had it firmly fixed to the front of the house just before we all moved out, and had a ceremonial unveiling which was reported in some of the papers. The plaque announced that: 'John Braine, Tom Greenwell, Stuart Holroyd, Bill Hopkins, Colin Wilson lived here, 1956-59.' Tom, I remember, thought it was a splendid stunt, an appropriate cock-a-snook ending to the 'angry decade'. His only regret, he said, was that the plaque wasn't a bit more elaborate, framed by cherubs blowing trumpets: 'their own, of course'.† I had often wondered how seriously Tom took the bunch of geniuses he had fallen among.

**The Stature of Man* in the US. — Ed.

†In fact, it was! (see Tom Greenwell's contribution which, I am informed by Bill Hopkins, is correct). The plaque bore the inscription: 'Hallowed be these walls' and one other name, that of Greta Detloff. Despite being firmly fixed it was stolen soon after erection. — Ed.

5

Aiming for a Likeness

BILL HOPKINS

It was a brilliant afternoon in May 1963, if I remember rightly, with
the sun filtering through the windows of the studio in Glebe Place,
Chelsea, which Pietro Annigoni was renting at that period to execute
the series of portraits that established him as the supreme portrait
painter of the time.

Watching the deft brush strokes placing paint on canvas was seeing
magic at work. The technique was uniquely Renaissance, challenging
the chaos of contemporary abstraction and reaffirming the figurative
approach in painting after its long abandonment. There in his studio, I
had no doubt about his significance in the future.

'This man Colin Wilson. He is an interesting mind, eh?' He went on
working as he spoke, not turning from the picture.

'You'll like him,' I said, pouring myself another glass of wine.

'Why should I travel hundreds of miles to meet someone you call
exceptional? Who is that, outside oneself? You think I need a Rasputin
perhaps, to tell me things I know already, like some gypsy with the
Tarot cards?'

'Did I say anything like that?'

'No. You say nothing, and make him mysterious. All I hear is that
he's one of the few men worth meeting. But you don't explain further,
or the purpose of meeting him. That, I'm supposed to guess. So you bait
a hook and I bite, you think!'

'You complain that the people in London bore you, yet when you
are offered the chance of meeting someone you won't, you bare your
teeth.'

'I'm a man of Florence. We always bare our teeth!'

I tried once more. 'Well, there's a seat in the car if you want it. It's
all arranged for tomorrow evening, and Tim and Sue are coming along,
too. It's about time you saw Cornwall, anyhow.'

This was a particularly adroit move since Tim Whidbourne was one
of his closest friends, and Sue Mandrake one of London's most beautiful
and intelligent models. I was not ignorant of the fact that he found her
beauty and joy in living irresistable.

'Why are you doing this to me!' Raising his hands and dropping them
with feigned despair, he said: 'Very well. I will come, too.'

At this point I should divulge the reasons behind this Machiavellian manipulation of my suspicious friend and enlist a little understanding. The grand plot in mind was to nudge him in the direction of painting a portrait of Colin without a fee; a portrait not only certain of finding placement in the National Portrait Gallery, but ensuring him of immortality at a stroke.

As I viewed it, the dreary succession of faces that Pietro was painting, Popes, Kings, Queens, ephemeral and expendable grandees of the world, could give way for one moment to a different class of person, and should. If it was a case of compelling the artist to see this alternative face in order to bring him to the boil, as it were, then I considered even a spot of hijacking legitimate in a good cause.

But just as Colin lacked a mighty portrait, I felt Pietro needed a major monograph on his vision, aesthetics and development. I foresaw the possibility of Colin remedying the omission once he had met the maestro and inspected a sufficient number of photographs illustrating the depth and virtuosity of his work. It was sufficiently off the beaten track to interest him, at any rate.

I also believed that over and above this projected *quid pro quo* there was also the distinct likelihood that both might find a new friend. That was the consolation prize if my attempt at adding to art history failed.

Musing on the satisfactory aspects of the *coup* if it succeeded, that night I telephoned Colin, warning him of the impending descent but saying nothing of my hopes.

'That's all right,' he said cheerfully. 'It'll be a pleasure to meet him. And Tim and Sue. So long as it doesn't mean that we're going to talk about painting all the time. I hope he's interested in a few other subjects, too? It might be a bit constraining otherwise.'

I reassured him. 'He's fairly wide-ranging. You won't be bored, I promise.'

The refreshing fact of our friendship over thirty years has always been Colin's good-natured acceptance of every inconvenience I have foisted on him. This time it was to be for his own good, even if he didn't know it.

When we arrived at Gorran Haven the following night, exhausted and travel-stained, it was too late for anything but brief introductions before heading for sleep. However, the following morning at breakfast all the omens were good. The conversation flowed easily with Pietro and Colin clearly taking to one another immediately.

As it happened, Colin was surprisingly conversant with quite a lot of Pietro's work, and Pietro, even more surprisingly, disclosed more of a grasp of our literature that I had hitherto suspected.

Eventually, when the conversation turned to the Italian Futurists and Marinetti, with both engrossed in the finer points at issue, I led the rest of the company off to the village, leaving them to become better acquainted. On the surface, that portrait and monograph seemed safely on course, with the rest just routine bookkeeping and a few navigational adjustments.

We stayed at Gorran for one more day, since we all had other commitments in London. The visit ended with Colin and Pietro clapping one another heartily on the back, exchanging autographed books with laudatory inscriptions, and expressing determination to meet again in the near future.

On the way back, Pietro held forth at considerable length on our host's intelligence, knowledge and vision. 'Here is a Titan,' he exclaimed. 'A man one is glad to know is alive!'

A few days later, in a telephone conversation, Colin expressed equally cordial views. 'A rare mind and eye,' he said reflectively.

But about that portrait, or the monograph, not a word on either side. Indeed, so far as I know, they have never met again, or gone one step further than that first introduction.

In the intervening years, I later discovered that Pietro had invited Sue Mandrake to Florence and painted many pictures of her, each one coveted by all who have seen them. In the same period, Colin has written extensive catalogue introductions for several impecunious painters who strolled into his life and out again.

It is no use complaining. I just put it down to experience.

6

'So Much Work to Do'

JOHN RETY

It is almost impossible to recall one's young days and to single out an individual. Looking back thirty years they all seem important. But in connection with Colin Wilson, one cannot think of him without Bill Hopkins. None of us doubted for one moment that it was Bill that typified the era, but what some of us did not know was that the world was not content with abstract achievements, it also wanted the usual blood and sweat. The world wanted the promise of solid achievement, something on paper like a collateral and plenty of promise of more to come. Some of us would have been satisfied with the illusion of greatness, the world wanted (and still wants) the solid monument. Some explanation is needed. But there is a nagging thought within me that the world owes *me* an explanation and not the other way round. We were talking about the new renaissance but it has not come about. What Bill warned us about is now true, the little men have taken over everywhere and will not let go until, in their ignorance, they have destroyed the whole caboodle. It would be difficult for me to write about what happened to that vast crowd which for a short time rubbed shoulders with Colin. Later on he was to write that he considered himself to be only 'the first through the hedge'. It was difficult to follow him. Many of us at that time had not yet had a chance to formulate our opinions; certainty was not in short supply, but it was inchoate, discussions had just begun. The movement that was created by the Press had nothing to do with us, the tag 'angry' was a clever device, but it was also an embarrassment and, after all, in John Osborne's play the point was made in an ironic way. Osborne was saying that there were no more ideals to fight for, it is not worth being angry about anything. It was not to be expected that any of those writers chosen at random would wish to offer a collective statement or would work together, not even in the sense that Chesterton and Wells at least disputed with each other in the same framework. Among the crowd behind it, and unknown to the press, there was a movement but it was swallowed up and harnessed. I don't even know whether it is worth mentioning it after thirty years, but Bill and Colin and Stuart Holroyd knew this was so. Those three at least were talking about fundamentals and wished for 'that evolutionary advance which alone would make all the tragedy and all the suffering meaningful'.

Many people benefited from that close-knit circle for not all were
certain of their own importance which 'had to be maintained in a world
that actively discouraged it'. But in that coffee house, where all of us
met, there was sufficient encouragement. Which brings me to the
Saturday Critic. I wonder if anybody still remembers the *Saturday Critic*?
Come to think of it can anybody still remember the Coffee House?
Behind its steamy windows there was the promise of a new life, some
undefeated people, it was peculiar then and would be peculiar now. I
suppose this was only so through my own distorted vision that dismissed reality, that would not accept reality; the people there, I suppose,
were no better than in any other steaming cosmopolitan crowd that
spends its stolen money in any of the filthy little holes of the town, safe
in each others company.

But there the coffee house was and through its doors strode William
B. Hopkins and the crowd hushed as he came in. Why he ever came in
to the coffee house, nobody ever found out for he only drank sweet
milky tea, the hotter the better and that was not to be got there, for
they must have been the first to experiment with tea bags. I think it
was Jean Fulton who introduced us and at the end of the conversation
he offered me some job on the *Saturday Critic*. He showed me the
cover of the proposed first issue with a drawing of a monocled character
in top hat with a finely drawn supercilious nose (come to think of it he
may have been holding a lorgnette).

'What will it do?' I asked. He replied, not so much addressing me
but the entire population of the coffee house and a tremendous crowd
in Trafalgar Square (which could easily be imagined through the coffee
house windows of nearby Northumberland Avenue):

'It will shatter the old order.' I was entirely pleased with his answer,
accepted the job, and looked forward with confidence to the future.

At that time I was still employed by an excellent, if old fashioned
publisher, who paid me the princely sum of £3 0s. 6d. a week and I had
a flat in Lisle Street, which I shared with two sex-maniacs who by now
I would have expected to be world famous for their crimes, but alas
must have slowed down a bit.

Lisle Street! I was the great writer and the sun shone out of my back-
side!

'What are you?' asked Bill. I told him I was a writer.

'What have you written?' he asked. 'I have written nothing,' I told
him, 'and I don't intend to write anything ever.' He pondered this for
a second.

'It won't do,' he said, 'we must all write a masterpiece each. Nothing less. You could say it is our duty.'

Duty?—I was shocked, if I wrote anything it would be sure to disappoint. As long as nothing is written down there can be no argument. I am a great writer and that is that. But once somebody, anybody, could see the evidence, a word of criticism like a cold shower could be directed on my deathly prose, worse still it could be compared to anybody's work, just anybody's.

'Don't worry,' he said, 'as long as the *Saturday Critic* is behind you, you need not heed any other criticism. Go home now and write your masterpiece!'

So that was when a typewriter was introduced into Lisle Street and for three weeks I was writing with great energy and enthusiasm. My room mates were anything but enthusiastic and Clifford (I think that was his name) told me that it caused his partners nothing but agitation. Underneath that skin of slush he was a true romantic. Today he would be rich enough to buy me a word processor to shut me up.

The next time I met Bill he was in Oxford Street near Tottenham Court Road and looked like a Colossus or at least like a film producer. He had four derelicts in his tow and he was directing them to greater and greater exertions. They were all, except Bill of course, carrying a massive great ornate door that was all that was left of Frascatti's, which had been demolished. I assumed that the door was meant for the gigantic offices of the *Saturday Critic*; I was astounded by his perspicacity. Indeed, no other door would do, that door could have been set up in an open field, anywhere, I could see that Bill was a master.

'When is the *Saturday Critic* coming out?' they asked me in the coffee house, day after day.

'Any moment now,' I said, 'we've got the door already.'

Then the word went round that we were all to meet at the *Critic's* printers in Tooley Street. This was an expedition indeed. In those days I never crossed the river, my knowledge of London is still hazy, having lived here for thirty odd years, but in those days I thought that South London was a different land, full of curious looking people, not entirely civilised or trustworthy. I was astounded to hear that William B. Hopkins also lived somewhere in Streatham and next time I met him I could see that he was tired and a little yellowing. I was glad that he was going to move to Notting Hill, it probably saved his life.

By the time I had found the *Critic* office in Tooley Street I was practically in tears for I have never seen a street more filthy in my life and, imagine my horror when on walking up four stone floors I found nobody there but a forlorn-looking ex-wrestler in the middle of this room of slanting print-holders on massive tables holding typefaces covered in decades of dust. Bill was nowhere to be found, but on his desk there was an attractive pile of manuscripts. I waited a couple of hours. There were no words spoken, nobody came or went. People talked about the end of the world, I have never been nearer to it. I don't know how I found my way back to the coffee house, but when I did the first person I met there was Michael Whyatt who had the most attractive laugh and such a beautiful mind. Wherever Michael walked there was Spring and he was such a beautiful mimic: Ah, how I wish he could cheer me up now as he did then:

'You big oaf,' he said, 'did nobody tell you, the *Saturday Critic* has been shelved.' I could have cried. 'No *Saturday Critic*, is there no God in Heaven?' I shouted.

'That idea has also been shelved,' said Michael and brought me a coffee.

The rest is history. There on the spur of the moment I decided to publish my own magazine, *Intimate Review*, which was to contain nothing else but poems by and articles about William B. Hopkins, probably the first fanzine in the world and, in production, just as shoddy as the ones to follow it. *Intimate Review* was to hold the torch and to deny that the world had come to an end, it was to fill in the gap until the real thing would appear, *Saturday Critic* in all its glory. Alas the world is still waiting.

To my horror *Intimate Review* became an instant success. No sooner was one issue published than people were asking when the next issue was coming out. I had no idea how to edit articles and was either too exhilerated or too proud to be willing to learn. The safest method in the circumstances was to print everything that was sent to me. Only once in the history of that periodical was it ever subedited, that was when an office boy acquaintance introduced me to another office boy, who was working for *The Manchester Guardian* and who, while I was asleep, went through the entire batch in my briefcase and put everything into the King's English. That young saboteur is now foreign correspondent of the year and, although I loved him very much, all my readers were astounded and several people cancelled their subscriptions. On top of that he read a twenty-page fan-letter which was addressed to me, replied and met the beautiful sycophant, without even telling *me*, who should have been the blessed recipient. Only after having married the young charmer and produced some delightful infants did he have the temerity to inform me of my bad luck.

I have hardly any issues of *Intimate Review* left and I suppose they

were eaten by worms at the British Museum for I cannot trace them in
their catalogue. I remember I had to send them five copies of each
issue as they were published, which amounted to a total loss of about
a hundred copies. Unless they are found the world has no access to the
pearls of wisdom of the following great minds who have contributed to
my magazine. Names that I recall include Michael Hastings, John
Comley, Raymond Matthews, Stuart Holroyd, Francziska Themerson,
Cressida Lindsay, Harold Jackson, John Glashan, John Pilgrim, Bernie
Kops, Tom Barling, and of course Colin Wilson.

It was again Bill who told me one afternoon in the coffee house: 'I
must bring you an article by a tremendous new writer. Never mind
what he says, just keep the front page open for him.' Bill had been
writing provocative articles for *Intimate Review* with titles like 'Is
Looseness Delightful: Or, Are Women To Be Taken Seriously?' or
'Should Parliament Be Abolished?' which called in a lot of correspondence in reply (the magazine was selling 12,000 copies an issue — a bit of
a mystery, for nobody I knew would be seen dead with it). When I
mentioned to him that I would like to meet Colin, he became very
evasive saying that Colin was very busy, screwing or sleeping on Hampstead Heath, that having finished a multi-million word novel he had left
it in a launderette, and such like, that I began to believe that Col was
a figment of William B. Hopkins's imagination and it was *he* who was
writing this article for the next issue under a pseudonym.

But then Jean Fulton, who was probably the only reliable person
in that crowd, told me that indeed there was such a person as Colin
Wilson and all the women were in love with him and that Colin spoke
on a World Syndicalist platform in Hyde Park and that she was rehearsing a play by him at the Garibaldi café and the play was called *The
Metal Flower-Blossom* and that I should hurry up with the next issue
which she might buy if Colin had an article printed in it.

Incidentally, the magazine never paid any of its contributors,
although I remember that Frank Norman, after his success with *Fings
Ain't Wot They Used T' Be*, claimed that his other great success was
having got seven guineas out of me. This caused me endless bother and
it was typical of my carelessness in financial affairs.

Like everyone else in that crowd I had one great affair after another
and although I had still not met Colin, he became a constant source of
irritation to me, for I was repeatedly told by one woman after another,
that not only was I an inferior writer to Colin, but a complete flop
after him in bed and that they all admired William B. Hopkins but were
overawed by his great charm and intellect.

I did enjoy writing and playing the little editor. I prided myself on being liberal minded and even encouraged hostile criticism in the journal. John Pilgrim (alias Malvolio), who was not only the most amusing jazz correspondent that I have ever read but was also to become a lifelong friend, even ventured into the field of literary criticism when in the pages of *my own magazine* he gave the worst review of my tossed-off master-piece *Super-Sozzled Nights: Or Htouy's Backward Youth* (published by Rubicon Press, again my creation, and financed by Joan Eccles, a very helpful friend I met at the Bal Musette in Oxford Street and whom I still see occasionally. Alas, Rubicon Press only published one other book, *Sincerity* by James Stuart, poems of love and amusement). My book was only reviewed in *The Catholic Herald* and *The Morning Advertiser.* Underneath my *bonhomie* I was nursing a wounded spirit. I thought I did my best and tried to be humorous.

The drawings for *Super-Sozzled Nights* by John Addyman were a delight. I met him at a Royal College of Art all-night do in South Kensington, a beautiful building full of truly beautiful people. I was in love with them all. John was a painter and so was his girl-friend and they invited me back to their flat and John kindly offered to illustrate my book. He turned up one day in Lisle Street, brought his pen, black ink and drawing paper with him and in one sitting drew all the exquisite illustrations, sitting there in the room with the sun streaming through the windows; a slim figure with such a sensitive face, shirt sleeves rolled up and drawing one masterpiece after another. It was enchanting but, unfortunately, as the book was ignored, so were the drawings.

So, the stateless little editor had a lot of pleasure out of that Bohem-ian crowd who, in Ironfoot Jack's phrase, 'does not mind working to live but he does not intend to live for work' (*Intimate Review*, vol. 2, no. 17).

In the same issue I find Colin's second article which he wrote for my magazine. The first appeared earlier that year, the third, about George Bernard Shaw, was printed in the final issue, his fourth article has never been published. I only possess a dummy copy, but fortunately the galley proofs remain.

Colin's article is on page 8, taking up the whole page. (Part of the editorial policy was that no advertisement appeared on editorial pages.) It was entitled (his own title), 'Where Are the Writers of the Future?' The first paragraph states the case:

If this article's title sounds as if I intend to ask you to send ten shillings 'without obligation' for our illustrated booklet, you are

mistaken. I am serious with the concentrated earnestness of the ego-
tist. You are being addressed by one of the writers of the future. My
question is prompted by the hope that I am being read by another.
Let me outline what I consider to be necessary characteristics of our
survival.

There is even an echo of Ironfoot Jack's aphorism in the article, but
of course Colin's priorities are on a higher plane: 'Should men live for
the sake of thinking or think for the sake of living?'

But what interests me most even thirty years later is that ominous
word 'survival'. What did he mean? Was the species of writers threaten-
ed by extinction even then? Certainly the situation has got worse since.

It is a pity about the unpublished article, it was bubbling with good
humour and good advice. He unashamedly enjoyed being lionized, he
always enjoyed going to parties and giving them, now he met 'all the
names in the school anthology of modern literature spread out in chairs,
or trying to support themselves against the piano, slopping champagne
out of their glasses!'

Colin thought everybody should follow him; he 'just happened to be
first through the hedge'. The rest of them should follow. There is more
need than ever before for a new school of writing—an attempt at a
commentary on modern life, an attempt to see a meaning in it. 'I am
only the first through the hedge, there may be many others—young
writers of my own age'. Then again: 'I do not hold the fashionable
heresy that some people can never do any decent work because they
are completely talentless . . . Talent and Will are one and the same (as
Novalis insisted). One needs nothing but self discipline and determination.

Everybody came to see Colin Wilson, he became one of the seven
wonders of the world. He had received good advice from all the famous
littérateurs of the day, even a letter from T.S. Eliot, a kind of Polonius
advising the young Hamlet to desist (but not so good as the original).
Colin quotes the letter adding characteristically: '(I quote without his
permission).'

The caravanserai got bigger and bigger. People who were beyond
one's horizon, now with Colin's outstanding success, appeared like dots
on a landscape, growing into recognisable shapes, that on approaching
did not flee but took on bodily contours. It was disconcerting for me
to find that the world was bigger than Soho and the population was
larger than could fit into the coffee house. I baulked at the mental
journey that was beckoning me and I stayed where I was. It could have

been asked, what was detaining me from fulfilling the deliberations
which was the task of the dedicated writer whose apprenticeship was
about to end. One aspect of authorship is, of course, the loneliness of
the monomaniac. Children are howling next door waiting for their supper, the telephone is off the hook, the newspapers are unread, the
writer at his desk is addressing an insubstantial audience, a quiet figure
surrounded by the debris of all our unlived yesterdays. 'The will was
there, but without feeling it becomes inoperative' (Wittgenstein).

Once you put your hand into that bag that holds the past, it comes
out trembling. The best you can do is to mention the events and names
like beads on a string. It is said that a good actor sees every member of
the audience. You may think that what you have seen was a great performance, but the actor knows better. It was a full house when it
started but as the curtain falls to rapturous applause, the actor sees that
some seats are empty, having been empty for the final act. I am sure
that Colin has his own list of missing people, like I have mine, and
some of the names coincide. I am only going to mention Charles
Belchier Russell, so that if there is an index at the end of this book,
his name will be included, for both Colin and Joy were very fond of him.
For many years he was adrift in Soho and then disappeared in Germany.
The beauty of being a writer, I now realise, is to write about the
people you are interested in, with whose lives and minds (like with
Colin's) one was intertwined in one's formative years. The beauty of
being famous is that you need not limit your interest and you can
begin to drop names that nobody has ever heard of. Until then you
write copy in which every paragraph tells: who did Michael Hastings
dance with at his homecoming party at Colin's flat? Why did Sandy
Wilson rush to relieve his stomach, pale and ashen faced?

If you substituted those two names for Bloggs, nobody would care.
But I am willing to bet that if you hide a good internationally recognisable story in a bumper book of private reminiscences it will be read
avidly by a multitude seeking after hidden treasure. 'I honestly believe
that any young writer who is totally unknown and unprinted today
could establish himself in one year from now, with no more than a
little discipline and determination,' wrote Colin in that same article.
Perhaps I should also have taken his advice, although many others have
benefited. Then I could enlarge upon things that interest me wholly and
fill my book with people unknown to you but with whom I still have
daily arguments, through an unrecoverable time, in the privacy of my
very own skull, where all those good and initially quite large people
fit and live amicably but who, in real life, would not lend each other

the ferrule off a shoe lace! (in John Glashan's phrase). And when I think
of all those towns and places crowded into that library that nobody
has ever seen, with all doors properly locked, but whose inhabitants,
at the slightest command, appear to continue the argument, the joke or
whatever, an uncontrollable fear begins to overwhelm me: that all is
going to *stay* locked within me, that any moment now I have reached
my allotted 3,000 words and I haven't yet said half the things I wanted
to say. For I wanted to divide my contribution (a) Colin and the epoch
(b) my own thoughts as a kind of 'birthday present' to him. I have been
delaying (b) until I have written myself in. This is how I always worked,
the machine is cold at the beginning, all my first pages are either
prissy, angry or unreadable. Gregory Corso once looked at a typescript
of mine and saw from where he was standing, about eight feet away,
that it was no good. He could see, even from that distance, that my
writing contained neat little paragraphs, scrubbings-out: the lesser brain
trying to control the major.

'How do *you* write?' I asked him.

'I write to the end of the line,' he told me, 'and then . . .'

'And then?' I asked him excitedly, thinking I was now going to be
given the key to the universe. But no:

'. . . and then I start a new line,' he said.

But, of course, Colin's great success meant that he had to leave the
slow ones behind. My only regret is that the first lap of the 'great surreal-
ist motor-cycle race' (James Molian's phrase and story from the *Intimate
Review*, 1955) has taken thirty years to run and I am only now in sight
of the leaders. If I tell you that Allen Ginsberg then was a thin young
man without the trace of a beard and that in a Paris café he jumped
over three tables just to take a bite at my left ear, it really brings back
the past with a vengeance.

'Whatever did you do that for?' I asked with all the bourgeois polite-
ness I could muster.

'Can't you see I'm hungry,' he replied.

I went into the Parisian night a changed man, only to return to the
Odéon Café with a pot of paint and a brush and write on that window
the now immortal slogan 'YANKS GO HOME!'

The night is getting longer and I can hardly remember where my bed
is, never mind what happened thirty years ago. This is the kind of excuse
that inexperienced writers come up with, for it is not very wise to give
in to the body's desire for rest, for the clockwork routine of eight hours
sleep, eight hours work and eight hours enjoyment of the socialist
utopia. So here is a thought that appeals to me and I hope will please

Colin. After each sleep we wake up to a changed world. As long as we stay awake the old world stays alive. We awake as the Babes in the Wood and the beans that we left for signs to find our way home are hard to trace in the long grass and fallen leaves.

Love and good company I scarcely mentioned, but it was as important to Colin as to myself and to all in that fabulous crowd. It is marvellous how many times we shared the same loves and lovers. This is where I get shy even to talk about it. The present age is the one to think about, for the young ones today look and behave so similarly. Perhaps they are our sons and daughters, for the love of freedom shines in their eyes. But my real companions are those inside my head and none of them will ever leave me.

There was a party in Hugh Schonfield's home down that dangerous slope by Highgate Underground station, to celebrate the forthcoming publication of *The Outsider*. What a lovely party that was, everybody so happy. Stuart was there and Bill and Laura and Carole-Anne; the drink was flowing. Colin was, of course, wearing his turtle neck sweater. In an armchair sat a big old man, with a large balding head and thick pebble glasses. Colin took me over to him and said:

'V.G., this is John Rety. He publishes *Intimate Review*, you should read my articles in it.'

Victor Gollancz said nothing, just sat quietly enjoying the hubbub, looking a bit like a character from a James Thurber drawing whose lead to his hearing aid is being cut by an enormous pair of scissors.

So this is where it stands. Colin became an overnight success, even a celebrity. And not many mornings after, we staggered into the dusty sunshine of Chepstow Villas in Notting Hill. He put his arm on my shoulder from a great height and leaned on me, with all of his twenty-five years, and said with a tremendous sight that could have split the very earth open (his husky voice was a most endearing feature): 'John, there is so little time and there is so much work to do.'

This came as a surprise to me, for I thought we were already doing too much. I could sense a parting of the ways.

7

A Literary Incident

ALLEN GINSBERG

Met Colin Wilson at Glastonbury 1978 for BBC Program—we'd not encountered before, though 'Outsider' and 'Beat' ethos had theoretically some sense of spiritual expansiveness and hermetic insight in common.

I'd hitch-hiked thru Glastonbury 1965 with US Poet Tom Clark—Now Mr Wilson conducted us through its historical mysteries. On parting companion Peter Orlovsky gave him a copy of his book *Clean Asshole Poems & Smiling Vegetable Songs* (City Lights, San Francisco, 1978).

Amazingly, a month later Peter received a long extraordinary letter of appreciation from Colin Wilson, who wrote (as I remember) that he hadn't enjoyed any American writing so much since he'd first read Kerouac decades before.

I was overjoyed because I do believe Orlovsky a natural genius. Though widely and fondly admired by many American Poets familiar with his eccentric spelling and wild verbal imagination and candour, and tho W.C. Williams had written 1959 that P. Orlovsky was the best Lyricist of our 'Beat' circle, I'd not encountered among English Intellectuals any such abandoned raw free perception and appreciation of Orlovsky's writing, eccentric as it is. It seemed a miracle of sympathetic imagination on Colin Wilson's part. How did he get that open mind?

8

Crisis and Revelation:
Some Personal Experiences

COLIN STANLEY

For some time now I feel as if I have been under a cloud. Nothing has gone my way. The whole world seems to have conspired to frustrate my ambitions. My physical health has suffered as a direct result and, in turn, has worsened my mental condition: a vicious circle.

In these times of mass unemployment, I suppose I should be grateful that I have a job at all but my position at Nottingham University library, it must be said, is undemanding, unrewarding, poorly paid and with no prospects for non-graduates such as myself. Numerous job applications to other authorities have met with little or no response and even my attempt to change my life by gaining a place on a three-year degree course at a local Polytechnic was foiled by the 'little men' at County Hall who refused me a grant on some technicality. Add to this the seemingly interminable delay in publication of my bibliography and guide to Colin Wilson's work—after several years of painstaking research and two time-consuming updates—and you may be able to appreciate my feelings of utter frustration. A claustrophobic feeling of stagnation has begun to hover around me and I have, at times, come close to understanding what it is that leads some people to 'give up on life' and allow themselves to slide into a state of despair, self-pity and even suicide. It would be so easy to just let go and wallow in misfortune.

But having written all that, whenever I feel like succumbing to this self-pity I am curiously unable to indulge myself whole-heartedly. This is because I know that it's all a charade. I know that I'm merely allowing myself to become dragged down and that *things really don't have to be that way*. Indeed, behind the veneer of self pity I feel a tremendous surge of optimism and well being which tells me that everything will be all right eventually. It's almost as if 'something up there' has got its eye on me and is determined to give me what I need when I need it rather than what I want when I want it. And this is something that I've felt for some time now. Looking back over the last fifteen years or so, I've been in similar situations before—in 1972, for instance, living alone in London, spending whole days in bed reading Sartre, Dostoevsky, Barbusse, Celine, etc. and becoming more and more depressed and alienated with every page. Then, when this reached a peak of desperation, suddenly two things happened almost simultaneously—I met my future wife and was introduced to the work of the philosopher Gurdjieff. My view of life was transformed almost overnight. Again, in 1976, I had reached another crisis when I had an experience which has been etched on my memory ever since. I recorded it in my diary, which was later published in a small booklet of poetry and ideas (*Objectively*, Paupers Press, 1983) as follows:

May 17th: an extraordinary experience. I concentrated on the flame of a candle for a few seconds and then closed my eyes. The image of the candle appeared before me and then became smaller until almost the size of a pin-head. Then it grew steadily larger and I felt a corresponding surge of energy and sheer joy within myself. In what must have been little more than a split-second this culminated in an almost blinding flash of light and the next thing I knew, I was lying on the floor with tears streaming down my face. Eventually I got to my feet and walked into the garden. It had been raining but the sky was now clear and the late evening sun was shining. Everything was fresh, clean and in its place. I felt as if I was positioned above myself, floating in the air, and yet able to feel my body precisely, as I had never felt it before. I was aware of every step I took, every movement around me and every sound carried on the air. I felt as if I was in total control not only of my body but my mind also. The seemingly ceaseless flow of unordered thoughts and impressions which, up until my experience, had clouded my perception had now ceased and I was, for the first time in my life, truly master of my own mind . . .

Although I was able to maintain this incredible state of consciousness for the rest of the evening, some four or five hours, I have never since been able to repeat the experience. Nevertheless, it is the memory of that extended glimpse of my potential as a human being that forms the basis of my underlying confidence in life. I do, from time to time, receive sudden glimpses of this potential, as if bubbles from this underlying pool of optimism spontaneously break free and float to the surface, bursting the veneer of triviality, momentarily allowing me to see life objectively. When I'm in good health, and everything is going well for me, I find I can induce these experiences at will by relaxing and allowing my mind to 'stretch out'[1] or just simply by means of a short period of meditation. (The connection here with Abraham Maslow's and Colin Wilson's ideas relating to 'peak experiences' will be apparent to students of their work.) But they are only frustratingly fleeting glimpses and when I'm in bad health I find the small amount of effort and discipline necessary to achieve this, an almost insurmountable obstacle. It's as if Colin Wilson's 'mind parasites' were a physical reality, desperately trying to stop me from experiencing the truth about myself and life.

But why am I diverted? Why should this obviously positive desire to evolve be distracted? Gurdjieff's 'law of octaves'[2] provides a clue into the mechanics of this. We often forget that, as human beings, we are part of Nature and one of Nature's basic laws is that all things eventually lose momentum, run down, die and are reborn. In short: everything proceeds in cycles, one situation giving way, in time, to its direct opposite. Sometimes this happens so imperceptibly that we fail to realise the change until we receive a sudden shock which makes us stop and think, 'What the hell am I doing with my life?' or something similar. The important thing, said Gurdjieff, is to learn to *introduce* these shocks *at the right time* in order to provide the necessary impetus to keep the evolutionary drive proceeding correctly. This, however, requires both insight and effort on a scale that most of us would consider impossible. So, in order to raise our consciousness it appears we must learn to *observe* and *act appropriately* but we *cannot* observe and act appropriately without *first of all* raising our consciousness—clearly there is a dilemma here. Gurdjieff attacks the problem from the bottom, so to speak, by teaching his pupils the discipline of self observation. Other philosophical systems, incorporating certain forms of meditation, concentrate on the direct Enlightenment of the individual, asserting that this will automatically *produce* 'right action'. It is up to the individual to decide which method suits him or her best. I favour the latter. Gurdjieff would no doubt insist that the personal experiences or 'shocks' I have described in the first half of this essay happened purely by accident. I, however, prefer to think they arose at precisely the right time and indicate an 'unconscious knowledge' resulting directly from my *desire to evolve*. For what better time to introduce a 'shock' of this kind than after a period of depression thus producing, as it were, an intense sigh of relief and feeling of tranquility. Sidney Campion quoted Colin Wilson as having said: ' . . . vastations[3] often seem to occur on the eve of success . . .'[4] This, too, has been my experience. And so, if things run true to form, any time now I am due for another great revelation, another 'shock' which will, once again, extricate me from this claustrophobic rut and reveal a new way forward. I'll try to keep you informed.

NOTES

1. Colin Wilson's 'pen-trick' as described in *Access to Inner Worlds* (Rider, 1983),

pages 37-8 can be useful here as an artificial stimulus if one is deemed necessary.

2. For those who wish to follow this up, read P.D. Ouspensky, *In Search of the Miraculous* (Routledge and Kegan Paul, 1950), pp. 124-37.

3. Terrifying feelings of absurdity – 'nausea'.

4. Campion, Sidney: *The World of Colin Wilson* (Frederick Muller, 1962), p. 125.

9

Floreat Colin Wilson

BROCARD SEWELL

In the summer of 1960, when I was on a visit to Launceston, my home town, my fellow-townsman Charles Causley asked me if I would like to meet Colin Wilson. His name was then considered a 'controversial' one, for echoes of the excitement aroused by *The Outsider* and *Religion and the Rebel* were still in the air. Causley told me that Wilson was living near Mevagissey, and that he would be visiting him in the next day or two and I was welcome to come along. Always ready to visit or revisit Cornish scenes, I was glad to accept the invitation. At that time Colin and Joy were living at Old Walls, a picturesque and somewhat 'Hebridean' property at Bodruggan, a mile or two inland from Mevagissey; a little later they removed to a more commodious if less romantic residence at Gorran Haven. They have been there ever since, and I should think are likely to remain there since it seems inconceivable that they could ever cope with the business of shifting the thousands and thousands of books that line every room in their house, or nearly so, and overflow into the chalet-annexe in the garden. Add to these Colin's huge musical library of records and cassettes and you have all the conditions for a more than monastic stability.

So I have now known Colin for twenty-five years. That in itself seems to me worthy of some small private celebration. Much more celebratory, however, is the double occasion of his 55th birthday and the 30th anniversary of *The Outsider*, and I am particularly grateful to Colin Stanley for inviting me to make some small contribution to this *festschrift* to mark these events. Colin Wilson has been so generous in giving time and effort to helping and promoting other writers that on this special occasion a hearty vote of thanks to him must clearly be the order of the day. This book is the symbol of that vote of thanks. Mr Stanley is its proposer, and the contributors its supporters. Needless to say, it is carried with acclamation, *nem. con.* The contributors, of course, represent and speak for a multitude of other wellwishers.

To reminisce, as the elderly are fond of doing: in 1960 I was editing *The Aylesford Review*, a literary quarterly that ran from 1955 to 1968, pursuing a harassed existence with only four hundred subscribers, no advertisement revenue, no subsidy, and an annual financial loss. The magazine attracted a number of distinguished contributors, who declined to take any fee for their articles, but our two outstanding supporters

were Colin Wilson and Henry Williamson. Colin's first contribution, in
1960, soon after I had met him, was an article on the Finnish writer
Alexis Kivi, of whom very few people in England had then heard, so
that his insistence that Kivi's novel *Seven Brothers* 'stands with *Moby
Dick* and *War and Peace* among the world's greatest novels' was a bold
challenge.

From 1955 until its demise thirteen years later *The Aylesford Review*
consistently championed the cause of Henry Williamson, whose un-
popular political sympathies had lessened his standing as a writer,
diminished his sales, and caused his new books, the opening volumes
of his masterpiece, *A Chronicle of Ancient Sunlight*, to be either
ignored or reviewed dismissively. The articles on Williamson by George
D. Painter, Malcolm Elwin, Middleton Murry, and other writers were
highly, even enthusiastically appreciative of his genius, so that Colin
Wilson did us a good turn in 1961 when he sent us an article on
Williamson in which appreciation and generous appreciation, was
tempered by certain reserves. For instance: 'The chief problem in assessing Williamson's achievement is that he is not a profound thinker;
consequently, his ideas cannot be neatly isolated and discussed separately.' And: 'Comparison with Proust . . . makes one aware of a factor
that has never been widely noticed – the lack of style in Williamson. He
can write superbly, as in *Tarka*, but . . . he is too inclined to be careless
and colloquial; and just occasionally his stylistic offences are agonising
and embarrassing.'

Naturally, this did not go down too well with Henry. He and Colin
knew one another, of course. Gorran Haven is not so far from Ox's Cross
(in North Devon), and there were occasional meetings in the BBC's
Bristol studios and at the annual reunions of the West Country Writers'
Association. Henry was a sensitive man; some might say touchy. So it
is significant that in the turmoil and upset of the collapse of his second
marriage it was to Colin and Joy Wilson that he immediately turned for
friendship and support.

On the occasion of this joint fifty-fifth and thirtieth anniversary,
Joy Wilson must not be omitted from the grateful flow of congratulation.
She is herself an excellent writer, and I think it is a very great pity that
she has published so little. In 1964 a very perceptive essay by her,
'T.F. Powys: "The Moods of God"', appeared in *Theodore: Essays on
T.F. Powys*, a symposium published by St Albert's Press. In this essay
she singled out for especial praise Powys's less well known novel *Mark
Only*. Her verdict on this writer is: 'No one could claim that Powys's
picture of rural life is closely realistic. Dodder and Madder and Folly

Down are not villages of the present day but of some indefinable time, when life is cruder, and closer to the earth. The villagers are close to allegorical figures; characters and motives are sometimes simplified to show more clearly Powys's vision of the changing pattern of human life coloured by the all-pervading "moods of God".'

There is also, I believe, the typescript, which Joy modestly says she cannot find, of an essay on William Beckford, a man whom one is surprised not to find in her husband's book *The Outsider*. This essay cannot fail to be of interest, so I hope that she will perhaps ask St Anthony — 'My saint,' as Beckford called him — to help her find it. But now, recently published, we have from her a short study in Cornish history or folklore, 'Cruel Coppinger: Who was He?' in *Westcountry Mysteries*, a symposium with an introduction by Colin Wilson (Bossiney Books, 1985) and 'Around St Austell Bay' from the same publisher (1986).

Now that the children, Sally, Damon and Rowan, are all, or nearly all grown up, I hope that Joy will find more time for writing, especially as she has now been for many years a keen student of Cornish history, tradition and archaeology.

In the introduction which Colin in 1968 invited me to contribute to the original version of his since revised 'preliminary' autobiography, *Voyage to a Beginning* (Cecil Woolf Publishers, 1968, reissued 1987). I said that 'If genius lies in the prosecution of great designs through unremitting hard work and refusal to admit defeat, then Colin Wilson has the basic qualities of genius. Perhaps also the genius is the man who never accepts boredom and unfulfilment.' It is a permanent puzzle to me how Colin has managed to write so many books — a totally time-consuming and exhausting occupation — and yet to have *read* so many. He is, I think, the widest-read person I know; and what he reads he retains. I cannot claim — and a Carmelite friar may perhaps be excused for saying this — to have read *all* his books, though I have certainly read every one that he has been so kind as to give me. Glancing through some numbers of *The Aylesford Review* I notice that in the summer number of 1966 I contributed a distinctly critical review of his *Introduction to the New Existentialism*, which concludes, however, by saying that 'Mr Wilson has written a lively, provocative and readable introduction to the new existentialism, and he should now go on to write a major exposition of the theme he now adumbrates.' Since then he has become, I think one can say, the nation's educator-in-chief: the successor in this role to H.G. Wells. He has not yet written *A New Outline of History*, but I feel confident that he will. (He has perhaps given us a hint of this in his recent *A Criminal History of Mankind*, a fine survey of human wickedness.) And he is likely to make a better job of it than Wells did of his *Outline*, which received a fearful battering from Hilaire Belloc in his *A Companion to Mr Wells's 'Outline of History'*. The fact is, Wells, a marvellous writer at his best, was singularly lacking in metaphysical sense, something in which Wilson has the advantage of him. Perhaps his most effective 'educational' book so far is *Starseekers*, a study in the history of astronomy and the astronomers.

For myself, I find that I can still read *The Outsider* and *Religion and the Rebel* with pleasure and profit, though they are so clotted with ideas and information that they are perhaps best taken rather slowly. But I sometimes wonder why it should be that Colin seems to have so little interest in and time for my own favourite outsiders: among them Baron Corvo, Montague Summers and John Gray. Reading again the other day the essay on Newman in *Religion and the Rebel* I was astonished to find the author saying that Newman was not an Outsider (in the sense of being 'a stranger in society'). This of John Henry Newman, to whom the visible world and all within it seemed almost as a dream, the priest who became a visible stranger in the church of his baptism and ordination, and left it for a church in which his gifts were not understood, and his offers of service despised: at least until the day when, in old age, he accepted the Red Hat. Even then he remained something of an outsider, seeking a dispensation from the duty of residence in Rome, remaining hidden away in the Birmingham Oratory, and preferring to stay, on his occasional visits to London, with the Dean of St Paul's rather than with his brother in the Sacred College, the Cardinal Archbishop of Westminster. Colin Wilson's view of Newman seems to me a real bizarrerie; but this does nothing to lessen the fascination of his essay. Always, he is a mentally stimulating and thought-provoking writer.

As I sit, a septuagenarian now, at my desk in my friar's cell, and contemplate the books ranged on the shelves before me—among them the works of Arthur Machen, Osbert Sitwell, Nancy Mitford, Virginia Woolf, Elizabeth Jane Howard, F.M. Montgomery and A.N. Wilson, as well as those of Samuel Johnson, William Beckford and R.S. Surtees—I sometimes wonder if the time has not come when I should dispose of all these works, leaving on my shelves, apart from the Sacred Scriptures and a few devotional works, only the greatest of the 'greats': Vergil, Dante, Shakespeare, Milton and Goethe. It may well come to that; but if it does I shall take care to exempt from the general edict of expulsion one or two of the works of Colin Wilson; possibly *Religion and the Rebel* or *The War Against Sleep*, *Voyage to a Beginning* and

Starseekers; but I hope I may live long enough to read his definitive autobiography, or at least the first of its successive volumes, to whose publication all his friends must now look forward.

In the meantime, *Floreat Colin Wilson. Ad multos annos!*

10

A Tribute to Colin Wilson

RENATE RASP

'The decision as to where to draw the line defining the subject one wishes to portray, must be a matter for the individual.' This teaching is given by the Academy of Fine Arts, to all students taking up painting, in their first term. The same applies to the personality within the picture which calls itself human society; man does not stop at the end of his hand or his right foot. He is smaller or larger than that. He comprises many facets, including not least those who portray their closest environment. Each paints his own picture – with a cigaratte if he has no brush – that is to say, each creates his own world, his own surroundings, a star searching for the sun. But when we reach the core of this fruit, then we find it divisible into four, after the example of Goethe's *Elective Affinities*. One of Colin Wilson's characteristics certainly finds a German echo. Were I to give a form to this characteristic then I would call it 'innovatory'. Did not Bill Hopkins say: 'A novel must be like an aircraft – it must fly.'

My English publisher, Marion Boyars, gave me Colin Wilson's address fourteen years ago, in London. 'You want to settle in Cornwall,' she said, 'you will need contacts there. Colin Wilson will help you.'

I met him for the first time in The Ship, a pub in Pentewan, which he has frequented regularly for twenty years. He had returned from a lecture tour and was met there by his friends. But what confused me at first was that behind the doors of the 'local', I found not just the author of *The Outsider*, but a cultural centre too.

It was a gateway to London, a road to Paris, a meeting place for people from around the world, a strange book which wrote itself. I found a formative world. People came together here to exchange ideas, to seek inspiration.

'What is new in this book? What have I not heard before?'

Colin Wilson teaches one to see with fresh eyes, to forget school learning, to look into the future. In *The Craft of the Novel*, he describes how a book is written on this basis. Generously, he allows his friends to take part in his intellectual expeditions, which lead to the origins of mankind.

One of the first evenings I spent with him and his wife will always remain in my memory. At that time, my English was not good enough for any long conversation. Colin Wilson had the idea of giving me a dictionary of forensic pathology, which was in German. He was then working on his book *The Occult*. Sorcerers came and went. The Germany of the Sixties had taught me to be sceptical of what could not be understood. I wanted to 'see' what could not be seen. The magic of his personality did not escape me then, although at that time I would have used a different word.

At that time, fourteen years ago, Colin Wilson's house 'Tetherdown', in Gorran Haven, was for me the only spot on a blank map representing Cornwall, to which I was drawn to realise a dream, to find a second destiny. 'The good life,' people say today. But then I was 'blind', a person who does something without noticing what it is. My blindness led me without question into another world. The library in Colin Wilson's home became the tiles of a Roman house. I discovered the 'Roman Empire' in his work.

I fantasised. My reality lay in the need to build up a life in England. Colin Wilson's *The Outsider* and *Schoolgirl Murder Case* formed the foundations of my English library. Since then, I have provided whole shelves for Colin Wilson's work. It seems that there is no intellectual territory which the author has not explored. The rows of books remind me of my visit to New York in 1980, when the Museum of Modern Art was cleared to make room for a Picasso exhibition.

'What do you actually do in Newquay all day?' he asked me when I next saw him in The Ship at Pentewan. Again it was Saturday and his friends had gathered together from Fowey and St Austell. It was like a party, as if there was something to celebrate. 'What do you do in Newquay?'

'I am trying, with my friend Jane, to make headway with Shakespeare.'

'You should acquaint your friend Jane with Goethe.'

I hesitated with my reply. Goethe himself considered Shakespeare as *his* source. I had come to England to find the sources. I wanted to forget Germany, to devote myself wholly to the new world, in order to let Shakespearean figures come into being around me. Colin Wilson reminded me of my roots.

'I feel myself related to Goethe,' he said, 'two hearts beat in my breast — a part of me is German.'

But Colin Wilson's circle, as it meets once a week, is not just a cultural centre where one can talk of Kleist; it is also the sorcerer's kitchen, the witches' cauldron, in which the work is brewed. In his books, situations are repeated in other forms. Take a basic feature of human society: strife. It may occur that Colin Wilson thinks: 'I need a dispute,' and somehow he finds it possible to change two men, within the circle of friends, into fighting cocks. It is hard to tell—is it in play or for real? I myself like to think it is feigned. Conflict is to be found in his work, in particular the preface to his *Encyclopaedia*. He quotes Raskolnikov:

> '...someone condemned to death says, or thinks an hour before his death, that if he had to live on a high rock, on such a narrow ledge that he'd only have room to stand, and the ocean, everlasting darkness, everlasting solitude, everlasting tempest around him, if he had to remain standing on a square yard of space all his life, a thousand years, eternity, it were better to live so than die at once.' It is precisely this knowledge of the value of life that the murderer lacks. But we all lack it to some extent. Only a few saints and mystics break through the hedge of daily trivialities to some partial awareness of the reality. Murder is a manifestation of the universal failure of values. As such, its study has for the existentialist the same kind of message that the lives of saints have for the devout Christian. (*Encyclopaedia of Murder*, Pan Books, rpt. 1984, p. 24)

Further on, he says:

> There is nothing, short of a conscious assessment of the value of human life, and a conscious effort to increase its intensity, that could make any difference to our present state. And this is the reason that I attach such importance to existentialism. (op. cit., p. 43)

'In the other preface, his co-author Patricia Pitman writes exactly the opposite,' said a German friend who visited me and to whom I gave Colin's books to read:

> I believe that we are fascinated by murderers not because they are so like the rest of us but because they are so utterly different. I believe that most people are born with an instinct against cold-blooded killing and that murderers lack this instinct. (op. cit., p. 50)

'But that is precisely the Cain and Abel situation which leads to murder,' I replied. 'It was a "creative act" of Colin Wilson to choose for this book a co-author who took quite a different view.' It does not matter that, at another point in his preface, Colin Wilson also takes the part of Abel: 'Criminality is essentially a socially immature attitude.' (op. cit., p. 36)

Perhaps too, Cain and Abel are to be regarded as one person, with Abel being murdered in the metaphorical sense, as not capable of surviving: a symbol of the pure, the unsullied, whose existence arouses aggression: the good conscience.

Every visit to Colin Wilson provides stimulation: his mind works quickly. It was one day in Autumn, shortly before my departure for Germany, where I return for half the year. We talked over Susan Sontag's book about the fight against cancer, in which she says that everyone has a house in the world of illness. Suddenly Colin said, urgently: 'Genius is trying to live as long as ever you can.'

In one sentence he conjures up the ghost, the fear of being unable to complete a work, of having to leave behind something unfinished, as Flaubert, the perfectionist, had to leave his last novel, *Bouvard et Pecuchet*. In his last letters he speaks of it with painful sorrow.

We went on to talk about my father, the actor Fritz Rasp. Colin had just seen a photograph of him as the beggar-king in G.W. Pabst's film of *The Threepenny Opera*. 'Why don't you write a book about it?' he said.

Colin Wilson reads many books and helps many writers. From all parts of Cornwall, young authors come to The Ship at Pentewan.'I will write an introduction for you. I will speak to my publisher.'

I hear it from him often, see grateful eyes, and well recall my own first attempts. He takes seriously everyone who is attempting to get closer to that taskmistress, Literature. Always he gives encouragement: 'Anyone can write,' I often hear. 'There's a book in everybody.' The most brilliant pieces of his work certainly include introductions to books, such as Valeri Briussov's *The Fiery Angel* (N. Spearman, 1975). He has a masterly understanding of how to view the personality of the other writer from his own angle. It is always a piece of himself; in the other writer, he finds a link with his own work, which stands on firm ground. He likes to follow the fantasies of others: 'You are a German romantic,' he once said to me, when I spoke of the four people that I believe I see in him. They lead me back to the starting-point of this tribute and open the door into the world of intellectual Russia before 1918. As a child, under Russian occupation, I have personal experience of Russian characteristics, such as generosity extending even to self-sacrifice.

'I am giving you the address of Bill Hopkins,' he said, before my return to Germany in 1975. 'He is my right-hand man in London.' I was to receive many more addresses, to get to know many of his friends. John Melling, who is more English than the English themselves.

David Ellis, who would be a gifted actor, if he had the desire to go on
the stage. A talent attracts other talents. In all his friends one can find
a little of Colin Wilson and likewise, perhaps, something of them in him.

He is an industrious writer, but will always find time for a conversation. When one enters 'Tetherdown', he conveys the feeling of living
outside time. My father, who learned magic for a Fritz Lang film, used
to say: 'Conjuring consists of tricks.' He never revealed the tricks.
Perhaps one of Colin Wilson's tricks is that he produces his own view
of life, a view of exceptional quality. In the middle of the countryside,
he has provided himself, like a Roman garrison, with cultural stimulation, and set up a base from which his works go out to all the
world.

My speech draws towards its close. Scarcely anyone understands how
to celebrate like Colin Wilson. Now I hope that he has not been bored,
while I have once again invited to this, my celebration, those whom he
so generously introduced to me. Without 'Tetherdown', without his
library where I found German books, without his friends, my 'English
adventure'—would certainly have turned out differently. I have taken
all our meetings as 'feast days'. There was the wine, a Mosel, from 1935,
the year of my birth, which he opened at one of my farewell visits.
There was the record of *The Threepenny Opera* which he put on, and
which I listened to in his house just as I had heard it as a child. Perhaps
it was the country air. The 'variety of faces' does not cease for those
who find themselves in Colin Wilson's company for a person changes in
his presence, develops abilities he would not otherwise have. The desire
to celebrate this gift has drawn me to those friends who here congratulate him on his existence. And if I now raise my hand, and fill my
glass with my own existence, then it is to toast him back over the years,
to wish that he tries, ' . . . to remain alive, as long as ever he can.'

Genius needs a form to express itself, and Colin Wilson has given it
this form. When he speaks of his work as 'the best', then it is to be
understood in this spirit. Certainly a great deal more could be said of
him and his circle, which is constantly expanding, growing, changing.
Thus everyone who came into contact with him can say he has been
able to look into a world which, without him, would have remained
closed. And when I, as a traveller between worlds, think of Cornwall
during the Munich winter, one name is always included in my thoughts:
Colin Wilson.

Birthdays always have to do with dying, too. They are days on which
one thinks back to one's mother, one's childhood, one's own children.
One thinks of the parting. Colin Wilson can look back on a rich life,

which is reflected in his work. Being used, as a German, to attributing to Goethe's life the same value as his work, it is no surprise to find the high points of Colin Wilson's life in his work. The time after *The Outsider*, his flight from the Press to find quiet for his work in Cornwall, has become 'history'. The fate of the young author, who achieved world fame with one book and must maintain his 'promise' is a book of its own. He has often spoken of it. 'Some are smashed to pieces, when this wave rolls towards them,' he once said during a lecture in Falmouth, 'but I thought I must stick it out.'

Colin Wilson speaks freely, he says just what comes into his head, lets himself be inspired by his audience. The author of *Werther* once had a similar fate: to overcome youthful fame, to pass from the *Sturm und Drang* phase to the classical, the romantic period. Colin Wilson had to free himself from the arms of the 'angry young men'. This he did gracefully.

Thus, in the eyes of a foreigner, his work is at the same time a piece of English literary history. 'The grand old man of English literature,' I recently heard from the mouth of a twenty-year-old. Now still too young for an 'old man', he has geared everything towards getting inside the part of this great aged figure. What was it I read in one of the many Goethe biographies: ' . . . a fine old man waited for him.'

After this picture, the brush in my hand changes into a cigarette. The figures turn to smoke. The feast is over. Friends, it is time to break up, to open the windows. But those who were there will pass it on. For a brief period I was able to be his companion.

11

Colin Wilson

JUNE O'SHEA

It has been twelve years since the first of many letters from Colin arrived amongst my usual heavy load of mail from university libraries. The excitement of receiving a letter from *the* Colin Wilson, my favourite living author, immediately turned to fear, panic and confusion. Feelings of awe and wonder were one thing; the realisation that I would be obliged to respond was another. For someone whose life is devoted to books, I must have resembled a nervous and awkward adolescent girl receiving her first love letter. At first, I decided to avoid that anxiety by writing to the customer in England who had taken it upon herself to get in touch with Colin. She had been purchasing crimonology books from me for some time, and we had become quite friendly. She had once asked me who my favourite living author was, and I had replied, 'Funny you should ask. It's one of your countrymen whom I admire the most, Colin Wilson.' And without telling me, she had written to Colin that there was a second-hand bookseller in the States specialising in crimonology who greatly admired his writing. I asked her what I should do, and she responded immediately, urging me to reply to his letter.

In his letter, Colin asked about several criminology titles. I replied with a thank you note and a catalogue. Not only did I send him books he requested, but in my search for titles, I would come across many others which I thought would interest him and send those along as well. I sent him the books he wanted as well as those I chose myself never intending to be reimbursed. I always had mixed feelings accepting money from him since I considered our dealings not only a pleasure but an honour, but he always insisted upon complete reimbursement. After sending that first letter, I began clipping out newspaper articles concerning bizarre criminal cases which I thought would interest him and perhaps be useful.

I never waited for a letter before responding, and our letters often crossed. But from our exchange of books and clippings grew a correspondence where we would write at least one letter a month, and I guess we've written each other more than a hundred. After such a long period of time, one must wonder if our correspondence ever became personal. Although our letters dealt mainly with business— book titles and clippings—they were always very cordial, but our relationship rarely went beyond books. We talked somewhat about our families, but I don't have any gossip. Colin once shared his frustration over the publication of the twenty-volume work on crime and punishment. He contributed several articles and was surprised to find, upon publication, that the editor had taken it upon himself to alter Colin's writing without asking permission. Colin hardly recognised it himself! However, we mainly discussed the crimes in the clippings, him asking my opinion, and sometimes we'd disagree. All in all, I felt I learned something.

Although I often sold Colin's works to my clients, I had only a limited number of his books in my personal collection. Our correspondence encouraged me to build up my collection, and finding his works for my personal library became a sort of vocation. Since he's such a prolific writer, there were certain titles I couldn't find or did not know existed. Besides writing books, Colin has also contributed to numerous periodicals on many subjects; however, Colin himself did not remember everything he wrote. I asked him for titles which were out of print and difficult to find, and he sometimes sent me additional books and eventually began sending me published and unpublished manuscripts for my opinion and as an addition to my collection. It took years to enlarge my Colin Wilson collection, but it is considered to be one of the most complete collections in the United States (although a truly complete one is impossible). My collection of Colin's works is currently being housed at the University of California at Riverside library.

One day I received a letter asking permission to dedicate to me a forthcoming science fiction novel, *The Space Vampires*, as thanks for my help to him. I was taken aback. Imagine, asking permission to dedicate a book to me. I experienced that same feeling as when I received my first letter from him which, at the time, I felt could never be surpassed. Well, I was wrong. This time I will go as far as to say that the euphoria experienced when *The Space Vampires* finally came out will never be matched. (Now I'm waiting for the movie, 'Lifeforce', which is being put out by a major movie company at a cost of over twenty million dollars.) I consider this the highlight of my career as a bookseller and collector.

As the years passed, Colin invited me several times to his home in Cornwall, and each time I politely refused. I hate to admit it, but I never wanted to meet him. Not only was I intimidated, but I feared such a meeting would somehow be demystifying. He seemed very nice, and I should never have felt that way.

Despite all the theories which influence the relationship between author, text and reader, I firmly believe that the text itself remains the meeting ground between author and reader. The author creates a product, his book, and then it is up to the reader to recreate the work for himself. As a bookseller, I am part of this process; I help to make such a meeting possible. However, it is a privilege to go one step further, to bypass the produst and establish some sort of *rapport* with the author. I have been this fortunate with Colin Wilson.

12

Colin Wilson

A.E. VAN VOGT

A non-fiction book by Colin Wilson has to be seen—meaning, read—to be believed.

The reader quickly becomes aware that here is a book that is the result of research on a level that one would normally expect from a university professor after a lifetime of teaching his speciality—but there's a difference. A Colin Wilson equivalent of a textbook is an exciting, intellectual-emotional experience, alive with high-level ideas, many of them originals by the author. And, although he wrote a number of such masterpieces, it is no exaggeration to report that his most famous work in this philosophical area continues to be *The Outsider*.

The meaning of the ideas that go with this title turns out to be something like: Just because you're different from the crowd doesn't imply something negative. It's all right to be different.

It is possible that a huge percentage of the individuals who, somehow, didn't 'fit in' received the equivalent of a psychoanalytic recovery of their self-esteem as that thought penetrated.

Was it a permanent 'cure' for those individuals who needed something like that? No statistics are available. But it has been my observation that most intelligent people pass through a period in their development where they can use a helping mind or a helping idea or a helping thought; and then they accept themselves as mature, capable—and better than normal.

It is difficult to establish for certain that an analysis of the universe by a philosopher is necessary. The average individual comes to awareness somewhere in his or her 'teens; it is necessary to prepare oneself, in the case of the boy, to make a living; and a girl realises that she is a potential child-bearer and should do practical things that take account of that reality. Millions of individuals seem to get by on that level of logic. The rest of us, the one per cent. or maybe the one-hundredth of one per cent., long ago read the writings of Plato and, since then, other great thinkers, and by that route felt better about the enigma of existence. That enigma can probably be stated as follows: the universe cannot possibly exist; there is no explanation for it. Yet here it is all around us. There are multi-millions who accept without argument that God made the whole place; which, of course, promptly brings us to the question: then who made God?

Those who believe at the level of simple acceptance, and those who seek answers, seem to live about equally long lives. They're born, they grow up, they grow older, they die.

But, still, we so-called intellectuals feel better after reading philosophical books, like those written by Colin Wilson. And, of course, that brings us to a special reality about writers of books. Every published writer has a communication line to the world so fabulous that if he or she were ever able to evaluate the implications—what?

One aspect: Just think, Colin Wilson lives in England, and I have lived in western United States since 1944. I don't know when he started to read my stories, but, since he's much younger than me, mine were around long before his. Yet by the time he visited the Los Angeles area in 1965 I had read his famous book, *The Outsider*, which was an instant best seller and has been read by just about every intellectual in the world.

He was in the US to give talks at universities. We got in touch. I contacted an SF group where someone was invited to deliver a speech one evening a month—free. And Colin was kind enough to come over and talk to us—free. Since he had other college lectures to deliver, he quickly departed. But our relationship never sank to zero. Back in the early sixties, I wrote a non-science fiction novel entitled *The Violent Man*. As a consequence Colin and I developed a sort of semi-mutual admiration society; and in the early 1980s when he was writing his history of crime he wrote asking me if I had any additional material on the subject.

I did. Because back in the days when I was 'studying' this type of male, I wrote half-a-dozen radio talks on aspects of this type—sometimes called macho—and a local radio station KPFK allowed me to give the talks in half-hour segments over their facility. (KPFK is the educational station in the LA area—it has no advertising and survives apparently by donations from well-wishers.)

Briefly, what I observed was a person I had begun to notice: the individual who has a . . . need to be right. When you feel 'right' in this fashion you can commit all the necessary in relation to what you feel right about. In explaining the 'criminals' Colin used aspects of my Mr Right 'violent male' hypothesis.

One would think that that would complete the association, aside from occasional correspondence or chance meetings, considering the distance that separates us in terms of geography. But, instead, something has come up in the last six months or so because—as most of Colin's readers know, and as the whole world is now finding out, he eventually wrote a novel entitled *The Space Vampires*—which Cannon Films has released under the title 'Life Force'. The novel (and the film, of course) features the author's variation on the recurring theme of Dracula.

Well, back in 1942, I wrote *my* variation on this theme — a long novelette entitled *Asylum*. This, together with a couple of sequels, eventually became one of my fix-up novels, *More than Superhuman*. Because of this background, at Colin's request, we are tentatively collaborating on a sequel to his book, to be entitled *The Return of the Space Vampires*. I say 'tentatively' because I am not completely convinced that I can be useful to him for such a project.

What I hope I have established in the foregoing is that Colin Wilson is in motion, mentally. His interest in philosophy, in the occult — too big a subject for me to deal with in a short article — and his mastery of the writing art in both its non-fiction and fiction forms, tell us that here is a man who will be remembered for a long time in the history of literature.

But no question: *The Outsider* was, and is, his greatest work.

13

Colin Wilson, the Best of Friends

DANIEL FARSON

Writers are not the nicest of people, they can't afford to be. Suffering from the tyranny of publishers, and their incompetence which is even worse, the persecution complex that so many writers suffer from is partly justified. Consequently, the writer lives in a state of resentment, against his agent, his publisher, and the literary critics, all of whom ignore his true worth. Far from fellow-feeling with other martyrs of this most uneasy and solitary profession, the writer usually lives in a state of bitter rivalry. He is at his happiest when he reads a damning review of a book by a close friend.

In all of this, Colin Wilson is the exception. I know of no writer so generous in his Forewords, or so encouraging to those who badly need encouragement. Though he is one of the busiest writers in Britain, he never fails in his support of other writers.

I met Colin for the first time in David Archer's bookshop, when Archer handed him the London *Evening News* and we read the first review of *The Outsider*. The next day, Sunday, came the historic acclamation from Toynbee and Connolly. By Monday, Colin was famous. That was a long time ago but he has changed remarkably little, which is a sign of true genius. He has been consistent to himself, and especially to his friends.

A dedicated, hard-working writer he deserves the success he enjoys, and honours our profession. And remains the best of friends.

14

Coming in from the Outside

DANIEL FARSON

Few writers begrudge Colin Wilson his success. They recognise the per-
severance which has kept him going; the hard slog since that too-brilliant
a beginning in 1956, which ended in a literary lynching less than two
years later. On Saturday, 26 May 1956 he was unknown. Next day
critic Cyril Connolly praised *The Outsider* as 'one of the most remarkable first books I have read for a long time', while Philip Toynbee
exclaimed, 'What makes it truly astounding is that its alarmingly well-
read author is only 24'.

On Monday, Colin Wilson found that he was famous, with all the
prizes and punishments involved. He was manna to the media: son of a
shoe-maker in Leicester, he had left school at 16 to bicycle to London,
working in the British Museum library by day, sleeping rough on Hampstead Heath at night. The perennial polonecked sweater was a trademark.
The room he moved into in Notting Hill, with an Einstein equation
scribbled on the wall, a pin-up of Nietzsche above a gas ring surrounded
by unwashed plates and chocolate biscuits, all became familiar.

Time magazine hailed *The Outsider* as an 'intellectual thriller', and
Life recreated the impoverished past, photographing him in his sleeping
bag under a tree. He was the subject—or was it the target?—of television
interviews. Labelled as an 'angry young man', he was in fact gentle. But
he talked too freely and too honestly about his genius, which no conceited person would have dared to do.

Sometimes the controversy was his own fault. When the Royal Court
Theatre rejected his play the following year, he reacted so indignantly
that he was labelled a 'petulant young man' and gave Ronald Duncan
the opportunity to make the unnecessary remark: 'He regards himself
as the new Bernard Shaw; what he should really be is a publicity man
for a detergent firm'.

Hostility turned to farce when a national newspaper claimed that
the father of the girl he was living with had burst into a private dinner
party brandishing a horsewhip with a strange accusing cry: 'You're a
homosexual with six mistresses!' This, it seems, had been caused by his
discovery of Wilson's Journal, the notes for Colin Wilson's planned
novel on a sexual psychopath. To the irate parent it suggested an appalling depravity. While Colin Wilson rolled on the floor with laughter,
some guests grabbed the father while another, Gerald Hamilton (Isher-

wood's 'Mr Norris') telephoned *The Daily Express*.

It all caused a sensation at the time; there were the carefully prepared images of grieving parents and Wilson's 'abandoned' wife and baby. Shocked by the nature of the publicity, Colin Wilson's venerable publisher, Victor Gollancz, implored him to take a job and not publish a word for the next three years. Daphne du Maurier predicted that he would not receive a good review for the next ten years. However, Wilson relied on his own judgement—and his girlfriend Joy Stewart's loyalty—and moved to Gorran Haven on the south coast of Cornwall. He continued with work on his second book, but when *Religion and the Rebel* was published 17 months after *The Outsider*, it was massacred by the critics, as if they could not forgive themselves their first outburst of enthusiasm.

Today Colin Wilson lives in that same village, with Joy as his second wife, her parents long since reconciled. They have two handsome sons, Damon and Rowan, his first daughter, Sally, lives in London, and two amiable labradors.

To begin with, the flight into Cornwall seemed reckless. The money from *The Outsider* had been lavished with the generosity of newfound wealth on lunches, books and records. He was able to pay 30 shillings a week for the cottage they rented from a friend; and when they had to move he was rescued by the royalties from the much maligned *Religion and the Rebel* and bought the house where they live today for £2,000. 'We were stony broke,' he says. 'Not even enough money for a bed. It was an empty house without furniture'.

He did not know that Victor Gollancz was suffering new agonies over his next manuscript, *Ritual in the Dark*, the novel about a sadistic murderer (the scribbles for which outraged Joy's father). Writing confidentially to a friend, Gollancz described it as 'a horribly nasty book indeed; I should go so far as to call it a foul foul book—one that I would not dream of publishing in any ordinary case'. However, he recognised Wilson's sincerity; Wilson received an advance of £500, heaved a sigh of relief and bought some furniture. Probably his most powerful novel to date, it sold 20,000 copies in hardback and has been in print ever since, but his name remained mud with the critics. 'Book after book of mine disappeared, like throwing stones down a well,' he says. 'Not even a splash.'

As Daphne du Maurier prophesied, the turning point came in 1966 with the publication of *The Mind Parasites*. The tide of hostility began to turn. Looking back on the years of rejection, Colin Wilson understands why Victor Gollancz urged him to take a job in a publishing house. 'But I hate working at something I dislike. Even after *The Outsider* I woke up sweating, thinking I had to go to the factory'.

He actually worked in a few. 'Boots and shoes, plastics, toys. Incredibly hard work. Even worse, it was boring. I dreaded that I would work in a factory for the rest of my life. I knew I could always make more money by writing. It was not simply faith in myself; I have always been obsessed by certain ideas. All my work is an expansion of one central idea'.

His output has been prodigious: 45 books, including 14 novels; six studies on the *Outsider* theme; six books on the occult; and three on murder. Then there are 15 pamphlets, such as his appreciation of the film director Ken Russell. Three books have been written about him; one, by the late Sydney Campion, 'was so fulsome, describing me riding around the lanes of Leicestershire on my bike "his long blond hair flying in the wind, his beautiful eyes blazing with madness" that I dropped it in the wastepaper basket and rewrote it from cover to cover'.

It could be argued that Wilson's output is too prolific; that there is a danger of dissipating his talent through his inability to refuse friends who ask for favours and reviews. He denies that his introductions to other people's books consume too much of his time – 'only two or three a year'. But he has written 30 altogether. He *wants* to help less fortunate writers, which makes him something of a rarity.

His lack of bitterness is a clear indication that he has left the rat race far behind. When he meets the train at St Austell he seems unchanged, still wearing a poloneck sweater and with a distinctive smile. A check tweed suit, too long in the trousers, contrasts disarmingly with a white hat which looks suspiciously plastic.

He heads for The Club, where his Muscadet is waiting, properly chilled. His youngest son, Rowan, appears from a back room, a beaming boy with red-gold hair. Later he heads for Tesco's, where he shops like a drunken housewife. The trolleys fill with soft drinks, masses of sweets, crisps, chocolates and fruit yoghurts.

'The children's friends drop in,' he explains blithely, adding three joints of meat and various varieties of canned food for the dogs. When the pramlike pyramids are pushed to the cash counter they cost a staggering £114.95. He admits it must be a reaction to his childhood, when they never had enough. Plainly it is a source of satisfaction that he is able to give his own family more than is necessary.

But while he made an astonishing £100,000 from *The Occult*, he lives in a constant state of overdraft. Books and vintage wine are another extravagance; otherwise he lives in comfortable chaos, with supper

served on trays in a sitting room which is happily lived-in. He watches
the BBC News, yawns and goes to bed at ten. In the morning he drives
Rowan to school and then goes back to bed for a while.

'I love my family very much. I am tremendously lucky to have Joy.
For I must be a difficult person to live with, and she is easygoing. She
understands that my work comes before everything. I love my home,
my books and living in the country and, of course, my children. My
father worked so bloody hard he had little time to give his love to us
kids.' His father died of cancer several years ago.

When Wilson was writer-in-residence at an American university for
two years he took his family with him. He is in demand for lecture tours
there – 'Hardest work I've ever done, five universities a week, flying from
one to another' – but returned more happily from a lecture in the Leban-
on, where he was presented with a magnificent camelhair robe.

Reappearing from his bedroom at ten, he examines the post, which
is startling by any standards. A letter from the economist Professor Von
Hayek suggests they meet on a forthcoming visit to England. A telegram
from the Organising Committee of the First Conference for Tafsir
Philosophy in Tripoli reads: 'Come and let participate in International
Congress to include writers who have exposed and criticised certain
aspects of the human behaviour'; this is only two weeks off and Wilson
declines diplomatically, dictating his instructions on tape to his part-
time secretary who lives at the end of the road.

There is also a letter from Ronald Duncan saying that Mrs Thatcher
has given them permission to include some of her material in their forthcoming book *Marx Refuted*.* But surely this was the man who rejected
his play at the Royal Court and accused him of . . . Exactly. It is astonishing how Wilson's enemies become his friends once they meet him.

As if to make amends for an earlier *volte-face*, Toynbee paid him
this compliment when reviewing *The Occult*: 'Colin Wilson has been
much battered by reviewers, including at times the present one. But
what nobody can deny is his staying power, his resilience, his indefatigable curiosity'.

How much of this is due to the 'peak experience' in which he believes
passionately? It is, at the very least, an affirmation of the optimism
Wilson feels. He believes that most people ignore the opportunities
open to them and are confined by boundaries which are unnecessarily
narrow. 'We are stronger, happier, healthier than we realise,' he says.

But how has his belief helped him personally? 'I felt trapped in my

*This was published in 1987 by Ashgrove Press. – Ed.

teens and contemplated suicide twice—nearly all suicides see life as an endless series of dreary obstacles. But the "peak experience" tells you that this is just not true. It can happen outside the gasworks or at the Parthenon; to a Proust or the person at breakfast who sees a ray of sunlight hit the cornflakes and realises how lucky he is'. He quotes Chung Tzu: 'He who follows that part of himself which is great will become a great man; he who follows that part of himself which is little, will be little. Genius is partly a matter of choice', he adds, 'though we may be born with talent'.

It seemed a boast in 1966 when he declared: 'I know that I have come further than any of my contemporaries. I would be a fool if I didn't know it and a coward if I was afraid to say so'. It is more acceptable now.*

*This article first appeared in *The Sunday Telegraph Magazine*, 7 December 1980.

15

The Human Future

NICOLAS TREDELL

We are moving towards 2000: the second millenium, a date that concentrates thought wonderfully about the future of humankind. There
is an almost intolerable contradiction between positive and negative
prospects: on the one hand, an astonishing level of technological
achievement which could, effectively applied, free human beings from
many of the burdens that have traditionally weighed upon them; on the
other, the gross human suffering of starvation and poverty, and threats
of world economic collapse, eco-catastrophe, and nuclear destruction.
The cultural and philosophical responses to the situation of humankind since 1945 have not been inspiring. Atheistic existentialism has run
into the sands; the plurality of religious belief makes it difficult for any
one creed to command intelligent assent; liberal humanism has found it
difficult to encompass the apparently irrational extremes of human
experience and behaviour; it is more and more difficult to maintain
faith in the emergence of a benign Marxism; neo-conservatism combines
a romantic enthusiasm for capitalism with a Hulmean pessimism about
the possibility of changing 'human nature'. Structuralism, post-
structuralism and deconstruction have displaced or eliminated the
individual human subject and aroused scepticism about whether it is
possible to make any true statement.

It is in this context that the by now considerable body of work
produced by Colin Wilson should be of interest to all those concerned
with the future development of humankind. Both his non-fiction and his
novels should be seen as contributions to the 'human sciences' – the investigation, in a variety of modes – philosophy, psychology, sociology,
literature – of human beings and human society. This is not to propose
Wilson as a prophet or saviour, who will lift responsibility from our own
shoulders; though he may sometimes have been cast in this role by others,
it is not one he has taken upon himself. On the contrary: his emphasis has
always been upon individuals assuming responsibility for their own 'salvation', their evolutionary development. His work is both a call to effort,
and an analysis of why, and in what ways, effort should be made.

Wilson's starting-point is his challenge to the 'passive fallacy' – the
notion of human consciousness as an inert observer of reality – which
has, he believes, dominated Western philosophy since Descartes. Wilson
draws on Husserlian phenomenology to argue that consciousness and

perception are 'intentional': that is, the human being 'subconsciously' selects his state of consciousness and perception; the way he feels and the way he sees the world. The subconscious workings of 'intentionality' confine us to a narrow state of 'everyday consciousness' for most of our lives; this is both necessary and useful; but it is also constricting, and, finally, dangerous. Wilson often compares human beings to blinkered horses: a horse is blinkered in traffic to stop it panicking and to enable it to provide motive power; similarly, human beings, especially in the West, are 'blinkered' and this has enabled them to pull civilization forward. But it has also tended to deprive them of the contact with the reality of meaning that is achieved in unblinkered, 'wide-angle' consciousness. Confinement in everyday consciousness can lead to a total collapse of meaning; this is what happens to Roquentin in Sartre's novel *Nausea* (1938); and this is the existential embodiment of the 'passive fallacy'; in Roquentin, we see 'Hume's scepticism becoming instinctive, all destroying' (*The Outsider*, p. 34). In Sartre's perspective, Roquentin's experience brings him into contact with the reality of contingency, of a meaningless universe; for Wilson, it is due to a subconsciously intentional narrowing of consciousness that loses touch with the reality of meaning. But such an extreme breakdown of meaning can also be the first step towards an intense positive vision, like a saint's dark night of the soul.

Wilson opposes to the total breakdown of meaning those intense experiences of meaning, value and purpose which can occur in a wide range of ways: in religious practices such as meditation and prayer; in intellectual and aesthetic activity — philosophy, mathematics, poetry, painting, music; in the sexual orgasm. It may also be provoked negatively, by suffering, crisis, the threat of death; one example which Wilson frequently cites is that of the whisky-priest in Graham Greene's novel *The Power and the Glory* (1940) who, as he is about to be executed, feels that 'it would have been quite easy to be a saint' (p. 211). It can also occur unexpectedly, in quite everyday circumstances, touched off by an apparently slight external stimulus; this happens in Proust's *Remembrance of Things Past* (1913-27), when the narrator tastes the morsel of a '*petite madeleine*' soaked in tea:

> No sooner had the warm liquid mixed with the crumbs touched my palate than a shudder ran through me and I stopped, intent upon the extraordinary thing that was happening to me. An exquisite pleasure had invaded my senses, something isolated, detached, with no suggestion of its origin. And at once the vicissitudes of life had become in-

different to me, its disasters innocuous, its brevity illusory – this new
sensation having had on me the effect which love has of filling me
with a precious essence; or rather this essence was not in me, it *was*
me. I had ceased now to feel mediocre, contingent, mortal. (p. 48)

It may be said that such 'privileged moments' are rare, and that it is
unwise to base a whole philosophy on them. Wilson has, however, drawn
upon the researches of the American humanistic psychologist, the late
Abraham Maslow (1908-1970), to suggest that such experiences may
be more common than we realise or acknowledge. Maslow called such
moments 'peak experiences', and his investigations led him to surmise
that healthy people in reasonably comfortable circumstances had 'peak
experiences' fairly often: for example, a young mother watching her
husband and children eat breakfast as a beam of sunlight struck through
the window went into a 'peak experience', a sense of overflowing joy.
It has been charged against Wilson, especially in regard to *The Outsider*,
that he is excessively concerned with the over-sensitive, the inadequate;
that the concept of 'the outsider' provides an excuse and justification
for eccentricity and weakness; but he has aimed, partly by drawing on
Maslow's researches, to create a psychology which, while it does not
ignore the negative side of existence (as American humanistic psychology
like Maslow's is inclined to), also acknowledges positive experience and
endeavour: a psychology of health which is concerned with states of
mind that are conventionally defined as 'extreme', but also with what
Wilson calls 'the mechanisms of everyday consciousness' (*The Occult*,
p. 763).

The meaning apprehended in 'peak experiences' is not, Wilson affirms,
illusory: 'meaning is an objective reality' (*Contemporary Novelists*, p.
1520); and apprehension of it generates a sense of values, of what is
worth doing; it is, if you like, an evolutionary message. The experience
of meaning is also an experience of a reality that extends beyond the
present moment: the reality, for example, of other times and places:
this capacity to reach beyond the present is what Wilson calls 'Faculty
X'.

At present, however, we cannot achieve the experience of meaning
at will. Our consciousness fluctuates: we are slaves to our moods and
emotions: the visionary gleam comes and goes. It is difficult to become
aware of and to control our 'intentionality'. We are split between
reason and imagination, a division partly built into the physiology of
our brains. We contain many 'I's', many conflicting, fragmentary selves.
It may be, Wilson suggests, that there are 'higher selves' within us, an

ascending 'ladder of selves', and that we can, in moments of intensity, extreme effort, crisis, experience 'promotion' to a higher self; but then we fall back again. Wilson also posits the existence of something in the nature of Husserl's 'transcendental ego' or Dr Howard Miller's 'unit of pure thought'; but we seem, for most of the time at least, to be out of touch with this. Too much of our existence is automatic, in the grip of the 'robot'. When we first learn an activity — typing, swimming, diving — we do so consciously, with difficulty; after a time, if we learn successfully, the relevant skills reach the level of automaticity: we no longer have to think consciously about them; a 'robot' has taken over, and applies those skills much better than we consciously could. But this 'robot' has taken over too many of our activities, cramping our consciousness.

The problem of the 'robot' is related to what Wilson terms the 'indifference margin' or 'St Neots margin' (so-called because he devised the concept when he was passing through the town of St Neots in Huntingdonshire): the fact that there is a margin of indifference where human beings can be stimulated by the threat, or the reality, of inconvenience or pain, but where pleasure fails to awaken any response. Somebody, let us say, is delighted when he moves from a cramped flat to a new, comparatively spacious house; but he soon comes to take it for granted; the 'robot' has taken over; it is only when the house nearly burns down, or the building society threatens repossession for mortgage arrears, that he suddenly, vividly appreciates it once more. The 'indifference margin' is illustrated by one of the first stories Wilson ever learnt at school — 'The Old Woman in the Vinegar Bottle':

> A passing fairy heard her complaining that she was too cramped, and transformed the vinegar bottle into a cottage. Passing by a month later, she stopped to see how the old lady was faring, and found her complaining that she was still too cramped. She transformed the cottage into a small house . . . and so on until the fairy has transformed the vinegar bottle into a palace; and *still* the old woman finds something to complain about. So the fairy turns the palace back into a vinegar bottle. (*The New Existentialism*, p. 122. Wilson's ellipsis)

Wilson remarks in *Voyage to a Beginning* (1968, 1987) that he finds this story 'symbolic of human nature — as symbolic as the story of the Fall of man' (p. 2).

Wilson believes, however, that human beings can redeem themselves. The need is to gain conscious control of 'intentionality'. It is necessary to unify the fragmentary scraps of one's 'personalities', to climb the 'ladder of selves', to try to get in touch with the 'transcendental ego'. Both analysis and effort are required: the descriptive analysis of subjective states, making use of a phenomenological method, and the effort of sustained self-observation and self-awareness (Gurdjieff's 'self-remembering') and of maintaining a high level of will and optimism. Effort, will and optimism are not merely, in Wilson's perspective, moralistic imperatives, but contribute to 'positive intentionalizing' that can lead to closer contact with the reality of meaning.

Wilson believes that the conscious control of 'intentionality' with the resultant power to move between everyday and expanded consciousness at will, should constitute a new evolutionary stage in the development of humankind: human beings who have such control will be able to enjoy far richer lives; they will have access to parapsychic powers, such as telepathy; they will be unlikely to engage in destructive behaviour towards themselves and others; they will, presumably, be able to make much more effective and equitable social and political arrangements; they will probably live far longer.

Of course, Wilson's position raises a number of problems. To posit the objective reality of meaning, the existence of 'higher selves' and a 'transcendental ego' seems, in today's sceptical climate, suspiciously metaphysical: 'meaning' looks like a substitute for God, the 'transcendental ego' for the soul. Wilson's creative evolutionism may seem, like Shaw's to be a fusion of residual religious notions that can find no mooring in traditional faith with a nineteenth-century humanist optimism about progress that can no longer place its trust in social and political development. The Christian might say to Wilson that he would do better to return to religion; the historical materialist that he would do better to see meaning and the individual subject as produced and altered by historical and ideological conditions, and to aim at changing history in order to give meaning and shape to the world and to our lives.

Wilson would acknowledge some similarities between his project and that of traditional religion; he has defined existentialism as 'a philosophy that asks the kind of questions that were once regarded as "religious": questions about the meaning of human existence, freedom and the existence of God' (*The New Existentialism*, p. 13); and his methods for working towards higher consciousness clearly resemble, in certain respects, the disciplines of saints, mystics, religious devotees. He has a number of objections to traditional religion, however. In *Voyage to a Beginning*, he notes: 'I was in total intellectual agreement with the "dynamic" religion of the saints . . . but had no sympathy for the

"static" religion that develops from it' (p. 116). He also disliked the
pessimism of such 'religious intellectuals' as Eliot, Greene, Marcel,
Bernanos, Kierkegaard, Simone Weil, and felt that modern religious
movements and sects, such as Billy Graham's evangelism, Frank Buch-
man's 'Moral Rearmament', the Jehovah's Witnesses, encourage the
individual to accept what the American sociologist David Riesman, in
The Lonely Crowd (1950), called 'other-direction': conformity to the
prevailing codes of a society or organization. The same could be said
of the belief that individuals are to be altered by altering society.

Wilson believes, in fact, that many of the problems of modern civilization can be explained in his terms. Even in this time of economic
recession, our society offers many of its members relative comfort and
leisure, although access to these remains unevenly distributed. But the
narrowness of human consciousness, the 'indifference margin', our
passive cultural premises, mean that comfort and leisure lead to boredom, and to attempts to relieve that boredom by external stimuli, of
which our society offers a great number – television, records, cassettes,
films, videos, the bright spectacle of consumer goods. As Wilson says,
we live in a society whose basic rule is: 'when bored, go out and buy
something' (*Mysteries*, p. 588).

The attempt to relieve boredom can lead to crime, even to the
extent of murder. Wilson sees crime as a form of what Sartre called
'magical thinking' – the imaginary dissolution of the real difficulties
and efforts that have to be faced to achieve one's goals. 'Crime in general is an attempt to take short cuts, to take the easy way out, to slide
out of responsibilities' (*Encyclopaedia of Modern Murder*, p. xvii).
This is seen at its most extreme in the apparently motiveless murder,
the murder 'for kicks', which seems to have become more frequent
in modern civilization; it is, Wilson provocatively suggests, 'one of the
more interesting forms of romantic revolt . . . In many cases it can be
seen as a crude attempt to achieve a kind of mystical self-fulfilment'
(*Essential Colin Wilson*, p. 12). But it is inevitably self-defeating, since
it contradicts the evolutionary imperative to more life. And the blame
for murder cannot be laid primarily on 'modern civilization': murderers are free individuals who have decided to kill as a result of a process
of 'magical thinking': they seek the easy way to intensity. The implications of Wilson's views for penal reform seem to be that criminals
should be encouraged to develop a sense of personal responsibility:
neither wholly repressive punishments, or behavioural or psychoanalytic 'treatments' are adequate.

For Wilson, however, 'the criminal is significant because he shows

us what is wrong with all of us' (*Essential Colin Wilson*, p. 12). The
need for the law-abiding individual is also to develop a sense of personal[ity] responsibility, an awareness of free will. Wilson's objection to
state socialism and to revolutionary ideology is that they are inclined
to erode the sense of personal responsibility. The kind of revolutionary
attitude which Wilson sees as originating with Rousseau's axiom 'Man
is born free but is everywhere in chains' leads to blaming other people
and things (society, capitalism) for one's lack of freedom: it is also the
source of modern terrorism. Wilson does not deny the importance of
political freedom: but he believes it is to be attained by clear thinking,
not misdirected resentment. Recently, he has given some endorsement
to E.F. Schumacher's ideas: 'in recognizing that it *is* possible to de-
centralize society, to live in much smaller units, Schumacher had made
an immensely important contribution' (*Essential Colin Wilson*, p. 222).
He believes, however, that Schumacher turned away from the social
aspect of the problem of freedom —which is, Wilson acknowledges,
very important—to reach, in *Guide for the Perplexed*, a conclusion
similar to Wilson's: that 'improving society has to start by improving
the individual' (*Essential Colin Wilson*, p. 223).

There are obvious objections to such a view. It may sanction a
retreat from political responsibility, a submission to what Christopher
Lasch calls 'the culture of narcissism', a preoccupation with the self
at the expense of social concern. It may also appear to apply only to
those countries of the West, and only to those individuals within such
countries, who enjoy relative affluence and personal freedom. For
others, it may be necessary to unite together in political action to
achieve even the first level of freedom, at which problems such as the
'indifference margin' become apparent. This is true; but it could be
argued that Wilson is tackling a problem that all individuals and
societies that advance to a certain stage will have to face. He does not
deny that 'there are many people in the world with real cause for
misery: poverty, starvation, physical pain' (*Essential Colin Wilson*, p.
242). But it is possible that, since the technological resources to remedy
poverty and starvation, and alleviate physical pain, are available, the
failure to employ them effectively is due, at least partly, to precisely
those problems of individual psychology Wilson identifies; the desire
for material prosperity well above the level of one's basic needs, for
instance, which hampers a more even distribution of wealth and
resources, could be attributed to the 'indifference margin', the failure
to appreciate what we have which makes us want more. Moreover, it is
clear that attempts to change the individual by changing society, at

least by large-scale action, can have bitterly oppressive results—as in Stalinist Russia—and can also, even when beneficial in important ways, seem bureaucratic and alienating—as with the British Welfare State. The lesson is that attempts at social and political improvement must take more account than hitherto of individual psychology; and the kind of psychology that is currently influential in social and political analysis, derived from the revision of Freud by the French psychoanalyst Jacques Lacan (1901-1981), reiterates the elimination of the individual already found in Marxism: it says nothing about will or personal responsibility. In these respects, the psychology offered by Wilson provides interesting suggestions. It has been said that Wilson's work is apolitical, or that it has 'fascist' tendencies. Neither of these charges can be sustained by an examination of Wilson's writing: it has important social and political implications, and it is concerned to promote, not authoritarianism and regimentation, but greater freedom.

Colin Wilson sees the emergence of the novel in the eighteenth century— as represented, primarily, by Richardson's *Pamela* (1740) and Rousseau's *Julie ou La Nouvelle Héloise* (1761)—as opening up a new dimension in human freedom; the novel can serve to free us from confinement in the present, to produce 'wide-angle consciousness': its basic mechanism is that of tension-and-release: it provokes the reader to clench, and then to relax, his consciousness, and this results in enhanced awareness. It can free us from confinement in the present moment, and bring 'Faculty X' into play, awakening, by imaginative analogy, a sense of the reality of other times and places. It serves as a 'thought-experiment': a way of projecting, exploring and testing hypotheses about reality, of asking, in effect: what if this were true? It is also an attempt by a novelist to create a clear self-image; not necessarily in the form of an autobiographical self-projection, though this may play its part, but by constructing an image of his own, and of life's, possibilities. At the highest level, a novel can bring us into contact with the reality of meaning. The novelist's task is, finally, 'a spiritual one: to free himself from . . . narrowness, to achieve "wide-angle" vision, and to convey this to his readers' (*Craft of the Novel*, p. 168).

In this perspective, the task of the critic is to judge how far a given novel realises the potential of the form to produce expanded consciousness. He should also judge the world-view that emerges, with whatever degree of explicitness, from a novel, by comparing it with the positive world-vision of evolutionary existentialism, and assessing how far it is valid or how far it is, in terms of that vision, a 'libel on life'. He may seek to show that what a novelist presents as the 'truth' about life is, in fact, carefully slanted and selected, a kind of 'literary faking'. Wilson advocates, in fact, an explicitly ideological criticism, akin to that which a Catholic or an older kind of Marxist critic might practice—'ideology' being understood here as denoting a particular system of beliefs and values rather than, necessarily, 'false consciousness'. The critic holds what he takes to be a correct, coherent and relatively explicit world-view; he assumes that a coherent world-view can be extracted from a text, and compared with his own.

This kind of explicitly ideological approach was, until recently, frowned on in English literary criticism. It was felt that it was likely to cramp and distort one's critical sensibilities. Lately, however, it has been argued that any literary critic will have an ideology of some sort, whether he admits it or not, and that it is more intellectually honest and rigorous to try to make that ideology as explicit as possible, so that its assumptions can be seen and questioned. Wilson certainly cannot be faulted on these grounds. The assumption that it is possible to extract a coherent world-view from a literary text (or indeed a philosophical text), and that this can be seen as an expression of the world-view of an individual 'author' has, however, been strongly challenged by deconstructionist, post-structuralist and neo-Marxist critical approaches that stress the contradiction and disunity of texts, and suggest that the 'author' is an effect of the work, rather than *vice versa*. While Wilson recognizes that parts of a literary text may contradict its dominant philosophy, he does believe that its dominant philosophy can be discerned, and accounted for, not primarily by historical circumstances, but by the temperament of the individual writer.

Wilson's theory of the novel and his conception of the critic's task mean that he finds much twentieth century fiction wanting: Joyce, Lawrence, Proust, Huxley, Greene, Sartre, Beckett, are all charged with 'life-devaluation', even though—as with Proust's madeleine dipped in tea—they may sometimes evoke moments of affirmation. John Wain and Kingsley Amis are seen, in their novels of the 1950s, as promoting a cult of the 'ordinary chap', and Angus Wilson as exclusively concerned for the lives of people within society. Colin Wilson has created an 'alternative canon' of twentieth-century novelists and novels for which he has qualified admiration: David Lindsay's *Voyage to Arcturus* (1920); H.G. Wells's *The World of William Clissold* (1926); John Cowper Powys's *Wolf Solent* (1929) and *A Glastonbury Romance* (1933); L.H. Myers's *The Near and the Far* (1943); the fiction of Herman Hesse, especially *Steppenwolf* (1927); Friedrich Dürrenmatt's *The Pledge* (1958); the novels of Nikos Kazantzakis. All these novelists can be seen, in their widely differing ways, as preoccupied with existential questions. Wilson has also shown considerable interest in the possibilities of genre fiction: he feels that modern literature has split into two streams, one esoteric and experimental, one of immediate appeal, and 'the free imagination has sought expression again in various types of fantasy: in ghost stories, detective stories and science fiction' (*The Strength to Dream*, p. 100).

Wilson sees his own novels as a vital complement to his non-fiction, 'a manner of philosophising' (*Voyage*, p. 160); they offer means of evoking and exploring the complexities of experience not available to discursive philosophy. All Wilson's novels are *Bildungsroman*, in the senses in which he defines the term in *The Outsider*:

> The *Bildungsroman* sets out to describe the evolution of the 'hero's soul'; it is fictional biography that is mainly concerned with its hero's reaction to ideas, or the development of his ideas about 'life' from his experience. The *Bildungsroman* is a sort of laboratory in which the hero conducts an experiment in living. For this reason, it is a particularly useful medium for artists whose main concern is a philosophical answer to the practical question: What shall we do with our lives? Moreover . . . as soon as a writer is seized with the need to treat a problem he feels seriously about in a novel, the novel automatically becomes a sort of *Bildungsroman*. The *Bildungsroman* is the natural form of serious fictional art, no matter how short the period of its hero's life that it treats (pp. 61-2).

We see here that Wilson suggests that any serious novel might be defined as a *Bildungsroman*: but his own are more clearly so than many English novels. They belong, as he has acknowledged, more to a European than an English tradition; they are 'novels of ideas', both in the sense that the characters explicitly think and talk about philosophical issues, and in the sense that such issues are explicitly dramatized in their narratives. His first two fictions—*Ritual in the Dark* (1960) and *Adrift in Soho* (1961) are relatively realistic, set in a carefully rendered 1950s London; this is also the setting of *The Sex Diary of Gerard Sorme* (1963), and its use of the journal form is a traditional means of producing verisimilitude: its frank acknowledgement of the possibility of occult phenomena marks, however, a move away from

realism. The provincial setting of *The World of Violence* (1963) is
barely evoked, without the detail that gives realistic vivacity, and the
retrospective, detached narration, which combines a good deal of
summary and analysis with relatively muted dramatization, means
that the reader is not involved in the immediate action; moreover,
while *Violence* contains 'thriller' elements, their potential to thrill
is not exploited.

The use of elements drawn from popular forms such as the thriller
is a central aspect of Wilson's later novels. *Necessary Doubt* (1964)
and *The Glass Cage* (1966) mix thriller and detective story elements;
The Mind Parasites (1967), *The Philosopher's Stone* (1969), *The Space
Vampires* (1976) and *Spider World* (1987, 2 vols) combine science
fiction and fantasy; *The Killer* (1970) is a kind of 'faction' novel,
which offers a composite portrait of a murderer based on details
from a range of real-life cases; it is a sort of sensation novel, a 'shilling
shocker', rather like a novelized version of a *True Detective* article.
The God of the Labyrinth (1970) draws on the mode of the pornographic novel, which, as Wilson points out in his 'Note' accompany-
ing *God*, 'has something of the symbolic rigidity of a ballet' (p. 284).
God is also something of a 'literary detective story', a hunt for the
manuscripts of an eighteenth-century rake and proto-evolutionist,
Esmond Donelly. *The Black Room* (1971) is a spy novel, and *The
Schoolgirl Murder Case* (1974) and *The Janus Murder Case* (1984) are
police detective stories *à la* Maigret. *The Personality Surgeon* (1985) is
a 'medical thriller', a combination of purported documentary and
detective story that tells of the quest to find a cure, not for a physical
disease, but for what is, to Wilson, our profoundest psychological
malaise: the failure fully to realize our positive possibilities.

The popular form elements in Wilson's fiction serve to give
scope to 'the free imagination', to provide some structure, and to contribute to narrative interest. Wilson's 'Note' to *God* claims that, in his
use of popular forms, he aims 'at an effect approximating to parody'
(p. 283) in order to achieve a kind of Brechtian alienation effect:
parody, disrupting novelistic illusion, should provoke readers to think
about the philosophical issues raised by Wilson's fiction as Brecht's
disruptions of theatrical illusion are intended to make his audience
think about the political issues raised by his plays. Wilson's novels do
not, in fact, establish a sufficient distance from the popular forms
which they employ to achieve parody very often; but a kind of 'alienation effect' is attained in two ways: firstly, by the non-exploitation
of some of the popular form elements which they adopt—for example,

the potentially exciting siege scene at the end of *The Glass Cage* is
played down, rendered in partly comic terms; secondly, and more
importantly, by the divergence between the concerns implied by the
popular form—those of espionage in *The Black Room*, for instance—
and the evolutionary concerns which are dramatized in the novel, and,
in most cases, embodied in the hero.

   In *The Age of Defeat* (1959), Wilson analyzed the phenomenon of
the 'vanishing hero' in modern society and literature, and suggested that
today's novelist should try to create a positive hero. He pointed out,
however, that since our age is one of unprecedented complexity, 'a
"hero" who possesses simple courage, or faith without intelligence,
would be a failure. The "hero" of the twentieth century would need
to be something of a metaphysician' (p. 82). How do the heroes of
Wilson's own novels measure up to this? Most of them are, in a fairly
direct sense, autobiographical self-projections, part of an attempt to
create a clear self-image. His most frequent persona is Gerard Sorme,
hero of *Ritual*, *The Sex Diary* and *God*, and Sorme sums up the
qualities of the Wilson hero: inwardly detached, retaining a certain
innocence, cerebral, 'something of a metaphysician', able to enjoy
peak experiences, optimistic, passive in his relationships with others,
but sought after by both women and men. Harry Preston in *Adrift in
Soho*, Damon Reade in *The Glass Cage*, Gilbert Austin in *The Mind
Parasites*, Howard Newman in *The Philosopher's Stone*, Kit Butler in
The Black Room, all have these qualities to varying degrees (though
there is also a number of subtle differentiations); so, to a lesser extent,
do the 'professional' protagonists—the prison psychiatrist Kahn in *The
Killer*, Inspector Saltfleet in the *Schoolgirl* and *Janus* murder cases,
the astronaut Carlsen in *The Space Vampires*. Charles Peruzzi, in *The
Personality Surgeon*, is a more fully characterized 'professional' hero:
a doctor with a real sense of purpose whose desire to help humankind
leads him out of conventional medicine and into a 'devil's pact' with
Ben McKeown, a ruthless millionaire businessman. McKeown provides
Peruzzi with the money to pursue his researches, but Peruzzi's essential
innocence and disinterestedness save him from corruption and he is
able to develop his 'personality surgery', which makes ingenious use
of video and computer technology to encourage people to fulfil their
latent potential—if they want to.

   In *The Killer*, the focus is on the murderer Lingard rather than the
psychiatrist Kahn, but the casebook format of this work, though sup-
plemented by novelistic techniques, means that we never really have
the impression of getting inside Lingard's mind as we do with, for

example, Raskolnikov in Dostoevsky's *Crime and Punishment*. Of all
Wilson's heroes, Karl Zweig, the elderly 'existentialist theologian' who
is the central character in *Necessary Doubt*, is the most distinct from
Wilson himself, and we do seem to get inside Zweig's mind; but Zweig
shares the characteristic Wilsonian detachment, and, at the end of the
novel, he too comes to commit himself to the evolutionary quest. With
the exception of Zweig, who if often wrong-footed by Gustav Neumann,
the man he is hunting, the Wilson hero is generally in a superior
position, in a psychological sense, to the other characters he encounters;
he often feels concern for them but he also stands back, judging and
placing them. In contrast to many of the protagonists of modern
fiction, he is not a victim who suffers frequent failure and humiliation;
his sensitivity and intelligence do not entail weakness. As we work
through Wilson's novels, we see that his heroes increasingly come to
trust that there is an underlying order in the universe, and this increases
their detachment and sense of security. This trust is expressed by
Damon Reade in *The Glass Cage*:

> ' . . . I believe like Whitehead that the universe is a single organism
> that somehow takes account of us. I don't believe that modern man
> is a stranded fragment of life in an empty universe. I've an instinct
> that tells me that there's a purpose, and that I can understand that
> purpose more deeply by trusting my instinct. I don't expect life
> to explode in my face at any moment . . .' (p. 46)

It is arguable that the Wilson hero, especially in the later fiction, is
too detached: it would be possible to regard that detachment not as an
elevated condition but as a self-centred and narcissistic withdrawal from
the complexity of reality. Wilson is, of course, aware of this—indeed, it
is dramatized in *The Glass Cage*, where Damon Reade is provoked out
of his reclusive solitude in the Lake District and goes to London to
track down a murderer. The qualities of insight and intuition developed
in his seclusion enable him to turn detective, to enter the world of action,
successfully. The detachment of the Wilson hero could be compared to
that found in post-modernist texts which refuse the concern with
personalities and personal relationships that has, in a liberal-humanist
perspective, traditionally characterized the novel. In Wilson's terms,
however, the hero's detachment involves a fundamental identification
with humanity; in *Spider World* it is Niall, the young man who develops
his inner powers of will and concentration, who is able, because of those
powers, to lead the human fightback against the master race of huge

death spiders—and who is, when the spiders are overcome, reluctant to remain for long as leader because he believes that human beings must learn for themselves how to develop the kind of freedom that is most important—inner freedom. This is the surest basis of liberty in the outer world. Detachment and withdrawal are not escape routes but roads to freedom, not only for one individual but ultimately for all humankind.

In Wilson's fiction, the hero often encounters larger-than-life figures who function as unofficial 'teachers', by example—sometimes bad—and precept; they serve to deepen the hero's insight and sense of purpose. This is the case with, for example, the rich, homosexual aesthete and murderer Austin Nunne, in *Ritual*; Caradoc Cunningham, the massive 'sex-magician' (based on Aleister Crowley) of *The Sex Diary*; the cool, strong-willed, strangely ambiguous Gustav Neumann of *Necessary Doubt*. The hero feels some interest in and identification with these figures; he may, even when their example is in some ways bad, be tempted by them. Indeed, one of the most disturbing aspects of *Ritual* is Sorme's temptation by Nunne, his attraction to what he believes Nunne, even in his acts of murder, represents. By contrast, in *The Glass Cage*, which in some ways echoes the plot of *Ritual*, Damon Reade is much more distanced from the murderer, though he still feels some kinship with him. But in *Ritual*, Sorme finally rejects Nunne, and though, in *The Sex Diary*, he learns from Caradoc Cunningham, he also sees his weaknesses. In *Necessary Doubt*, however, Karl Zweig does not reject Gustav Neumann: Neumann, in fact, reconverts Zweig, who has succumbed to the temptation of Christianity, to evolutionary existentialism. It is notable that Wilson's 'larger-than-life figures' are always men: the relationships between men are given more attention in his novels than the relationships between men and women: women are in the background, passive, submissive, serving the hero's needs.

Nunne, Cunningham, and a range of other, sometimes lesser figures— the bohemians in *Adrift in Soho*, for instance—all embody various kinds of romantic revolt; indeed, the whole of Wilson's fiction could be read as an investigation of the varieties of romantic experience, as a critique of Romanticism: it accepts and aims to deepen the romantic vision, which is seen as an authentic evolutionary intimation, while evoking and analysing a number of destructive and self-defeating ways of pursuing that vision. The attractions and limitations of Romanticism are perhaps best summed up in one of Wilson's most evocative pieces of writing, Sorme's vision of Nunne as Nijinsky which closes Part One of *Ritual*:

The bedclothes were thin and light, but he was not cold. He slept for a little, but woke again, feeling that it was somehow a pity to sleep and waste the feeling of certainty. A few seconds later he slept again anyway, and dreamed of Nunne: Nunne was standing on the rooftop of a house in Berkeley Square, and shrieking like Petrouchka at the night sky. He woke abruptly, deeply aware of Nunne, feeling his presence in the room. There was no one. Nunne had stood there, his arms flailing, shouting something at the sky; below, the crowds watched his protesting silhouette; many shouted, urging him to jump. But Nunne would not jump; Sorme was certain of it, and the certainty made him glad. In the empty house below, he hurried up uncarpeted stairs, hoping to reach the roof before it happened, feeling a happy excitement, certain now that there would be a light of prophecy over London, from Islington to Marylebone, from Primrose Hill to St John's Wood, and hanging like a red sun over Kensington Gardens. Nunne wouldn't jump. He would stand there, Austin, Vaslav, Petrouchka, above the rooftops. But he was not in an empty house. He was in a brothel, lying in an attic room. And Austin was there.

He was standing by the window, staring out. In the faint dawnlight, the big naked body looked like a marble statue. The shoulders were broad; rounded muscle, a dancer's shoulders.

Sorme could not see his eyes. They would be stone eyes, not closed, immobile in the half light, nor like the eyes of the priest, grey in the ugly gargoyle's face. When he closed his own eyes he saw the dancer, the big body, moving without effort through the air, slowly, unresisted, then coming to earth, as silent as a shadow. It was very clear. The face, slim and muscular, bending over him, a chaplet of rose leaves woven into the hair, a faun's face, the brown animal eyes smiling at him, beyond good and evil.

Cold the dawnlight on marble roofs, more real than the jazz. You're gonna miss me, honey. Glass corridors leading nowhere.

And then the leap, violent as the sun on ice, beyond the bed, floating without noise, on, through the open window.

The excitement rose in him like a fire. The rose, bloodblack in the silver light, now reddening in the dawn that blows over Paddington's rooftops. Ending. A rose thrown from an open window, curving high over London's waking rooftops, then falling, its petals loosening, into the grey soiled waters of the Thames.

He wanted to say it, with the full shock of amazement: So that's who you are!

Certain now, as never before, the identification complete.

It was still there as he woke up, the joy and surprise of the discovery, fading as he looked around the lightening room. He said aloud: Vaslav. (pp. 181-2)

Colin Wilson's novels are rarely mentioned in discussions of post-war English fiction: this is regrettable. It is true that their imaginative reach can exceed their stylistic grasp; this is especially evident in the attempts, in *The Mind Parasites* and *The Philosopher's Stone*, to evoke the consciousness of men who have made the evolutionary breakthrough. It is also true that his fiction can be insufficiently dialectical – that is, it does not explore and dramatize opposed viewpoints enough. But it is, nonetheless, interesting and disciplined, and does imply directions in which the novel, as a form, could develop in the future.

Wilson's autobiography, *Voyage to a Beginning*, is also worthy of note. Like some other post-war autobiographies – most famously, Sartre's *Words* (1964), Malraux's *AntiMémoires* (1967) and Barthes' *Roland Barthes* (1975) – it is, in a sense, an anti-autobiography. It does not promise personal revelation: 'the events of my life do not interest me enough to make me attempt [a formal autobiography], except where they can be used to illustrate an idea' (p. 1). It implicitly raises the issue of whether autobiography is possible:

One of the strange paradoxes of this world is that the quality of living experience has nothing whatever in common with the quality of a story told in retrospect. Other people's lives may be a 'story', may have an epic or romantic quality; but sitting here, now, looking out of a window or reading a book, every human being knows that the present is not a moment in a story; it just *is* (p. 10).

In this perspective, any autobiography must falsify: it is the point made by Sartre in *Nausea*, and reiterated in *Words*: one retrospectively confers order on events that had no necessary order in their unfolding. But in Wilson's terms, the order of existence is not, as it is for Sartre, an illusion, a subjective, retrospective projection, but a reality: we might suggest, then, that an autobiography could reveal an order, a meaning, in a life that was actually there, but, due to the narrowness of one's consciousness, unperceived: it calls to mind T.S. Eliot's lines in *Four Quartets*: 'we had the experience but missed the meaning'. The retrospective ordering of autobiography may disclose, not impose, meaning, provide illumination rather than falsification. *Voyage* could thus be said to reveal Wilson's life as an existential-evolutionary quest;

writing for him is not, as it is for Sartre, a neurosis which separates him from reality (though it could, no doubt, be analyzed in this way); it is a means of pursuing that quest. *Voyage* also offers a positive hero, 'something of a metaphysician', who triumphs over physical and philosophical obstacles; it conduces to wide-angle consciousness. In these respects, Wilson's autobiography fulfils his criteria for the novel; but this does not mean that it can be assimilated to fiction, in the sense of falsification; rather, it brings the reader closer to what is, in Wilson's terms, the reality of meaning. The triumph of Wilson as hero is not the obvious one of worldly success, though that plays a part in it: in a way, *Voyage* is the story of a working-class lad made good, a stirring tale of self-help; it is also the story of a writer who breaks through to fame — and Wilson tells us, in *Voyage*, how he always raced through writer's biographies to get to the moment of breakthrough—and how, the more spectacular the breakthrough, the more he read and re-read it, 'to get its savour' (p. 126). But his own breakthrough, of course, was to have an ironic dimension.

Voyage also, in addition to its anti-autobiographical elements, also calls upon an older autobiographical model—though this, in a sense, contributes to its anti-autobiographical effect. The model is that of the nineteenth-century 'intellectual autobiography'—John Stuart Mill's, for example. Since, however, *Voyage* also deals with, for instance, Wilson's boyhood shoplifting activities, his adolescent sexual experiences, his factory and office jobs, and his sleeping-bag-on-Hampstead-Heath days, it gives the 'intellectual autobiography' an added dimension. It suggests, in a way alien to English culture—though we find it in *Roland Barthes*—that ideas, intellectual analyses, are as much a part of 'life' as unreflective experience, that anecdote and analysis can fruitfully complement each other, that the gap between 'thought' and 'experience' is, in a sense, artificial. Autobiography has become a topic of considerable theoretical and critical interest in recent years: *Voyage to a Beginning* is a fascinating contribution to the genre.

In conclusion, it is worth considering why Colin Wilson's work has not received more serious attention in our culture. In part this is no doubt due to the lingering folk-memory of the brouhaha surrounding *The Outsider*. A more significant reason is that Wilson is difficult to 'place' on any conventional kind of intellectual or literary map. His work shows scant respect for academic etiquette; it does not conform to those codes which currently signify academic rigour. Similarly, his novels do not clearly signal their superiority to the popular forms they employ; they embarrass the traditional literary critic. But he cannot easily be dismissed, even by those who might like to do so, as, in the pejorative sense, a popular writer. His work has a consistency of its own; like Wells and Shaw, he wants to reach a wide audience, to communicate, to exhort, to improve; his spirit, in this sense, is that of the Victorians and Edwardians; his clear, forceful prose has an effect like that which he ascribes to Shaw's, 'of determined clarity . . . obviously inspired by a conviction that any problem will yield to a combination of reason, courage and determination' (*The Genius of Shaw*, p. 227).

These are unfashionable virtues: and they bring us to the most important reason for the relative neglect of Wilson's work: its attack on some of the most deeply entrenched features of contemporary culture: a pessimism about the human prospect beyond that justified by our real and undoubtedly acute difficulties; the scepticism about the possibility of finding any sure ground of meaning, value and purpose evident in deconstruction and in the 'antifoundational' pragmatism of the American philosopher Richard Rorty; the prevalence of neo-determinist systems of thought—psychoanalytic, marxist, structuralist, post-structuralist, deconstructionist—that exalt the unconscious, or history, or ideology, or structure, or discourse, over individual will and effort—all, in a Wilsonian perspective, perpetuations of the 'passive fallacy'; the pursuit of sensation and intensity without a recognition of the need for discipline and work. Given these cultural features, it is hardly surprising that Wilson's writing, though it has found many readers, has had relatively little acceptance. The assimilation of his ideas would be part of a major cultural shift; but it may be we can make this happen. Wilson has affirmed: 'the prophets of decadence and the "decline of the West" were wrong. We are living in one of the most important epochs in human history' (*Bernard Shaw*, p. 298). Indeed we are; and whether those prophets are proved wrong depends, as Wilson rightly insists, upon us.

REFERENCES

This lists books quoted in the essay, in alphabetical order of title. Publishers and dates of the first English editions are given, and also of later editions where quotations have been taken from these.
BY COLIN WILSON
The Age of Defeat (Gollancz, 1959)
'The Age of Murder: An Introductory Essay' in *Encyclopaedia of*

Modern Murder, 1962-82, ed. Colin Wilson and Donald Seaman
(Arthur Barker – Weidenfeld and Nicolson, 1983)
Bernard Shaw: A Reassessment (Hutchinson, 1969; Macmillan, 1981)
The Craft of the Novel (Gollancz, 1975)
The Essential Colin Wilson (Harrap, 1985)
The Glass Cage (Arthur Barker, 1966; Village Press, no date)
The God of the Labyrinth (Hart-Davis, 1970; Mayflower, 1971)
Introduction to the New Existentialism (Hutchinson, 1966. Now en-
titled *The New Existentialism*)
*Mysteries: An Investigation into the Occult, the Paranormal and the
Supernatural* (Hodder and Stoughton, 1978)
The Occult (Hodder and Stoughton, 1971; Mayflower, 1975)
The Outsider (Gollancz, 1956; Picador, 1978)
'A Personal View' in *The Genius of Shaw: A Symposium*, ed.
Michael Holroyd (Hodder and Stoughton, 1979)
Ritual in the Dark (Gollancz, 1960; Panther, 1976)
The Strength to Dream: Literature and the Imagination (Gollancz,
1963; Abacus, 1976)
Voyage to a Beginning: A Preliminary Autobiography (Cecil Woolf,
1969)
'Wilson, Colin (Henry)' in *Contemporary Novelists*, ed. James Vinson
(St James's Press, 1976)

BY OTHER AUTHORS

Greene, Graham, *The Power and the Glory* (Heinemann, 1940; Penguin,
1971)
Proust, Marcel, *Remembrance of Things Past: Volume One: Swann's
Way*, tr. C.K. Scott Moncrieff and Terence Kilmartin (Chatto and
Windus, 1981; Penguin, 1983).

16

Writing *Ritual in the Dark*

SIDNEY CAMPION

Although *The Age of Defeat* was published several months before
Ritual in the Dark, it was written when the novel was almost completed.
Ritual is the logical continuation of *Religion and the Rebel*, the attempt
to deepen its conclusions and extend its notions of existence-
philosophy.

The first version of *Ritual* was begun in 1949, before Colin went
into the R.A.F., and travelled with him to France. Because it passed
through so many metamorphoses, it may be worth tracing its
development from this early version.

Ritual began as a short story about a man who murders a prostitute;
its original title was *Symphonic Variations*. The subject of the story
was frustration, and the idea that a man who is completely inactive
can have no identity; his 'identity' can be discovered by himself only in
action. Through all its transformations, this has remained the basic
theme of *Ritual*. In the original story, Sorme is the murderer, who
kills a prostitute as an expression of his disgust at the meaninglessness
of life. He feels that the world is inscrutable, giving no clues to its
laws of good and evil, rather like Eddington's picture of the final in-
scrutability of nature:

> For I was thinking of a plan
> To dye one's whiskers green
> Then always use so large a fan
> That they could not be seen.

Sorme hopes that, by committing a 'definitive act', he will have
lifted his life permanently—for better or worse—above this sense of
not having started. In fact, the murder is the last act in a complete
breakdown with hallucinations; in a dream he sees an old man who
assures him that he is not real, that nothing is real. At the end of the
story he attempts to commit suicide, but his stomach rejects the
poison; after vomiting he is left staring at the wall, aware that life is
still inscrutable; his actions have changed nothing.

The most important point in the story is a speech made by Sorme
to a girl to whom he confesses the murder. He speaks of a strange
weight inside him, a lump of unexpressed emotion that he can find no
way of releasing. He speaks of it as being like a child wanting to be born;

but something prevents its birth; at last it begins to come away in pieces, a hand or a leg at a time. The speech probably expresses Colin Wilson's own emotional state at the time of writing the story; it certainly expresses the disgust he had come to feel at the 'cumulative ignobility' of being a civil servant, and doubting his final ability to escape to some more meaningful way of life.

After completing the story, Colin decided to turn it into a full-length novel. To emphasise the sense of being trapped in unreality, he now made it doubtful whether Sorme had really committed the murder, or whether he only imagines he has committed it. At the time of writing the new version, Colin was reading a great deal of Pirandello, and was impressed by Pirandello's way of suggesting that truth is relative. In *Cosi é se vi pare*, for example, the audience is left in doubt as to which of the characters is mad and which is sane; Pirandello tries to imply that no one can know. Colin found this unsatisfactory; in the situation posited by Pirandello, one of the characters would quite definitely be mad, and it would be possible to determine which, even though the audience is not let into the secret. The completely relative nature of truth could be better demonstrated in a novel in which everything is seen through the eyes of a man suffering from delusions.

Unfortunately for this early version of *Ritual*, the technical problems were immense. The essence of the novel was the idea that when the world is not surveyed through a curtain of action, it appears to be meaningless. So everything depended on *having nothing happen*. At this point, the novel was given the title *Things Do Not Happen*. But a novel in which nothing happens is hardly satisfactory (although Robbe-Grillet has since attempted something of the sort). Sorme sat in his room, took a walk in the local cemetery (based on the cemetery at East Finchley), sat in cafés drinking tea, talked with friends with whom he felt no sense of contact. The technique consisted in emphasising Sorme's sense of having no contact with the world; this is increased by the continual emotional self-delusion practised by most people with whom he comes into contact. It is present, for example, in the palpably untrue or sentimental inscriptions on the gravestones in the cemetery. Sorme has a hard, dry sense of reality, but it brings him no pleasure; only freedom from the illusions under which others labour. He studies Saint John of the Cross, who describes this sense of complete emotional suspension as the first stage of the way to sainthood—it is the 'dark night of the soul'. Unfortunately, his contact with a Catholic priest is no more satisfactory; he feels that the man's faith is based on illusions, although he may be closer to reality than some of Sorme's other contacts. And still somewhere in the background, there are echoes of murder that arouse a response in Sorme; he broods on Gauguin's comment: 'Life being what it is, one dreams of revenge'.

Woven into the basis of the story, even at this early stage, were references to Nijinsky. In reading about Nijinsky, Colin had come to feel that the dancer is the most extraordinary example of the modern 'self-division'. A half of him was god-like; when he danced, he was in contact with 'the power-house'. But in his everyday affairs, he was inarticulate, bullied by Diaghileff, and regarded with faint contempt by the 'intellectuals' in the company. Often, he identified himself with Christ. Colin writes: 'I was told that some of his jumps defied gravity, like Christ's feat of walking on water. Another man who seemed to me to possess the same kind of power was Grigory Rasputin, and certain stories told of him attest his ability to perform miracles. Unlike Nijinsky, Rasputin experienced no self-division; he was betrayed from outside, not from within. Nijinsky and Rasputin were basic to the symbolism of the story; they were hints of the man-god'.

But writing a novel without a plot proved difficult, and Colin's discovery of the *Egyptian Book of the Dead* made a considerable difference. The *Book of the Dead* was compiled by Budge from funeral texts on the walls of the pyramids. The Egyptians believed that the soul of the dead man takes the day of his death and the whole of the following night to reach the Egyptian underworld, Amentet. In the course of this journey, he meets with many perils—various monsters, vampire worms, evil spirits, etc. The prayers of the *Book of the Dead* were charms, to be repeated by the 'soul' to defend it against these perils. (The procedure in the Tibetan *Book of the Dead* is, of course, very similar, except that the 'perils' are delusions of the soul entangled in Maya.) The dead man is known in the texts as 'the scribe Ani' or 'Nebseni', and he frequently identifies himself with the god Horus or Ra to escape the demons.

Colin found in this scheme a possible structure for his own novel; he regarded it as a kind of omen when he discovered that one of the titles of the *Book of the Dead* is *Ritual of the Dead*, one of the early titles of the 'Sorme-book'. (*Ritual* is referred to consistently in journals as 'the Sorme-book'.) Sorme is also travelling through a kind of night— the dark night of the soul; his hero Nijinsky, like the scribe Ani, had repeated, 'I am God, I am God'. The symbolism was beginning to accumulate; he was studying *Ulysses* and James's collected prefaces to try to find the clue that would help to unify the book. He writes: 'It seemed to me that the novel has not even begun. With his preface

(*The Art of the Novel*) James did for the novel what Newton did for physics with his *Principia – and yet people go on writing the same old-fashioned, rule-of-thumb novels as if James had never existed.* What I wanted to do was perhaps absurdly over-ambitious; I wanted to produce a Dostoevskian novel, using the techniques made available by Joyce and James'.

In order to give the novel a plot, the story about the seduction of the Jehovah's Witness was utilised; so was an episode from the earlier *Ritual of the Dead* about a painter who feels an inexpressible desire for his ten-year-old model. In the story *The Mirror*, one of the characters had said: 'There is often no way of satisfying the appetite for certain kinds of beauty. When I first saw the Lake of Geneva from a hilltop, it aroused an inexpressible agony, for I knew its beauty was untouchable. I could not feel it by swimming in the lake or by drinking its water; it was a desire with no real object.' This is still the most important theme of *Ritual in the Dark*; Glasp's agony comes from his realisation that the feeling aroused in him by Christine is not a physical desire, and cannot therefore be assuaged in the normal way.

But most important of all was the reflection of this theme in Sorme's sexual explorations. In a letter about *Ritual*, Colin wrote:

No man has ever experienced sex in its purity. The violence of sexual desire has nothing to do with having an affair with a woman, taking her to bed. It is instantaneous. In a love affair, the personalities make contact, and the love-making is essentially personal. Turner expressed this when he wrote in *Epithalamium*:

> Can the lover share his soul
> Or the mistress show her mind;
> Can the body beauty share
> Or lust satisfaction find? . . .
>
> Marriage is but keeping house
> Sharing food and company,
> What has this to do with love
> Or the body's beauty? . . .
>
> I have stared upon a dawn
> And trembled like a man in love,
> A man in love I was, and I
> Could not speak and could not move.

It might seem, therefore, that a man could attain that violent,

instantaneous contact ('can lust satisfaction find') in lust-murder or
necrophilia, where the personality of the woman becomes unimport-
ant. . . . The question, of course, is why on earth should anyone want
this kind of 'purity of violence'? My answer, I think, would be that
the sexual orgasm is the nearest that most men ever come to an unify-
ing vision of the world, to the affirmation of the saint. Sorme is
most impressed by the *impersonality* of sex on the occasion when he
fails to make love to a communist tart he is sleeping with; he says:
'She reminded me of mathematics'. This is why he comes to excuse
Nunne's crimes; he feels that perhaps Nunne is simply a reflection
of himself, with the courage to carry his theorising into action.

Sorme is obsessed by a feeling of the ambiguity of reality; in its early
version, the novel simply documented a series of his contacts with
people who seem to be unaware of this ambiguity, who all feel that the
world is a simple and straightforward place (as Broadbent does in *John
Bull's Other Island*). There are various degrees of self-delusion, ranging
from the priest's insight into human weakness, to Miss Quincey's simple
belief in a future heaven on earth—a belief which she is too intelligent
to accept wholly.

I asked Colin why he had chosen the Jehevah's Witnesses. Miss
Quincey would seem far more plausible as a Catholic or even a Method-
ist. His reply was: 'It seems to me that there is one valuable and true
element in their beliefs; they hold that *this world* will become Paradise
after the Last Judgement. This is a curiously mystical belief for such a
literal-minded sect, and it corresponds with the views held by Traherne,
Dostoevsky and Blake. Life is actually good; the world *is* heaven; hell is
man's subjective states. If we were freed from delusion, we would know
that men are gods and the earth is paradise. It is because the life-current
that flows through us is so low that we live in misery and boredom. But
there *must* be some way to increase the current.'

From its very earliest versions, the style of *Ritual* is deliberately flat,
two-dimensional. This was also the reason for excluding inverted com-
mas. Shaw has defined style as 'effectiveness of assertion', and remarked,
'He who has nothing to assert has no style.' In the earlier versions of
Ritual, Colin was in revolt against his own early style (borrowed from
Poe) and against tortuous psychological language—a heritage from
James. His story of how this change first came about is amusing and
worth quoting:

I was asked to read a story to the Vaughan Literary Society (Leicester) when I was seventeen; my friend Alan Bates was also asked to read a story. He produced some work in which a pianist falls asleep at his piano as he reads a score of Chopin, and has a dream in which he becomes Chopin, sitting in George Sands's house. I decided to use the same theme, and turn it into a psychological study of 'vision' in the manner of James's story, *The Great Good Place*. The evening was a fiasco. Alan read his story first, then I read mine; everyone was prodigiously bored, and started up conversations before I'd finished. Afterwards, I heard a woman friend of mine describing it to another girl: 'Oh it was *ever so* soulful—all about a garden or something. . . .' I went home in a miserable rage, feeling humiliated and sick of my own work. I started to read Dostoevsky's *Possessed* again; the savagery of his portraits of Stephan Trofimovich and Varvara Petrovna gave me a feeling of relief; it was the way I felt about the Vaughan Lit. Soc. Then I started to write a sort of fantasy in the manner of the Night Town scene in *Ulysses*, in which I tried to obtain an effect of irony by contrasting the trivial with the violent and horrible. From that time onward, I dropped the 'Jamesian' style and tried to write flatly, without charm, with an undercurrent of violence.

A further elaboration of this manner was the determination to do without the usual novelist's devices of switching from character to character and giving the reader 'inside information' on what his characters are thinking. Instead, Sorme was treated as if he were a camera with a built-in tape-recorder; nothing is observed except what he could have observed. (Joyce takes this technique to its logical extreme in the Aeolus chapter of *Ulysses*—in the newspaper office.) In later versions of the novel, however, this extreme rigour was abandoned, and the 'narrator' occasionally comments on Sorme's feelings.

Little by little, sub-plots were introduced into *Ritual* to try to carry the 'metaphysics'. The close adherence to the scheme of *The Book of the Dead* was dropped, although its essentials were kept. The final effect of this, as Colin admits, was to give the novel far more plot than it needed. There are half a dozen themes; the relation with Nunne, with Miss Quincey, with Caroline, with Glasp, with the priest, and with the old man in the room above (introduced for comic relief). There is also, of course, Sorme's 'relations with himself'—and these were primarily the reason for abandoning the 'camera' scheme of writing; to describe such episodes as Sorme's 'vastation' in the basement flat, his visions of affirmation on the roof of the house, the narrator *has* to take over,

unless the episode is restricted to Sorme's thoughts (which might fairly
be 'picked-up' by the tape-recorder).

A rather late—but nevertheless important—influence on *Ritual in
the Dark* was Berg's opera *Wozzeck*. For the greater part of the opera—
a pathetic story of a soldier who murders his mistress and then com-
mits suicide—Berg remains completely detached. Other composers—
like Puccini—allowed the audience to feel their own emotions, to feel
the composer's pity for Butterfly or Liu. Berg, with his charmless
atonal music, presents the irony and tragedy with no personal involvement. His involvement only occurs at the end of the opera, in the final
interlude in the key of D flat, in which the composer's pity for Wozzeck
and Marie can suddenly be felt. (This is the only part of the opera with
a definite key.) Colin was struck by the method—conveying violence
and horror in an 'alien' language, free of the emotional overtones that
have slipped into ordinary language through imprecise use. He spent a
great deal of time brooding on the possibility of a literary counterpart
to the style of *Wozzeck*. The result of this study was a careful revision
of the novel, removing any words that seemed tinged by emotion, attempting to produce a 'flat surface', broken only by the events, not by the
author's intervention.

But the centre of the dialectic in *Ritual* is the problem of sex. One
reviewer referred to Sorme as 'the usual promiscuous young ruffian', but
there is more than ordinary promiscuity in Sorme's relations with
Caroline and Gertrude. Just as, in the earliest version of *Ritual*, Sorme
committed murder to try to produce in himself a certain sense of having
broken the laws of nature, so in the later version, he seduces both the
aunt and her niece as an experiment in immorality. In fact, the result
puzzles him. He believes himself completely unattached to Caroline, and
yet suddenly feels himself to be in love with her when he goes into her
bedroom. After a night with Gertrude, he feels in love with her, and
confesses to her about Caroline. The problem seems to be solved; it is
Gertrude he is really in love with. Then, at the end of the book, Caroline
rings him, and he realises that things cannot be simplified so easily; the
emotion he feels for Gertrude is not exclusive; he can also feel it for
Caroline; it is even remotely possible that he may come to feel it for the
child Christine (with whom he is preparing to embark on a new
'experiment' at the end of the book). As the novel ends, he realises that
the complexity must be accepted; it is not like a mathematical equation
that can be reduced to simplicity by allowing some of the elements to
cancel themselves out. The contradiction might be resolved if Sorme
reaches an altogether higher level, if he attains some new maturity; but

on the level upon which he lives in the book, there is no simple answer, and certainly no solution in simply choosing Miss Quincey or Caroline.

Finally and most fundamentally, *Ritual* is a *Bildungsroman*, an attempt to trace a certain moral evolution in its central character. This, in a way, might have been expected from Colin Wilson, considering the importance he attributes to the *Bildungsroman* as a form in his 'philosophical books'. In *Religion and the Rebel* he writes: 'In the twentieth century, the only serious form of literary art is the *Bildungsroman*'. What is emphasised in *Ritual* is the importance of the idea of maturity, of education in the processes of living. Sorme, who began as a murderer with no sense of values, achieves one certainty in the course of his involvement with Nunne and Gertrude: that maturity *is* an ultimate value. 'Ripeness is all.' The world *is* inscrutable and unchanging; only man's perception of it changes as he matures.

This leads to an important observation on *Ritual* that, as far as I know, has been noted by only one critic. P.N. Furbank wrote in *The Listener*: 'One expects a prophet of anti-humanism to be filled with agony and pessimism in the face of everyday futility; but what, in fact, shines out in this book is a buoyant Edwardian optimism'. In fact, this is precisely what distinguishes Colin Wilson from the majority of his contemporaries. Many reviewers of *The Outsider* spoke of it as a typically gloomy book, full of suicide, madness and despair. Certainly, he is in every way aware of the contemporary material utilised by Kafka, Eliot, Joyce. His work is an attempt to fashion a philosophy of optimism from the material of 'contemporary chaos'. 'The stupidest literary heresy of our time,' he writes, 'is the belief that Shaw's optimism has been superseded by the more realistic vision of Eliot, Joyce and the rest. (Pound stated this in a particularly silly article on Joyce and Flaubert's *Pecuchet*.) In fact, Shaw's vision is a great deal deeper and wider than that of any contemporary pessimist. I see my problem as this: to start from Eliot's "sense of his age", to take into account everything that he took into account, and still to finish with an overwhelmingly affirmative vision'.

17

Introduction to *The Outsider*

MARILYN FERGUSON

The Outsider, first published in 1956 when Colin Wilson was only twenty-four, is a prophetic book as well as a literary *tour de force*. By tracing, analyzing and giving a context,to the disaffection and struggle of creative thinkers from William Blake to Ernest Hemingway, Wilson anticipated many developments of the 1960s and 1970s. The trajectory of Outsider consciousness led naturally to the rising interest in Eastern philosophy, the human potential movement, and the proliferation of techniques designed to help individuals transcend a sense of alienation from self and society.

Wilson summarizes the problems of that alienation:

> The Outsider wants to cease to be an Outsider.
> He wants to be integrated as a human being, achieving a fusion between mind and heart.
> He seeks vivid sense perception.
> He wants to understand the soul and its workings.
> He wants to get beyond the trivial.
> He wants to express himself so he can better understand himself.
> He sees a way out via intensity, extremes of experience.

Surveys and polls in the United States reveal Outsider values in a significant and rapidly growing minority of the population. The 'inner-directed' are the fastest-growing consumer group. Increasingly people say that meaning is a more important consideration in their work than economic incentives. Self-fulfilment and self-expression are high on the list of goals.

The atmosphere of conformity that made the Outsiders feel different from their peers is now under attack from the mainstream. Social norms are changing rapidly in the direction of greater personal freedom.

Those seeking the experiential, the spiritual, and the numinous are no longer a handful. Millions have recognized that they are harbouring within themselves another dimension of consciousness and that many old social structures are deadly to this other self. The phenomenon Blake called 'twofold consciousness' has become an increasingly common experience.

To an observer the way of the Outsider may appear excessive, difficult, even reckless. Wilson shows us, by example after example, why the Outsider cannot accept society as it is, why he 'sees too much and too deep'.

Outsiders seek to heal divisions: between conscious and unconscious, intellect and intuition, mind and body, self and society, spirit and sensuality. 'The Outsider's chief desire is to be unified. He is selfish as a man with a lifelong raging toothache would be selfish.'

Refusing to resolve life's difficulties by withdrawal or denial, Outsiders seek transcendence through headlong involvement. They believe with Herman Hesse's Steppenwolf that 'the way to innocence leads . . . ever deeper into human life. Instead of narrowing your world and simplifying your soul, you will have at the last to take the whole world into your soul, cost what it may.'

The Outsider's intensity is expressed in Goethe's poem, 'The Holy Longing', with its image of the butterfly drawn to, and transformed by, the flame:

> And so long as you haven't experienced
> this: to die and so to grow,
> you are only a troubled guest
> on the dark earth.

Most of us accommodate to the cultural trance, but Outsiders continue to be appalled at inauthenticity and mechanicalness. They see through their act and that of others. 'The problem of the Outsiders is the unreality of their lives. They suddenly realize they are in a cinema. They ask: Who are we? What are we doing here? . . . They are confronted with a terrifying freedom.'

Because they have glimpsed another, deeper dimension to life, they are not satisfied to be automatons. They are driven to self-discovery, even self-inquisition. They put themselves to tests of imagination and action that awe more 'sensible' people. 'I doubt whether such pain improves us,' Nietzsche said, 'but I know it *deepens* us.' And Rilke wrote, 'May I, emerging at last from this terrible insight, burst into jubilant praise. . . .'

The Outsider, Wilson points out, does not wish to accept life merely because fate is treating him well at the moment *but because it is his Will to accept*. He wants to control his responses through understanding, to build affirmation into his vision. Freedom of response is the only authentic freedom. This search is essentially spiritual, but 'religious truth cannot exist apart from intellectual rigour'. The Outsider's stubborn intellect seeks to understand the whispers of his intuition.

For a hundred years or more, Wilson said, Outsiders have been slowly creating new values by implication. 'The real issue is not whether two and two make four or whether two and two make five, but whether life advances by men who love *words* or by men who love *living*.'

A thoughtful reading of *The Outsider* gives us a profound sense of our collective modern struggle: how to restore the timeless and visionary in a culture that has prided itself on divorcing reason from feeling. Understanding the historic roots of this struggle gives us a deeper understanding of the Outsider in ourselves.*

*This article first appeared as an Introduction to *The Outsider* (J.P. Tarcher, 1982).

18

Murder as Existential Act

HOWARD F. DOSSOR

Someone—was it the American novelist James Drought—developed the argument that human beings die from one of only two possible causes: they either choose to die or they are killed by another person.

The French philosopher, Albert Camus, understood that if his philosophy was to become relevant to contemporary life, it would have to embrace a theory of suicide. For Camus, suicide was the ultimate absurdity in a world where absurdity abounds. He did not advocate or condone suicide: he insisted that it must be rejected as a mature response to absurdity since it simply added to absurdity.

But what is man to think and say in the face of murder?

Colin Wilson has demonstrated a profound interest in the philosophy, sociology and psychology of murder since 1961. In that year, his *Encyclopaedia of Murder* (jointly written with Patricia Pitman) was published by Arthur Barker. Since then, his studies on the subject have included *A Casebook of Murder* (Leslie Frewen, 1969), *Order of Assassins* (Hart-Davis, 1972), *Encyclopaedia of Modern Murder* (with Donald Seaman) (Arthur Barker, 1983), *The Psychic Detectives* (Pan Books, 1984) and the vast *A Criminal History of Mankind* (Granada, 1985). His novels, *Ritual in the Dark* (Gollancz, 1960), *The World of Violence* (Gollancz, 1963), *The Schoolgirl Murder Case* (Hart-Davis, 1974) and *The Janus Murder Case* (Granada, 1985) should all be regarded as important steps in his analysis of the subject. His 'fictive' work, *The Killer* (*Lingard* in the United States) (New English Library, 1970) is virtually a cornerstone of his investigations. Nor should we overlook the Phoebus Publishing Company's *Crimes and Punishment* of 1973, a partwork for which Wilson served on the Advisory Editorial Board. Although this work is now out of print and very difficult to obtain in a complete set, it remains an impressive testimony to Wilson's determined efforts to embrace the world of murder within his philosophy.*

A student of Wilson's criminology should not ignore the significant contribution he has made through essays published in a wide variety of journals. Among these, the most significant are probably *Crimes of Freedom and Their Cure* ('Twentieth Century', London, Winter 1964-65), *The Violent Void* ('Cavalier', May 1965), *Towards a New Criminology*

---

*All Wilson's essays for this work have now been published as *The Mammoth Book of True Crime* (Robinson, 1988) with an introduction by Howard F. Dossor.—Ed.

('Crime and Detection', November 1966), *The New Trend in Murder*
('Edgar Wallace Mystery Magazine', vol. 3, no. 29, 1966), *The Dominant Killer* ('Men Only', vol. 38, no. 5, 1973) and *A Doomed Society*
('Journal of Human Relations', vol. 21, no. 4, 1973).

We know that Wilson was interested in murder before 1961. In his childhood and youth he read avidly the copies of 'True Detective' and 'True Crime' passed on to him after she had read them by his mother. But this interest did not mature until the 'fifties and early 'sixties when he began to develop his theory of a New Existentialism which found expression in his Outsider cycle. Wilson noted that the Outsider was possessed of certain characteristics which he held in common with the murderer. It was not that the Outsider *was* a murderer so much as that he was prone to becoming a murderer. Thus it was through his extensive examination of the psyche of the Outsider that Wilson came to plunge into the depth of the criminal.

I remember once trying to explain Wilson's Outsider to a Supreme Court Judge in Australia. When I had finished, the Judge nodded in an indication of comprehension and then commented that the person I had described was a fair replica of many of the prisoners who had stood in the dock before him charged with criminal offences, including murder. The similarity is not an accident. In Wilson's terms, the Outsider who fails to move *beyond* himself is indeed prone to commit an act of violence.

In tracing the development of Wilson's philosophy of murder, it is interesting to note his sources. It is not to the traditional criminologist that he turns—although he does not ignore him completely. It is, rather, an Abraham Maslow or an A.E. van Vogt who attracts his attention. Maslow's observations about *peak experiences* have been important to Wilson in his thinking about murder and it is of some interest that Maslow himself used his own insights to help rehabilitate alcoholics. The van Vogt portrait of the *violent* or *right* man has likewise provided Wilson with an important stepping stone to understanding. It seems that important developments within a scientific discipline are presaged by insights attained outside that discipline and then transferred to it by an alert intelligence.

It was while in the process of compiling his contribution to the *Encyclopaedia of Murder* that Wilson identified a number of significant patterns in the history and geography of murder. He noticed that murders in various countries differed in kind and frequency and that there had been a notable change in their nature over the past eighty years or so. Whereas murder in the mid-nineteenth century had been largely economic in its aetiology, by the contemporary period it had become associated with a pervasive sense of boredom and a low self-esteem on the part of the perpetrator.

Just as Viktor Frankl found the roots of a certain psychological disorder in a sense of meaninglessness which could be dealt with in what he called Existential Analysis, so Wilson has found that boredom is a critical factor in the debilitation of human emotions. So critical is boredom in destroying an individual's self-image, that it is important to understand something of its origin.

Boredom occurs when our daily living is taken over by the *robot*. Wilson's robot is that part of our personality which attends automatically to the task at hand while another part of our self focusses on higher issues. Thus the robot drives our car to the lecture theatre while we compose and refine the opening few sentences of our lecture or frame that smart question which will disclose our intellect to the assembled company. At this level, the robot is a useful device for if we could perform simple functions only with total concentration upon them, life would be uneventful and dull. But the robot has a tendency to exceed its brief. Instead of remaining content to drive the car or prepare the vegetables for the evening meal, it begins to eat the meal itself, thereby depriving us of the satisfaction of our taste buds. As Wilson points out, the robot can even make love to our wife!

It will be understood readily that when the robot exceeds the authority we intended to vest in it and begins in fact to live our lives for us, we are inevitably deprived of what Maslow called *peak experiences*. There is no longer any rich reward for our best behaviour. There is no stimulus from our environment since it is the robot rather than ourselves who interprets the world about us. At this level, the robot is a dangerous interference with our living and as a consequence we succumb to a sense of boredom.

The *St Neots Margin*, named after the town through which he was being driven at the time he conceived the notion, is, perhaps, Wilson's most important single idea. The St Neots Margin, which has also been called *The Indifference Threshold*, is akin to a blinkering of consciousness with the result that the capacity to grasp experience is lost. It is a state of drift in which we are profoundly untouched by the events and things around us. An image may help. A young toddler is walking along a pathway with his father. Suddenly, the toddler stops and points his fingers. His father stops and looks but sees nothing until the child takes him by the hand and leads him forward twenty paces where he now sees what it is that has attracted the child's attention. A brightly coloured butterfly flutters lightly on the grass at the path's edge. Yet, having seen it, the father remains unmoved as if he has still not seen it and continues his walk while the child stoops in silent wonder.

The St Neots Margin is a loss of the sense of wonder: an incapacity to respond to stimuli. It is consciousness in a void: it is a form of life-devaluation and it inevitably produces an overwhelming sense of boredom.

In dealing with the myriad inexplicable events that impinge upon human experience, Wilson has given close attention to the phenomenon of multiple personality where as many as sixteen 'characters' have apparently been located within a single human body. As a consequence of his study of such cases, Wilson has concluded that each individual is composed of a ladder of selves. According to this theory, we have a simple, primitive self but also a series of successively more sophisticated selves with, perhaps, a self at the top which we have never yet realized. In fact, we oscilate between a lower self and a mid-level self for most of the time without entering what Maslow called 'the further reaches of human nature' very often, if at all.

The notion of a ladder of selves has clear implications for a psychological theory which emphasizes the consequences of boredom. Obviously, if I am performing at an infantile level of self, my juvenile level of self will be frustrated and this frustration will commonly find expression as boredom. It may well be the case that the greater the disparity between the actual self at a given moment and the highest realizable self that I may be, the greater will be my frustration and boredom.

In recent years, Wilson has given considerable attention to the matter of the bicameral nature of the human brain. He has noted that the left hemisphere of the brain has a logical, computational function while the right hemisphere is given to intuitive and imaginative speculation. The left brain speaks, counts and plans: the right brain dreams, paints and composes. Nor has Wilson lost sight of the fact that in the contemporary West the former type of mental activity is valued more highly than the latter. This value judgement poses considerable problems for those whose right brain behaviour is more pronounced than left brain activity since it represents a contrary bias. The sensitive individual in our Western civilization is perforce an Outsider whose essential needs are being frustrated. The not uncommon result is a descent into boredom which may find ultimate expression through alcoholism or even criminality.

At the very least, the concepts of the robot, the St Neots margin, the ladder of selves and the bicameral mind are all most useful symbols in our attempt to think through the question of boredom. There is some hope that they may be more than this: they may well become diagnostic tools which help lay the foundation for a more appropriate psychology and sociology of crime.

In contributing to the publication of *Crimes and Punishment*, Wilson was attempting to identify the essential nature of the single, local murder. Perhaps one of the greatest mistakes made by professional criminologists is that they interpret murder as a universal affront against humanity. Of course it is that but it is within the local, individualized act that the real nature of murder will be discovered. Wilson is at least sensible enough to recognize that the death thrust that ended the life of Sharon Tate was categorically different from the explosion that killed Lord Mountbatten. In a sense, one can comprehend the Mountbatten death because it was in accord with the laws of political assassination – no matter how unpalatable they might be. But what of Sharon Tate? How account for the flow of her blood. There was no political motive: only the desperate need of an individual named Charles Manson to assert his own identity in the face of a world which, at least in his mind, had denied his reality.

The essential view held by Wilson with respect to modern murder is that it is, paradoxically, an attempt at self-affirmation. By taking a life, the murderer places himself centre-front on the stage of the mass media and thus mollifies his sense of boredom.

The twentieth century has seen an increase in the complexity of the threats confronting the human individual. Cascading sociological and technological changes make it difficult for the individual to maintain a sense of purpose and a positive self-esteem. In our large cities there is a dehumanizing influence abroad and individuals are locked in a cocoon of loneliness. Not the least significant aspects of this loneliness are the devaluation of intellect and the elevation of an ultimately unsatisfying hedonism. The media numb us with their crassness and the institutional establishments virtually complete the process of dehumanizing us. We are taught and encouraged to accept the most bland and peurile *mores* of our age.

There is, in Wilson's understanding, a high level of intellectual frustration in the mind of the murderer. This is not to deny the reality of emotional despair or even the deficiencies in emotional makeup but it is to reassess the emotional factor in crime as being only a component in the complex making of the murderer.

Wilson is well known as a student of the occult and in his recent *The Psychic Detectives*, he weds his understanding of the mysterious to his study of murder. Although he is cautious – he points out that he is unable to identify a single case where the intervention of a psychic was directly responsible for the apprehension of a murderer – he compiles credible evidence that psychometry may well have a place in the homicide investigations of the future. If we demythologize the terms 'occult' and 'psychometry', we can see that what Wilson is suggesting is that the study of murder might benefit from an admission of *intuitive* understanding alongside rational analysis. Such an admission constitutes an important element in Wilson's criminology. Some 'psychic technology' of the future will no longer be dismissed contemptuously by those who remain open to the full armoury of detection. At least, every facility available to us which will assist us, not merely to solve individual murders but to comprehend the essential character of the murderer, must be utilized.

To conclude: Murder may be the quintessential statement of our time. If we pay lip service to the sanctity of human life and yet live in an age when countless lives are taken at the blow of an angry fist or the passionate frustration of a thwarted lover, then we are forced to ask where we stand. At the centre of Wilson's philosophy of murder is his understanding that it is an *existential* act. Murder as a social phenomenon has much to say to the totality of the human condition and as long as we ignore it we fail to comprehend something essential about ourselves. We are indebted to Wilson that he has persisted in asking the question.

19

Control of Consciousness ~ Mental Freedom, Not Bliss ~ Colin Wilson's Ultimate Objective

K. GUNNAR BERGSTRÖM

Some thirty years have elapsed since Colin Wilson's first book, *The Outsider*, was published. It was at the time of the 'angry young men', among whom, against his will, Wilson was included. In the United States, the 'beat generation' was at its peak. In 1957, Jack Kerouac's book *On the Road* was published. Its title suggests the bohemian nature of the beatniks. No doubt, Kerouac played his part in creating the beat ideology, but so probably did Colin Wilson by *The Outsider*. In Chapter Seven of his *Order of Assassins*, Wilson states that the chapter in *The Outsider* dealing with Herman Hesse's work had a strong influence on the beakniks.

Although Colin Wilson thus influenced the 'beat generation', one cannot say that he approves of its life style. Wilson is by no means a friend of the bohemian life or the use of drugs. It is true that his aim is to enhance consciousness but the means by which this is to be achieved is, according to him, not drugs but mental discipline. He strives to create a psychology of consciousness.

Like many others, Colin Wilson thinks that our every-day consciousness perceives only a fraction of reality because, most of the time, we are too worried, distracted and fatigued to register more. We can, however, according to him, achieve a fuller and richer consciousness. It may appear quite suddenly as a benign grace of God but Colin Wilson thinks that man should be able to learn to switch on this kind of consciousness by an act of will. We have only to realize that we are not puppets but puppeteers, in control of what is going on. 'Once you *know* that "you" should be in control of consciousness, and you make a determined effort in that direction, the rest follows inevitably,' Wilson writes in one of his latest books, *Frankenstein's Castle: The Double Brain: Door to Wisdom* (1980, p. 123).

A conviction that you yourself are in control of consciousness and an intense mental effort are then, according to Colin Wilson, the keys to the broader, richer kind of consciousness. In *Frankenstein's Castle*, this

kind of consciousness is described from the point of view of the recent
theory of man's two brain halves: our left brain half being the seat of
the intellect and our right brain being the seat of our feelings and
intuition. The richer kind of consciousness is achieved when the two
brain halves work together in harmony. The left half must, however,
take the initiative for this co-operation, Colin Wilson claims. The right
half which, according to Wilson, also seems to control our supply of
energy must be enticed, as it were, into releasing its resources. This is
done by an act of will, by our conscious *I*, the seat of which is the left
half of the brain..Drugs can also make the right half of the brain release
its resources, but then we have no control of what is released, and Colin
Wilson strongly advises us against the use of drugs. He has always
preferred the difficult way to the easy one, and has always
advocated will, effort and discipline. Consequently, he warns against
sloth and drugs.

In his book *Roboten och meningen* (*The Robot and the Meaning*)
the Swedish diplomatist and author Kaj Falkman criticises Colin Wilson
for over-stating what the American psychologist Abraham Maslow calls
'peak experiences'. But Colin Wilson has made it perfectly clear that it
is not the peak experiences themselves that are important, but what
may accompany them: the illumination, the insight, the broadening of
and sense of control of consciousness. 'The point of phenomenological
existentialism is not the "peak experience"; it is the control of consciousness *and its extension by language*,' Wilson states in the last chapter of
his autobiography *Voyage to a Beginning* (p. 174). Colin Wilson's aim
is not the heightening of feeling alone but feeling and insight: education
or *Bildung*. Man should acquire insight into his own psyche, and learn
to control his feelings and his consciousness. He should learn to be
mentally free. That mental freedom—control of one's mind, not bliss—
is the ultimate objective, Colin Wilson makes quite clear in both his non-
fictional and fictional work, and this is one of the two reasons why I
have called my dissertation on his novels *An Odyssey to Freedom*
(Uppsala, Acta Universitatis Upsaliensis, 1983).

The other reason for the title is that reading Colin Wilson's novels
has been like an odyssey to freedom for me. Take, for instance, the
first book by Wilson I ever read, his first novel *Ritual in the Dark*. At the
time I read this book, I was living with my family in a small place near
Gävle in Sweden. I was working as a teacher. Feeling that I was a failure
both as a teacher and a husband, I was deeply depressed. Colin Wilson's
book was a great relief to me, in spite of its somewhat gloomy nature.
It tells the story of a young man who is depressed but gains a kind of

insight into man's psyche through his experiences and his moments of vision. This story kindled a hope in me that change was possible and that, maybe, I could learn to free myself from depression, or, at least, learn to understand it and live with it. Each book by Colin Wilson that I read confirmed and strengthened this hope in me.

Rather like Socrates admonishing us to learn to know ourselves, and trying to make us gain control over our minds—Colin Wilson has without doubt extended man's freedom. His writings began some thirty years ago with *The Outsider*—when he was only twenty-four. Let us now look forward to another three decades of productivity on his part.

20

Wilson's Occult

ALAN HULL WALTON

Colin Wilson is a controversial writer. Inescapably so; since in an age of talented mediocrity, he is blessed with far more than talent—he is blessed with insight, sincerity, humility, an extraordinarily wide learning (comparable to that of the 'universal man' of the Renaissance), and also manifests something of the breadth of genius of a Goethe. He is interested in many things, many subjects; but his interest is not a surface interest; it goes deep. He questions, investigates, ponders; anf then comes up, not only with what may well be the right answers, but with some fascinating and original theories.

He has, moreover, the rare faculty of concentrating into a limited space—with the utmost clarity and readability—that which would demand of the average author more than twice the amount of print.

His new book on *The Occult* (Hodder & Stoughton, 1971) is by far and away his best work to date, and worthy to be placed on the same shelf alongside William James, F.W.H. Myers' monumental study of *Human Personality* (in its complete two-volume edition), and Frazer's *Golden Bough*. And it has something of the thoroughness and erudition of Havelock Ellis's celebrated *Studies*.

It is important to state at the outset, that in a review of a thousand words or so, one cannot do justice to a book of this calibre; and one certainly cannot involve oneself in the why and wherefore of its frequently original basic theories. But one thing is certain: it is an essential volume for every public and university library, as well as for all readers interested in any way whatsoever in the wide spectrum of inter-related occult subjects which he discusses with such penetration and intelligence.

But to get down to the book itself: unlike the zany cranks on one hand, and over-intellectual philosophers on the other, Wilson's approach is that of the careful scientist, convinced of the reality of unusual facts and happenings previously dismissed by the strict materialist as due either to imagination, or explicable on the basis of superstitious misinterpretation.

Nor is this said lightly, since I have spent many years studying the subjects under consideration; and my own opinions are not infrequently very similar to those of Mr Wilson. In fact my private library of about 8,000 volumes contains seven or eight hundred devoted to occultism, parapsychology, and allied areas of investigation.

The volume is divided into three parts. Part One forms a general survey of the subject; Part Two constitutes a History of Magic – one of the best and most illuminating I have yet come across: and Part Three devotes itself to an intriguing study of Man's Latent Powers. Each part is subdivided into several lengthy chapters. The Bibliography is extensive (though one feels that many more works were consulted than those listed), and the Index well compiled.

From the points of view of scientific theory, the metaphisical approach, and the interpretation of facts, the first and third parts are certainly the most important. These occupy almost one half of the total 608 pages of the book, and are unusually well done.

Of course one of the main preoccupations of Wilson's life has been the investigation of means of expanding human consciousness beyond its narrow, and virtually self-imposed limits. And here he outlines various solutions to the problem.

'The trouble,' he says, 'is the narrowness of consciousness. It is as if you tried to see a panoramic vision through cracks in a high fence, but were never allowed to look over the fence and see it as a whole. And the narrowness lulls us into a permanent drowsiness, like being half-anaesthetised, so that we never attempt to stretch our powers to their limits . . .' Then he quotes William James, who said: 'Our normal waking consciousness is but one special type of consciousness, whilst all about it, parted from it by the filmiest of screens, there lie potential forms of consciousness entirely different.'

He believes, and I think justifiably, that 'scientific rationalism has turned man into a thinking pygmy'; and suggests, with a wealth of superbly reasoned argument, that the human mind is undoubtedly gifted with incredible powers – which once were ascribed to supernatural agencies. Primitive man, and many of the higher animals, possess seemingly unlimited capacities for telepathic communication; not to mention the homing instincts of birds, fish, and insects. Civilised man has lost – or repressed – these powers. Yet Wilson suggests an even more important one, Faculty X: the power of the mind to establish direct union with Reality in its truest sense (probably produced by the reaction of a chemical called Serotonin on the pineal gland). Even animals may possess this faculty to some extent; and Wilson believes it is the ground for a vast amount in occult experience.

Magic was dismissed during the eighteenth and nineteenth centuries as the result of ignorance and superstition. Undoubtedly a lot of it was silly nonsense. Yet, as the author so convincingly argues, much of it was

the result of the natural employment of the hidden faculties inherent in
man – faculties which, fortunately or unfortunately, remain latent in all
but approximately five per cent. of the civilised population. But at last,
during the late twentieth century, such studies are becoming respectable, and the faculties under consideration are slowly being recognised
by legitimate science.

During the course of Wilson's text, many old, and not a few new
characters come in for detailed investigation. The list is surprisingly
lengthy. We have Cornelius Agrippa, Paracelsus, Boehme, Dr John Dee,
Grandier, Pythagoras, and Apollonius of Tyana. Not to mention Levi,
Home, Edgar Cayce, and many others such as Gurdjieff, Ouspensky,
Crowley, and Cagliostro (on whom he casts new light). He recognises
Madame Blavatsky's vast learning; and, while admitting her regrettable
lapses into showmanship, realises, like Keyserling and others, that she
was undoubtedly possessed of considerable psychic and magical powers
of a genuine order. Mary Baker Eddy is included, and the validity of
Christian Science admitted (with some possible reservations). Moreover,
various forms of spiritual healing are discussed in a number of separated
sections. Yet all these curtailed indications give only the briefest idea
of the far-ranging scope of the book as a whole.

Reincarnation is accepted (perhaps reluctantly) as a very likely
probability – but see also, on this point, Sri Aurobindo's *Life Divine*,
and the very important and favourable works of Arthur W. Osborn
(not to be confused with Arthur Osborne, another excellent writer on
oriental religion).

For those with insight, this stupendous volume is the natural sequel
to *The Outsider*, and *Religion and the Rebel*. This second (and excellent)
title is, alas, out of print in hard-cover, and has not yet been published in
paperback. Why it hasn't appeared in this form I cannot imagine; for
there are countless hundreds with limited purses who would welcome it
in a reasonably-priced edition*

To conclude, *The Occult* is a valuable 'must' for anyone with the
remotest interest in the future of civilised man.†

---

*This has now been published in paperback by Ashgrove Press, 1984. – Ed.
†This review-article first appeared in *Books & Bookmen*, December 1971, pp. 50-1.

21

Colin Wilson's *Magnum Opus*

ALAN HULL WALTON

Since we are about to deal with a book of the first importance, *Mysteries* (Hodder & Stoughton, 1979), it might be helpful to suggest something of the literary calibre to which the volume under review assuredly belongs.

In order to achieve this aim, let us consider for a moment the scope and excellence of three vital and permanent 'classics' in their chosen fields—each quite different in subject, yet each equally monumental. The titles alone are sufficient to conjure up a clear idea of what I mean: Frazer's *Golden Bough* (twelve volumes, with a supplementary thirteenth); Toynbee's *Study of History* (another twelve-volume work); and F.W.H. Myers's formidable *Human Personality* (two heavy and bulky tomes in its *complete and unabridges* text, as published by Longmans). Such is their importance that no library could afford to be without them.

It is in this especially distinguished category of immaculately present-ed, scientifically objective, well-marshalled, carefully reasoned, logical, incredibly informative, and compellingly readable non-fiction, that Colin Wilson's new book, *Mysteries: An Investigation into the Occult, the Paranormal and the Supernatural*, now takes its honourable place. In effect it might be described as the second volume of a long and scrupulously detailed study, which began with *The Occult* (Hodder & Stoughton, 1971); and it marks a new 'high' in Wilson's prodigious out-put, placing him in the top rank of serious contemporary investigators of the paranormal.

The detail and wide range of the book (well documented) defies analysis in these few pages. But each and every example and subject is described, probed and weighed-up with such an eagle-eye that the volume immediately becomes 'definitive'. Moreover, the flow of writing is so natural and unaffected that nothing could be easier to read. There is, I think, only a single word which adequately sums up the qualities of this enormous *opus* of over 260,000 words—already a 'classic' in its own right—and that word is *superlative*. I might add that, after many years of study of such works, my opinion is a carefully considered one. And it is a volume one 'simply can't put down', but must go on reading, and read-ing . . . and re-reading.

Having said these imperative things, let us now turn to the basic contents of the hardcover arousing such praise; or at least as much of those contents as there is space to deal with reasonably adequately.

That, unfortunately, means being 'selective' . . .

During the early Seventies Wilson had been grossly over-working, with the result that towards the end of 1973 he began to fall victim to repeated 'panic' attacks accompanied by unpleasant physical symptoms. He describes these in some detail in his Introductory chapter, and quite terrifying reading they make. They came on in the early hours of the morning, usually, and he realised that he was close to a nervous breakdown. They seemed to be the result of some undefined fear, and without obvious cause. Anyway, with his usual courage he turned down medical aid and drugs, and undertook controlling the panic by analysing it, by a calculated attempt to uncover the mechanisms behind it. It took six months to achieve this end — but it worked wonderfully.

This self-analysis threw considerable light on many problems which had been bothering him for a number of years: telepathy, out-of-the-body experiences, precognition, poltergeist phenomena, so-called 'second-sight', and many other things; all of which remain undeniable facts, yet concerning which no theory, so far, has been able to offer all-round adequate explanation.

Readers will well remember that when they were at school, just before lessons commenced, the many different personalities in the classroom would be squabbling loudly. But as soon as the master or mistress entered a silence would fall immediately, and the little demons would become a quiet, subdued and manageable 'body' of children — the disrupted 'parts' would become welded into a team-like 'whole', perfectly united. As a result of this, Wilson summoned a higher level of his personality (or consciousness), nicknaming it 'the school-mistress'. He was also enabled, at the same time, to observe (from outside himself, as it were) other levels of personality with a distinct identity. These he compared with the rungs of a ladder. All of which fitted in with another curiosity which has bothered psychologists for over a century — the condition known as 'multiple personality', in which, under stress, or during illness, some people split into two or three totally different personalities, as though these different personalities were taking turns in inhabiting the same body, and often fighting to retain possession ot it. Tests have shown that these 'personalities' even have different brain-rhythms (as revealed by the electro-encephalograph).

Following an incredible series of researches Wilson has applied himself to bring together some proof that his 'ladder of selves' can be utilised in explaining an astonishing range of paranormal phenomena, from dowsing, to ghosts, astral-travel, pre- and retrocognition, psycho-kinesis, and the like.

Now, although the author has come—by his own route—to this conclusion of a multiplicity of 'selves' existing (almost always in secret)
within each human body, the idea, in somewhat different form—and
with extended consequences—has for centuries lain hidden in many of
the esoteric sacred tomes of the East, in India, Tibet, China. And nothing
could be more scientific or accurate (in non-Western terminology) than
the conclusions arrived at in Vedanta, and its offshoot, Tantra; or in the
mysteries to be discovered in a number of exceptional Tibetan treatises,
and Chinese expositions. In fact almost everything said in the Vedas
(and much in Tibetan works) is incontrovertibly borne out by our
contemporary higher physics.

For example, *everything* is made up of energy alone—which applies
equally to rocks, plants, and people. The atom contains electrons,
neutrons, positrons, and, of course, the proton, which are looked on as
'particles', but in reality are simply waves, or vibrations, the behaviour
of which gives the impression that they are 'particles'. The various length,
rates, and patterns taken by these 'vibrations' which condense energy
into matter, are governed by one infinite universal mind, an infinite and
perfect, and omnipotent intelligence which is beyond time and space
(which in truth do not exist), but which creates time and space by
manifesting its living self as matter—infinity cannot be measured or
limited; but *seemingly* concrete matter can. The everlasting, without
beginning or end, is devoid of time. It is an ever-present 'now'; yet,
descending into the impermanent illusion of the material universe, a
form of 'time' is created, alongside the notion of measurable 'space'.
Thus to put it in religious terms, God exists outside and beyond time
and space, which have no true reality; but he manifests *in* time and space
—Unity in multiplicity, multiplicity in unity. Under the surface everything is ultimately one.

And this is because, as Nicholas of Cusa said (1401-64): 'God is a
circle, whose central point is everywhere, but whose outer circumference
is nowhere.' Or: 'God is a sphere, whose central point is everywhere at
every moment, but whose outer shell is nowhere.'

From this we may easily realise that all *seeming* solids are generated
by the movement of points. Yet, as dear old Euclid said, a point is something which has neither parts nor magnitude—it cannot be measured—
thus it is as total an abstraction as any spiritual nucleus. From this we
can also realise that what is known at one time and place can be known
at any time and place—although, in practice, only by a few gifted
individuals, or those with a capacity for long and arduous training by
an enlightened 'Master' or Guru. Much can be explained on this remark-

ably sound basis, and one is tempted to go on. For it bears some
affinities with what lies beneath Wilson's discovery of the different
levels of consciousness or personality.

It seems to be perfectly obvious that his conclusions are entirely his
own. But they have their analogies in, let us say, the *Upanishads*. The
Chandogya Upanishad, for example, indicates a plurality of selves. And
there is an oriental yogic technique which looks upon the individual as
an 'onion'. Here the 'selves' are the different layers of the onion, and
each layer (or self) is different in one way or another. By peeling off
each layer one finally arrives at the centre – *infinity*; asking, all the
time: 'What am I? Is this me?' The personalities, the rungs of the
ladder, are mere masks. The true 'Me' is pure consciousness. And, of
course, it should be possible (at least in theory), to return from pure
consciousness into everyday living as quite a different 'me'.

Wilson, however, never gets so abstruse and abstract as this – thank
heaven; and writes in a style which any intelligent man or woman can
grasp quite simply. Indeed his lengthy examples and explanations have
all the compulsion and thrill of a masterly *who-done-it*?

He opens his investigation by delineating the career and theories of
an exceptional Cambridge don, Tom Lethbridge, who retired to Devon
after many years as a successful archaeologist and historian. There he
plunged into the mysteries of dowsing and ghosts, not to mention other
supernatural phenomena. And he made the discovery that the pendulum
can be used, not only as an alternative to the twig in dowsing, but to
discover exceptionally detailed information on virtually any subject
one cares to think of. Fascinating examples are given. Moreover, he discovered that he had a neighbour in his village who was a true witch. She
taught him a lot! And his scientific mind proved the validity of what he
learned . . .

Taking, then, Lethbridge's investigations into ghosts and ghouls,
giants and witches, the forces of the earth, and precognitive dreams, as
a fecund starting point for his own individual and conclusive – one might
say 'definitive' survey, Wilson then enters into the impeccable details of
the results of his own search for the validity behind, and the reality of,
every aspect of psychic and occult phenomena. These lead to some
remarkable results and conclusions, with a stronglv scientific backing to
support them.

The journey is long, the chapters many; yet time flies as we read them,
dealing vividly, as they do, with so many curious things which have
baffled Western man over the centuries; things which scientists once dismissed as 'nonsense', but which they now (in the higher echelons, at

least) are finding proper and profitable subjects for serious, precise, and careful study. They previously disliked such phenomena, of course, because their existence made them uncomfortable, disconcertingly spoiling a simple, almost crude, nineteenth-century materialistic-mechanistic view of man and the universe.

In fact one of the reasons why this book covers so extraordinarily wide a range of subjects—becoming, in the process, a kind of *Principia* of the paranormal—is because the author is fundamentally, insatiably curious, as to why a majority of scientists have exploded with astonishingly unreasonable indignation and argument, when faced by enigmatic processes and events which, owing to their own extremely specialised, and therefore frequently 'narrow' education, they are unable to explain. Or is it because so many of them have an unconscious dread of 'the widening of boundaries'? Many of them claim that *psi* phenomena can not be fitted into their picture of the universe, much less of the world. Therefore, what Wilson has so courageously attempted (and, I think, achieved), is to present a new paradigm, or pattern, 'which fits all the known scientific facts', at the same time leaving plenty of latitude for the explanation and acceptance of the many and uncomfortably varied things which science has, up to the moment, been unwilling to admit.

I have suggested, above, that some of the best and more perceptive scientists (mainly, I think, physicists, of the calibre of, say, Raynor Johnson) are already beginning to accept 'the unusual' and paranormal, and to investigate them. There has always been a handful of such men of insight: Lodge, Jeans, James, Eddington, Einstein, Lyall Watson, to name a few. Yet Wilson is correct: the vast mass of scientists still remain unwilling to leave their comfortable cubby-holes or take off their blinkers. Which is one more reason why this book is so important. It will give all such individuals a severe jolt—and cause them to think again . . .

The volume contains eighteen chapters, together with a significant appendix by Peter Maddock: *The Electromagnetic Induction of Psi States*. Analysis of the chapters cannot be undertaken here (besides, that would spoil the book!); but as an appetiser here are a few of the headings: *The Timeless Zone*, *The Curious History of Human Stupidity*, *How Many Me's Are There?*, *In Search of Faculty X*, *The Rediscovery of Magic*, *Descent into the Unconscious*, *Worlds Beyond*, *Powers of Evil?*, *Evolution*, *Messages from Space and Time*, *Other Dimensions*. And there is the fascinating mystery of Mary Ann South's *Suggestive Inquiry*.

The chapter on *Evolution* is paramount, crammed with information and the stimulus to further thought (as, indeed, is an earlier one on

Alchemy). Darwin's theory has always been misinterpreted by the less
educated populace – and sometimes even by the educated; and, with the
passage of time, some of his ideas, like those of Freud in a different
context, have been discredited or modified. Wilson, however, begins to
get evolution into true perspective, selecting his considerable material
with sound insight and scientific acumen. He quotes, for instance, Stan
Gooch (*Personality and Evolution*, 1973), whose main objection to
Darwin is the theory of random mutations, and having explained Gooch's
ideas, proceeds to carry his logic a stage further . . . He also shows how
he believes that Gooch's 'notion of man's three brains' provides us with
a basis for 'explaining the strange phenomenon of multiple personality';
considering, immediately afterwards, Robert Ornstein's opinion that
the left and right sides of the brain constitute separate entities . . .

The long final chapter, *Other Dimensions*, distils the essence of what
has preceded it, and has a great deal to offer.

> It is tempting to regard the whole field of the paranormal as a realm
> of weird phenomena and peculiar people – Uri Geller, David Dunglas
> Home, Madame Blavatsky, Aleister Crowley, Rasputin, Nostradamus,
> Cagliostro – all demonstrating utterly inconsequential powers . . .
> Understandably, most scientists find it easier to condemn the whole
> thing as a kind of fantasy.
>   In this book I have attempted to show that one simple hypothesis
> can bring a certain amount of order into the confusion: the notion
> that the mind of man possesses many levels . . .

Several pages later he points out that there is a part of 'our being
that knows far more than the conscious mind. And the evidence of
mystics through the ages suggests that there is a part of our being that
knows even greater secrets than this.' What we need, he suggests, is 'increased control over the robot' – that is, the lower, every-day 'mechanical'
man which most people are. Thus the book ends, and on an optimistic
note:

> Control seems to suggest some ugly, assertive will-to-power and
> ultimate breakdown. But we are forgetting what all the evidence of
> this book unmistakably suggests: that we already possess this control.
> It already exists on deeper, or higher, levels of our being. How we
> have come to lose it is something of a mystery; the only thing that
> seems clear is that it has to do with the development of consciousness.
> 'Conscious' man is a pygmy, a mere fragment of his true self. That he

once possessed such a conception seems clear from the occult traditions of alchemy and cabbalism. Our problem is that we know this intuitively . . . Consciousness is intentional; its destiny is to become more intentional. Through a gradual deepening of intentionality, it will re-establish contact with our 'lost' levels. The higher levels *are* there, as I discovered from the 'schoolmistress effect'. They can be summoned when we need them. But unless we know they are there, we make no attempt to summon them.

What will happen seems to me perfectly clear. Human beings will one day recognise, beyond all possibility of doubt, that consciousness *is* freedom. When this happens, consciousness will cease to suffer from a mistrust of its own nature. Suddenly, the 'profits' will be clear and self-evident . . .

When that happens, the first fully human being will be born.

The book opens with a fourteen-page *Analytical Table of Contents*—a bonus of inestimable utility. It also contains a useful series of Notes, ten pages of Bibliography, and an Index of thirteen pages (which, I feel, offers room for expansion).

Faults?—one minor printer's error, that's all; and something for which we should be more than grateful these days, when almost every volume published contains at least half a dozen (or more) misprints. Oddly enough, this seems to be restricted to the book-world, since periodicals appear to be blessed by an immunity to such defects.

And now, if the reader will turn to Wilson's *Magnum Opus*, I think he will agree with me that it reflects an almost super-human amount of research and magically ruminative thought, both of which belong to that quality defined as 'genius'.*

*This review-article first appeared in *Books & Bookmen*, March 1979.

22

Toward an Existential Realism: the Novels of Colin Wilson

R. H. W. DILLARD

> We fight not for ourselves but
> for growth, growth that goes on forever.
> To-morrow, whether we live or die, growth
> will conquer through us. That is the law
> of the spirit for evermore.

—H.G. Wells, *The Food of the Gods*

There is no need to recount the literary career of Colin Wilson. It follows an all too familiar pattern and unfortunately has a great many counterparts; the encomiums of praise and delight upon the publication of a writer's first book and the quick critical turnabout when a second book is released. The exceptions are few today, and the damage is severe. A young writer has fame thrust upon him and snatched away before he has assimilated it and adjusted to it; too many writers never recover from the shock. And if a writer keeps working, his readers still suffer, for once he has been dismissed by the critical press, his later books are seldom even mentioned; he becomes an invisible man. Like Melville, he may be 'discovered' much later, but only after he has been lost to his contemporaries who simply have no way of knowing what he is doing and writing.

Colin Wilson's example is, of course, more exaggerated than most. His first book, *The Outsider*, published in 1956 when he was twenty-four, was an amazing critical and popular success. One critic wrote that 'Not since Lord Byron woke up one morning and found himself famous has an English writer met with such spontaneous and universal acclaim.' When his second book, *Religion and the Rebel*, appeared the following year, it was as universally condemned. The eighteen books which followed over the last ten years have received a small and varied response, but on the whole they have been more ignored than attacked or praised. To the great majority of the reading public, Colin Wilson has become, at thirty-five, a finished man, remembered only for his early success and not for his work which has continued beyond that success and despite its attendant critical reverse.*

*This article was published twenty-one years ago in *The Hollins Critic*, vol. 4, no. 4, October 1967.

The publication in England of Wilson's seventh novel, *The Mind Parasites*, last spring roused, however, a revival of critical interest. Hilary Corke announced in *The Listener* that it was time the literary world stopped ignoring Colin Wilson, and Robert Nye, in *The Guardian*, called Wilson 'one of the most earnest and interesting writers of his generation.' In this country, *The Mind Parasites* was published in July by Arkham House, the small publishing house in Sauk City, Wisconsin, founded by August Derleth to print the works of H.P. Lovecraft and other books in the Lovecraft tradition. Since the tiny advertising budget of such a small firm and the force of critical inertia will probably preclude much serious mention of the novel in the American press, I should like here to greet its appearance and to discuss Wilson's novels and his development as a novelist of independence and real ability.

Of course, Colin Wilson thinks of himself primarily as a philosopher, and the bulk of his writing has been critical and philosophical, from *The Outsider* to his most recent *Introduction to the New Existentialism*. Although his 'Outsider Cycle' (*The Outsider*, *Religion and the Rebel*, *The Age of Defeat*, *The Strength to Dream*, *The Origins of the Sexual Impulse*, *Beyond the Outsider*) is a sustained attempt to define a new synthesis of evolutionary humanism and phenomenological existentialism, he is no systematic philosopher. He is rather a man thinking through his ideas in print, a philosopher who feels, to use Emerson's description of the wise writer, 'that the ends of study and composition are best answered by announcing undiscovered regions of thought, and so communicating, through hope, new activity to the torpid spirit.'

Like Emerson, he sees man as 'a god in ruins' who must only be awakened in order to fulfil his godly potential, but because he is 'Anglo-Saxon and empirical' by nature and heritage, his is a more specifically rational philosophy than Emerson's, depending more upon the analytical faculty than creative intuition. By phenomenological analysis, he argues, man can capture and extend moments of vision like Nietzsche's on the hilltop in the storm or the mystic's vision of unity with God, can expand human consciousness, and can chart 'a geography' of 'the world of the inner mind.' As he fulfils his own identity, he will also find himself part of a larger identity, life itself; he will be able to attune himself fully 'to purpose and evolution.' Perhaps the clearest statement of his aims is this brief account in the *Introduction to the New Existentialism*:

The 'new existentialism' accepts man's experience of his inner freedom as basic and irreducible. Our lives consist of a clash between two visions: our vision of this inner freedom, and our vision of contingency; our intuition of freedom and power, and our everyday feeling of limitation and boredom. The problem cannot be reduced to simpler terms. The 'new existentialism' concentrates the full battery of phenomenological analysis upon the everyday sense of contingency, upon the problem of 'life-devaluation'. This analysis helps to reveal how the spirit of freedom is trapped and destroyed; it uncovers the complexities and safety devices in which freedom dissipates itself. It suggests mental disciplines through which this waste of freedom can be averted.

His is an attempt to satisfy man's absolute need for religion with a rational understanding of his own nature. His method is one of synthesis, a bringing together of science and art, of reason and imagination. He is striving to reach a new synthesis of the ideas of William James Husserl, Wittgenstein and Whitehead on the one hand, and Blake, Dostoevsky, Wells and Shaw on the other. It is a bold attempt, and it is not my place to evalutate it here. What does interest and concern me is that more and more, like his direct literary forebears Wells and Shaw, he has discovered the limitations of exposition and is turning to art rather than philosophy to shape and transmit his ideas and belief – a shift similar to his earlier turning from science to philosophy. He has recognized, as he puts it in the postscript to the new edition of *The Outsider*, that 'There are things than can be said in a work of fiction that are unsayable in a work of philosophy,' and although he has by no means abandoned his philosophical writing, he has turned strongly to fiction (and drama) to bring his ideas artistically alive.

'What I would like to do,' Wilson said in a preface to one of his novels, '– what I feel it will one day be possible to do – is to write a white dwarf of a book, a book that is so dense that it can be read fifty times. Not a book of ideas, in the sense that my *Outsider* is a book of ideas, but a book that deals with life with the same directness that we are compelled to live it.' His novels show him to be searching for a form, a proper metaphor, a true hero to give his ideas the directness of life. And the direction of his search has been toward more imaginative and artificial means which convey truth by effect more than by statement, by art more than by philosophy. Of his seven novels, the first three use the traditional form and methods of psychological realism, the fourth breaks out of those strictures by exploiting the freedom of the diary form, and the three most recent use openly artificial popular forms (detective and science fiction) to develop metaphoric and parabolic novels of vital imagination, of what Wilson calls 'existential realism'.

The creation of a hero has progressed as steadily as the search for a proper form. The thesis of *The Outsider* is 'that religion begins with the stimulus which heroism supplies to the imagination,' so that the hero is essential to the religious intensity necessary to evolutionary purposiveness. He is a hero detached by the condition of a complex and possibly dying civilization from the social and political problems of that civilization. As a part of an evolutionary vanguard, he must strive for essential power and disregard temporal power; he serves a saintly function by awakening us to our true selves by persuasion and example. He is a personification of the vision of inner freedom, of human possibility as Wilson describes it in the *Introduction to the New Existentialism*:

> He has glimpses of a joy that is beyond anything possible to the born coward: the ecstasy of power and freedom. He knows about the miseries and insecurities of human existence, about weakness and contingency. But he does not believe in them, since he is certain that freedom is an absolute power. He knows that man is only subject to pain and misery insofar as he allows himself to be dominated by the coward, and that most human misfortune is another name for stupidity and self-pity. Consequently, he is inclined to suspect that even death may be a disguised form of suicide, and that human contingency will prove to be an illusion in the light of ultimate freedom. In short, he is totally the optimist and the adventurer; he cannot believe that human reason, powered by the human will to freedom, can ever encounter insurmountable obstacles.

The hero is any man who can see the 'exit' from the human dilemma, and 'is capable of making the choice that the insight demands.' To create such a hero, to make him artistically plausible requires a newer and more imaginatively flexible art than that afforded by ordinary realism, so that properly the development of the hero progresses along with Wilson's search for a form; he takes on substance from novel to novel as Wilson searches for metaphors strong enough on which to build heroic novels. All of the novels are concerned with the same basic theme, an awakening and activating of the slumbering god in man, so that to some degree they are repetitive, but they are better seen as variations and developments of a theme, each one growing out of the preceding ones. Together they reveal the steady growth of Wilson's talent and his progressive creation of a viable hero for an existential realism.

Ritual in the Dark (1960), *Adrift in Soho* (1961), and *The World of Violence* (1963, in America: *The Violent World of Hugh Greene*), Colin Wilson's first three novels are all novels of initiation, of a young man's first painful encounters with experience and reality, and of the heightened awareness he gains from that initiation. They are concerned with the birth, the first real awakening of the hero to his evolutionary purpose. As in most religious initiation rites, the subject of the ritual is primarily passive, acted upon by the experience which will ultimately allow him to act himself in experience. Missing, however, is the wise older man who traditionally guides the youth through the initiation, for Wilson's hero is alone, existentially isolated, able to seek advice from his elders but forced finally and always to discover and decide for himself. The three young initiates in these novels are all thinkers, budding philosophers to whom learning is in great part living; they are involved in understanding, while the more fully developed heroes of the later novels are involved in transforming understanding into action, idea into being.

Gerard Sorme, in *Ritual in the Dark*, is a young man possessed of an incubating vision, but he is not sure of himself so that his moments of vision are matched by feelings of vastation and utter meaninglessness. 'There was a futility about physical existence that frightened him,' but, as Wilson was to describe it later, he 'sits in his room and hurls his mind at the problem of the *negative nature of freedom*.' Gerard is an outsider, a man who has instinctively rejected everyday reality, 'feeling that it is somehow boring and unsatisfying, like a hypnotized man eating sawdust under the belief that it is eggs and bacon.' He is an outsider with a growing subjectivity, a developing harmony with the life force itself, and his initiation consists primarily of his confrontation with another outsider who is being destroyed by his sense of alienation and frustration. In *Religion and the Rebel*, Wilson described the novel, then in progress, as one 'about two Outsiders, one based on Nietzsche, and the other on Jack the Ripper.' Gerard, like the young Nietzsche, is on the brink of transforming his alienation into creative awareness; Austin Nunne, like Jack the Ripper, is releasing his frustration in a brutal series of sex murders. Nunne succumbs to and is destroyed by 'the insanity of the age,' the life-negating despair which convinces modern man too often of the loss of his freedom, while Gerard transcends his sense of limitation, develops an active subjectivity which makes the living world around him truly his, and expands his consciousness and vision to accept the complexity of experience and being (a continuing epiphany akin to Wordsworth's mystical moment on Westminster Bridge).

The confrontation is a dramatic one, for it takes place in the last weeks of Nunne's freedom and the terror resulting from his fear of that freedom. At first, Gerard sees Nunne as a fellow spirit, a rebel against the pervasive futility of ordinary life, and this belief continues even after Gerard discovers that Nunne is the Whitechapel murderer. But stimulated by his sexual affairs (*loving*, but not really *love* affairs) with Caroline, a young drama student, and her aunt Gertrude, Gerard gains a human insight into and feeling for Nunne and at the same time a sense of superiority to him, for Nunne is not truly a rebel against disorder and meaninglessness, but only a victim of his own belief in disorder and his inability to impose meaning upon experience. But Gerard remains detached despite his new understanding, for he expresses that new vision not by decisive action but by a passive acceptance, a refusal to despair. He has learned from Nunne's failure, but he has not taken part in correcting the wrongs caused by that failure nor the wrongs that gave rise to it. But he has made the first step; he has not given in to complexity, but has rather decided to be of complexity; he does not choose between Gertrude and Caroline but maintains his involvement with both:

> In spite of his tiredness, he felt a curious sense of certainty, of order. It was as if he could see inside himself and watch processes that had been invisible before. There was no longer a desire for simplicity; an accumulation of self-knowledge had made it less important. . . . A curious elation stirred in him, an acceptance of complexity. He stared at his face in the mirror, saying aloud:
> What do you do now, you stupid old bastard?
> He grinned at himself, and twitched his nose like a rabbit.

Adrift in Soho picks up the lightness and comic spirit of Gerard's mime in the mirror. In it, Harry Preston is initiated into free life and complexity by the bohemians of Soho whose careless lives attract Harry away from the problems of life and ultimately release him again to those problems but with the strength and desire to solve them. He rejects the bohemian way ('For better or worse I am a bourgeois'), but he gains from his experience an insight into himself which frees him for a life larger than the self, an understanding that the future is an extension of his belief in himself, that the future flows from within. He realizes that 'there is no such thing as future success. It is either there all the time, or it is non-existent.'

The novel is slighter than *Ritual in the Dark*, but it does develop the moral understanding a step further, pressing acceptance toward affirmation:

It was true that the only thing wrong with the world is human beings. But perhaps one day there would be a new type of human being who would understand that time is the same thing as eternity, that life is a million times more desirable than any man ever realized; that there is no such thing as evil, because the only reality is the power house, the dynamo that drives the world.

Although Harry finds an artist, Ricky Prelati, who approaches the 'new type of human being', his real victory is, like Gerard's, the gaining of an insight into possibility, a glimpse of the dynamo. He manages, also, to move beyond acceptance to choice, even if his choice is one of rejection. That rejection is a necessary second step toward action and vocation.

If the dynamo that he sees is essentially Shaw's life force, the idea of the new man is very much H.G. Wells', as he stated it in such novels as *The Food of the Gods*, *In the Days of the Comet*, *Men Like Gods*, *The Croquet Player* and *Star Begotten*. It is appropriate, then, that Wilson's third novel, *The World of Violence*, which carries the hero a step closer to the new man, should sound very much in its first half like one of Wells' social novels (*Tono-Bungay* or *The New Machiavelli*). The tone is serious and comic at once, a wry Wellsian tone which is both warmly human and curiously detached and objective. The novel even comes complete with a set of eccentric uncles, each of whom has a distorted but true glimpse of the nature of things and all of whom influence young Hugh Greene in an intellectual and human way:

> My grandfather had died of delirium tremens at the age of forty, and there is a tradition in the family that his uncle . . . was either Jack the Ripper or Peter the Painter (the leader of the Sidney Street Gang). My father's Uncle Sam (of whom I shall write later) was definitely peculiar, but had a talent for making money, so that the family never tried to have him certified. But Uncle Nick had once spent a year in a mental home, after he declared that he was a bird and jumped off the roof.

Springing from a background of madness and violence, however comic it may have been, Hugh Greene, the narrator of the novel and a young mathematical prodigy, becomes obsessed early with violence and the search for pure truth in chaos. Mathematics offers him an intellectual escape from the external violence and chaos, but it cannot free him from the fact of his own human inner darkness. His obsession and the frustration he feels in being able to do nothing about the way things are lead him into a Nietzschean belief in the will to power beyond good and evil, and also into an adolescent attempt to combat senseless violence with a murderous but seemingly purposeful violence of his own. His narrow escape in a scrape with a gang of Teddy boys which ends with his shooting one of his assailants, and his first sexual experiences, and his meeting with a half-witted sex criminal and murderer (modelled after Charley Peace), startle him out of his obsession and enable him to under-stand the lesson of his mad Uncle Sam who locked himself permanently away in a dark attic in order to 'treat directly with God in behalf of my fellow human insects.' He learns that to fight violence with more sense-less violence is to surrender the real fight with the real problems inherent in and beyond violence, those of man's evolution and his sleeping con-sciousness. Like Gerard and Harry, he transcends his early intuitions and attitudes in a discovery of vocation, a conviction that he, too, like his Uncle Sam, should take up man's struggle in the presence of God. His way is to aid in the evolution of a new science of man in the universe by thinking and by writing such books as *The Structure of Language* and *Mathematics and Phenomenological Analysis*. Hugh carries the hero from acceptance through new conviction to action, but his action is of description and understanding rather than doing and being. His is still a transitional stage in the development of the hero and the new man.

All three of these novels, then, develop a single initiatory metaphor of human awakening similar to one of Emerson's in 'Self-Reliance', a fable 'of the sot who was picked up dead-drunk in the street, carried to the duke's house, washed and dressed and laid in the duke's bed, and, on his waking, treated with all obsequious ceremony like the duke, and assured that he had been insane,' which 'symbolizes so well the state of man, who is in this world a sort of sot, but now and then wakes up, exercises his reason and finds himself a true prince.' But the success of the novels rests in great part not on the metaphor but on the details of the narrative, the bits and pieces of colour and flavour which are essential to realistic fiction. Wilson's purpose suffers, as he recognized, by the limitations of traditional realism, which suffices as the tool for fashion-ing novels of awakening but is useless, with its dependence on the present and the known, for the creation of metaphors for the shape of things to come, the world of action beyond the awakening.

Man Without a Shadow (1963, in America: *The Sex Diary of Gerard Sorme*) is Wilson's first attempt to break out of the fetters of realism. Using the form of the philosophical diary and the sex novel, he found the freedom to present his understanding of the life force in an elemental form. 'The sexual urge,' he has written elsewhere, 'particularly in its purer forms, seems to reveal an underlying purpose. In the light of sex, we can occasionally glimpse the purpose of history.' Gerard Sorme, already 'awake' and trying to shape vision into experience, meditates in his sex diary on the insights gained from sexual experience on his vocation of overcoming the temptations of freedom and of disciplining himself for the task of beginning to map the unexplored inner mind. Caradoc Cunningham, a sex magician modelled after Aleister Crowley, is Gerard's foil in this novel. Both have discovered the revelatory orgasmic power leading through and beyond sex, but Cunningham is prey to his own weakness and an over-awareness of society; he is concerned with surfaces. Gerard, on the contrary, finds meaning beyond society ('I am evolution made conscious,' he says at one point) and uses the sexual power for his own ends; he is concerned with essentials.

The novel is one of Wilson's most interesting, for the ideas are at the surface, and the sexual intensity drives them along. Gerard settles in, at the end of the novel, to his vocation (and his new wife, an example of his ability to exercise choice which he lacked with Gertrude and Caroline), but, like Hugh Greene, his vocation is primarily intellectual and descriptive. He is the author of *The Methods and Techniques of Self-Deception*, not the new hero who must act in the world without self-deception. He is a transitional hero, as his diary is a transitional novel, for in his three most recent novels Wilson moves into new forms which plunge their heroes from thought into action, from understanding into being. The new active heroes and the more imaginative modes of fiction all reflect Colin Wilson's own determination to carry his beliefs into action, to move from philosophy and criticism to art. Or, as he put it in an essay in *Eagle and Earwig*, 'intellectual discussion becomes a bore; only some form of action can redeem the existential thinker. And the only form of action that is meaningful is creative.' The three novels, *Necessary Doubt* (1964), *The Glass Cage* (1966), and *The Mind Parasites* (1967), two detective novels and a science fiction novel, are his most imaginative, and they carry his hero from awakening into purposive and creative action. They are, to my mind, his best novels.

The title, *Necessary Doubt*, of Wilson's fifth novel is borrowed from the theology of Paul Tillich, and the central character is an ageing existential theologian, Karl Zweig. He has become a television personality in England (on a show called 'Ask the Experts'), although he is still an active thinker after thirty years of writing, but both his Christianity and his existentialism have failed him, have led him 'to feel stoical about my life—to accept defeat as inevitable.' By a series of coincidences, he finds

himself involved with a motley set of associates in a private manhunt
to stop one of his former pupils (the son of an old friend and associate)
from continuing a series of murders of old men which he has apparently
accomplished by means of a new habit-destroying drug and powerful
hypnotic suggestion.

The stimulus and tension of the chase along with the sexual tension
and desire which he feels and satisfies with Natasha Gardner, the wife
of one of his colleagues in the manhunt, shatter Zweig's complacency
and prepare the way for a new awakening. As events progress, Gustav
Neumann, the quarry in the hunt, appears to him less and less a murderer and more and more a genuine 'new man', working on the fringes of
legality and morality to discover for the human race a means to new and
higher conditions of consciousness. Neumann, cornered but not desperate, explains to him how the drug, neurocaine, was of his father's making
and how, after his father's death, he has continued to experiment with
it to discover its capabilities and proper uses. The drug destroys habits
of thought and frees the brain from its fetters, but it gives its user 'a
sensation of existing in a desert of freedom' which is destructive to a
mind weak in will and belief. The old men were, then, victims of themselves rather than of Neumann.

Reawakened to a new youth of insight, Zweig turns from his life's
career as a theologian, which he recognizes has always been a shield to
protect him from the necessity of acting, and joins Neumann in his
quest for a method of freeing the mind from its purely physical limitations to a new consciousness and vitality. As he explains it, 'You
remember what Gustav said as he went out: "I need your help." His
way can provide the vision, but what good is vision without purpose?
A man needs a lifetime of discipline to make use of such a vision.' Age
and youth, reason and imagination, purpose and vision, all are united in
heroic action as detective and 'murderer' break together the conventions
of a limited consciousness in order to free that consciousness to its own
future. The novel is a metaphor for thought's freeing itself by necessary
doubt to creative belief, an artistic rendering of an 'unsayable' moment
of truth.

The Glass Cage is also a detective novel and a reworking and development of the basic situation of *Ritual in the Dark*. In it, Damon Reade, a
Blake scholar and recluse, is initiated and awakened by his love for a
young girl and his need for human communion, and, like a medieval
knight, he puts his love (and his new awareness) to the test of action; he
goes to London from his home in the Lake District to solve a series of
brutal sex murders which have involved the scrawling of quotations from

Blake on walls by the bodies. Where Zweig was a man of reason, Reade is, like John Cowper Powys to whose memory the novel is dedicated, an instinctive nature mystic, and his success as a detective (and as a hero) is a product of a fusion of vision and reason, of ratiocination and imagination like that of Poe's Dupin.

The murderer in *The Glass Cage*, George Sundheim, is, like Austin Nunne and Carodoc Cunningham, a distortion of the new man; modelled after Rasputin, he is a man of enormous congenital energy and gargantuan appetites, who is so afraid (and, as it turns out, for no reason) of inheriting madness that he has crippled his mind and become a victim of his imagination and energy rather than their master. Damon Reade tracks Sundheim through the urban world which he abhors, solves the crime, and, like Inspector Barlach in Friedrich Dürrenmatt's *The Judge and His Hangman*. manipulates events so that justice is served in the best and most humane manner, tempered by his understanding of the true nature of the 'evil' being punished. The reclusive mystic acts in the human world on the strength of his vision, and Damon Reade becomes himself a hero, being and doing, no superman but a real man. The serpent who changes his skin in an ordeal of pain and illness to be born anew (Sundheim's pet boa constrictor for which Reade assumes responsibility at the end of the novel) is at the centre of the novel's metaphoric structure, appropriately the emblem of evil become the emblem of change and the promise of the future.

Written at the suggestion of August Derleth, *The Mind Parasites* moves further from realism and is built upon a most effective and comprehensive metaphor. Wilson outlined it earlier in the *Introduction to the New Existentialism*:

> To express the problem in science-fiction terms: it would seem that there is some mysterious agency that wishes to hold men back, to prevent them from gaining full use of their powers. It is as if men contained an invisible parasite, whose job is to keep man unaware of his freedom. Blake called this parasite 'the spectre'. In certain moments of vitality and inspiration, the spectre releases his hold, and man is suddenly dazzlingly aware of what he *could* do with his life, his freedom. . . . On the other hand, if man can become fully conscious of the enemy and turn the full battery of his attention on it, the problem is solved. Man will solve the problem of 'alienation from the source of power, meaning and purpose,' and a new phase of evolution will have begun, the phase of the truly human . . .

The novel is both Volume III of the *Cambridge History of the Nuclear Age* (2014) and the new gospel of Gilbert Austin, an archaeologist who, in communion with a handful of colleagues, defeats the mind parasites and sets man on the next leg of his evolutionary journey, only to 'vanish in such a way that the human race could never be certain of his death.' The novel both parodies and develops the manner and situation of H.P. Lovecraft's *The Shadow Out of Time*, and uses the full panoply of science fiction devices—rockets and space travel, ESP, telekinesis and even a 'neutron dater' lifted from John Taine's *Before the Dawn*. With good humour (one of the characters did 'a term on Wilson and Husserl' at college) and real imaginative force, Wilson combines the familiar pieces of science fiction in a new way to form his own myth, a metaphor for his own vision of human destiny. His heroes commune to become a larger self; from the new perspective, they are able to view other men both as apes and as brothers; they form an evolutionary vanguard for the future and leave the account of their victory (the gospel according to Gilbert Austin) behind to guide their fellow men in taking the evolutionary leap. In some ways less emotionally powerful than *Necessary Doubt* or *The Glass Cage*, *The Mind Parasites* nevertheless is the fullest picture of the new hero as he can be and an apocalyptic parable of Wilson's insight into the nature of things. It and those other two most recent novels are meaningful examples of an imaginative and transforming art, an artistic existential realism.

The novels of Colin Wilson are, then, a developing and growing expression of the serpent's statement in Shaw's *Back to Methuselah* that 'every dream could be willed into creation by those strong enough to believe in it.' He has used literary forms as he has needed them to create love and life from the crude materials of sex, violence and death, and, as he says in the preface to *The Mind Parasites*, speaking of his use of detective and science fiction, 'In every case, it has been my aim to raise the form to a level of intellectual seriousness not usually found in the *genre*, but never to lose sight of the need to entertain.' He has succeeded in that purpose, and his novel in progress, *The Black Room*, a spy novel and therefore less cosmic than *The Mind Parasites*, will, as the excerpts published recently in *The Minnesota Review* indicate, also make effective and meaningful use of a popular form.

Wilson once said that 'a good novel can't be faked,' for it can only show 'what it is actually like *to be* the writer.' If doing and being are somehow one, his novels, with their developing manner and matter, their movement toward a viable existential realism of inner as well as outer truth, show Colin Wilson to be a young man of real vision who has never ceased to grow and whose promise, for that reason, outshadows even his present achievement.

23

The Novels of Colin Wilson

JOHN A. WEIGEL

Colin Wilson's first book, *The Outsider* (1956), was almost instantly an international best-seller. It quickly became one of the most controversial items in recent literary history. Wilson's significance still depends to a large extent upon what one thinks of this book, its sequels, and avatars in the way of essays, biographies, critiques of literature and music, dramas, encyclopaedias and many novels.

Wilson believes that fiction is an appropriate vehicle for exploring philosophical concerns. In 1958, in 'Beyond the Outsider', published in *Declaration* (1958), the young author wrote that if he 'were to prescribe a rule that all future philosophers would have to obey it would be this: that no idea shall be expressed that cannot be expressed in terms of human beings in a novel.'

Wilson was born on 26 June 1931, in Leicester, England. Aware at an early age of what he called in his autobiography (*Voyage to a Beginning*, 1969) the 'vegetable mediocrity' of his working-class background, he chose greatness, feeling that his choice was limited to that or nothing. He wasted little time in getting started. Leicester offered basic schooling, books and movies. After the age of sixteen Wilson was on his own. He knew he was different from others, dared even to think of himself as a genius in order to bolster his courage. After a series of menial jobs and a short time in the Royal Air Force, a marital disaster, and other evidence of his own outsiderism, Wilson settled in London, and during the years 1954 and 1955 determinedly educated himself. Much was made later, after the publication of his first book, of his study habits. For months he slept on Hampstead Heath in a sleeping bag and spent his days reading in the British Museum. The Wilson legend was beginning to take shape.

Strongly motivated to do something important and increasingly informed by his prodigious if erratic reading (including mystics such as St John of the Cross, Jan van Ruysbroeck, Giovanni Scupoli and Jakob Boehme), Wilson began to write the book that became *The Outsider*. He was confident of the value of his book, judging it 'the most important book of its generation.' And indeed for some time after its publication in May 1956 many others agreed with him. Rave reviews by important critics, some of whom later recanted, and enthusiastic promotion by the publisher, Victor Gollancz, made the work an instant best-seller. Wilson became famous, and along with John Osborne, whose play *Look Back in Anger* had opened the same month in London, and several other young rebels, he was placed among England's 'angry young men'. (The label was more or less repudiated promptly by the young men, but it became a popular and correct name for the newness in the air.)

What then happened to young Wilson was what he calls in his autobiography 'a grotesque parody of success'. Although he had in his reckless enthusiasm appointed himself the 'heir of Eliot and Joyce' and unabashedly identified himself with Nietzsche, Nijinsky and Shaw, he had, he admits, never foreseen 'being treated like a film star, an intellectual prodigy, a boy wonder'. The reaction soon set in, however, and a half year after its publication *The Outsider* was reconsidered. 'It was the general opinion among English intellectuals,' Wilson dispassionately notes, 'that *The Outsider* had been a craze that had died a natural death, and that I should now be returned to the obscurity from which I had accidentally emerged'.

Depressed but not defeated by the backlash, Wilson in 1957 left London and moved to a cottage in Cornwall, where he began to solve the 'success problem' by getting back to work. He wrote another book, a kind of sequel to *The Outsider*, called *Religion and the Rebel*, published in October 1957. Then the massacre began. Philip Toynbee, who had originally praised Wilson's first book by comparing its author to Sartre, was evidently anxious to redeem his *faux pas* and called the second work 'a rubbish bin'. Perry Miller wrote: 'To call these essays sophomoric is to dignify them.' The American press joined in the manhunt, and Wilson's publisher advised him to stop writing and to take a regular job, at least for a year or two.

Wilson refused to consider such a retreat, despite the fact that his play, *The Death of God*, had been rejected the same year by the Royal Court Theatre. His contemporaries, the other so-called 'angry young men', were also being rejected. Kenneth Allsop describes them as they appeared to hostile critics: 'This peasant army (all the group, I think, grew up in provincial industrial towns) have had the temerity to clump into the academic closes where the trainee priests are learning their catechism from A.J. Ayer and Bertrand Russell, and break in with a loud boy's whistle. "Throw your logical positivism out of the window and stick up your hands," they shouted. They have irritated and offended the orthodoxy.'

Happily enough, during the ensuing years Wilson worked all the harder at offending the orthodoxy. His third volume in the Outsider series appeared in 1959. *The Age of Defeat* (published in the United States as

The Stature of Man) was reviewed rather politely. Apparently Wilson 'was here to stay,' *The Times* reviewer sighed. The young writer agreed and began at once to show how serious he was about enduring. His first novel, *Ritual in the Dark*, aooeared in 1960, and the Wilson production line got underway with about two books a year—on subjects diverse enough to verify his genius, or, as the hostile hinted, to underwrite his dilettantism.

Soon after the publication in 1956 of *The Outsider*, its author was invited to lecture at Cambridge University. For a week after the visit, so the story goes, all Cambridge debated the proposition: Colin Wilson— bloody fool or great writer? There was no formal decision, and the debate, on a reduced scale, still continues although Wilson's industriousness has won him a grudging respect from most of his former detractors. Also, changes in the philosophical climate have redefined Wilson's significance as a thinker who has persistently opposed pessimism and the existential- ism of Jean-Paul Sartre. Sartre had warned cheerful human beings that their cheerfulness was bad faith. The evidence clearly pointed to a dis- crepancy between the way things are and the way things could be. People were asked to consider this evidence seriously, to come to terms with absurdity. All optimism was fraudulent insofar as it made things seem better than they are. Wilson's ideas dominate whatever *genre* he frankly exploits for its idea-conveying potential. His many novels and fable-like fantasies are for him devices for promoting his commitments. Predictably many of his writings have been misunderstood and discount- ed for the wrong reasons—and sometimes praised for equally wrong ones.

The Outsider, which is still probably the most famous of Wilson's books, despite the assaults it has rather badly weathered, contains most of his virtues and most of his faults. *The Outsider* is an enthusiastic synopticon of an earnest youth's eclectic and extensive reading. As an autodidact Wilson did not hesitate to copy passages directly from his notes into his work-in-progress, sometimes inaccurately, sometimes without properly crediting his sources. A host of characters from liter- ature, life and history are made to bear witness to a thesis which is constantly altered—at least in details—as the result of the accumulating testimony.

Wilson's thesis posits a common difference in a small group of people which makes the members of the group outsiders to those not in the group and often outsiders to one another. Capitalizing the name of the category, he specifies the ways in which the Outsider manifests his dif- ference. An Outsider, for example, knows he is sick partly because he lives in a sick society. (The society, however, lacks awareness of its sickness.)

Wilson's reading was esoteric, eclectic and extensive. He found many books that had been overlooked, he believed, by his elders: a novel by Henri Barbusse about a man who looked through a hole in the wall; H.G. Wells's autobiography, *Mind at the End of Its Tether*, a chronicle of increasing despair; Sartre's novel, *Nausea*; Albert Camus's *The Stranger*; Evan Stroude's *Secret Life*; and Herman Hesse's *Demian* and *Siddhartha*, to start with. As he went on reading he accumulated testimony from such disparate 'thinkers' as T.E. Lawrence, Vincent van Gogh, and Vaslav Nijinsky. Everywhere he found a paradox. The Outsider possessed an inner source of power, but he was not happy, and frequently he failed in reaching his real goal. The Outsider's power was also his source of weakness. The Outsider, Wilson theorized, *must* believe in the relevance of his insights and sensibilities; yet those very insights and sensibilities tell him that his insights and sensibilities are probably irrelevant. Because the Outsider has greater awareness and sensitivity he is capable of ecstasy and despair. Unfortunately, however, because of his special awareness he is incapable of the ordinary evasions that help the mass of men survive their quiet desperation. Apparently intellect alone is not enough.

Wilson wholly endorsed the advice of William Blake: 'Go and develop the visionary faculty.' In addition to Blake, Wilson endorsed the teachings of George Fox and his resistance to those who regarded his visions as evidence of insanity. Outsiders, however, can end up as Insiders because of too much and too early success. Wilson cites in this category D.H. Lawrence, Charles Dickens, Bernard Shaw and Rainer Maria Rilke. Ironically, says Wilson, none of them reached ultimate self-realization simply because they did not need to struggle long and hard enough.

Among the Outsiders that interested Wilson in his search for understanding were famous suicides. Apparently, in Wilson's view, those who kill themselves care enough to act, to do something about their despair. Murder is also an act of the will, and in some cases is an intensely creative act, as Wilson tries to demonstrate in much of his fiction.

It is not surprising that Wilson became interested in the ideas of George Gurdjieff, an eccentric philosopher who believed that the planets are alive. Wilson credits him with finding the first ideal *Existenphilosophie*. Those persons capable of being awakened into a fuller existence must not be allowed to be lulled into security and mediocrity. A kind of elitism begins to show its equivocal head at this point. Not all men can be awakened — perhaps only five per cent., the truly gifted or potentially gifted. Wilson, finding himself temporarily left of this particular centre or right of the same centre, is uncomfortable at times in identifying with a minority. If Outsiders were in the majority they would not, of course be on the outside. Morons are also a minority, however, as are potential demagogues.

Obviously Wilson needed time to resolve such problems, or at least to face them. After the success and subsequent failure of his first book Wilson saw ahead of him the need to study religion, psychology, more literature and philosophy—in fact practically everything, including witchcraft. His second philosophical work, which followed hard on the now slightly run-down heels of *The Outsider*, was an attempt to resolve and fill out. *Religion and the Rebel* examines the decline of Western Civilization—with capital letters—and proposes certain remedies. Authorities cited include Ludwig Wittgenstein, Alfred North Whitehead, Sören Kierkegaard, Vilfredo Pareto among innovators, and the old guard such as John Henry Newman, Blaise Pascal and Emanuel Swedenborg. Nobody was too big or profound for the young Wilson to wrestle with, and he certainly felt he won every match. Inevitably he generalized hastily, made special pleas and annoyed many specialists whose areas he was invading or who had never heard of most of these authorities.

Incredible as it now seems, in 1956 Kingsley Amis admitted in his review of *The Outsider* that he had never heard of Sartre, Camus, Nietzsche, Hesse, van Gogh—and Hemingway! How much more hostile were the ignorant when Wilson began to publish novels overlaid with his learning *and* 'pugnacious ignorance'.

In 1960 his first novel, designed to support his determination, appeared. Of the many works by Wilson *Ritual in the Dark* is in some ways still the most ambitious book. As an attempt to invoke the dark mystery, he claims for it an intricate and solemn genesis as it went through several major revisions before being published. Wilson has claimed that his first novel is to *The Egyptian Book of the Dead* what Joyce's *Ulysses* is to the *Odyssey*. Be that as it may, the novel is carefully structured to reveal its purposiveness. The authorial point of view, never present as first person, is nevertheless divided between several young Outsiders: Gerard Sorme, a writer; Austin Nunne, a dilettante and murderer; and Oliver Glasp, a painter. Secondary characters include a German psychiatrist, a Scottish detective, and an aged priest. Final significances, however, are filtered through Gerard Sorme: ultimately only he remains a reliable witness.

The story exploits a search for who-did-the-murders without ever trying for either mystery or tension. No one is surprised when Austin is identified as the killer of four women. The interest focusses on why he kills rather than on whom or when. Gerard Sorme partially succeeds in justifying Austin's killing four prostitutes by stabbing them brutally. Even murder is a creative act when done by a superior person, for the act releases a sense of power. Gerard confesses to having some of the same impulses at times. 'I belong among the Enemies,' he tells his murderer-friend: 'certain men whose business is to keep the world in a turmoil—the Napoleons, Hitlers, Genghis Khans.'

Finally Gerard sees Austin as truly insane—not 'supersane'—and no longer condones the killings, telling himself that such killing is 'a complete negation of all our impulses. It means we've got no future.' Wilson, however, unlike his Gerard, remains very much interested in murder, and the subject comes up frequently in his writings. Specific works include an *Encyclopaedia of Murder* in 1961 (with Patricia Pitman), a second novel on the subject called *The World of Violence* in 1963 (*The Violent World of Hugh Greene* in the United States), *A Casebook of Murder* in 1969, another novel called *The Killer* in 1970 (*Lingard* in the United States), and *Order of Assassins* in 1972, a psychological analysis of killers as Outsiders—to name only the most substantial works on the subject.

Wilson's output has remained prodigious for many years, as if the prodigy cherished the root meaning of the label derived from *prodigium*: omen and/or monster. In the survey of his later work which follows here, emphasis and selectivity are not necessarily his, for he has often considered rather small items in his canon as of special significance. Indeed, he has never disowned any of his creations, so that any selective discussion does injustice to his fervour and dedication. One suspects that he has written much more than he has published. One knows that some of his projects have been aborted by reluctant publishers. The 'case', however, of Colin Wilson still remains very much in his own idiom which is at the service of his commitment to defeat defeatism.

The novels that followed *Ritual in the Dark* vary in themes and techniques from one of the first 'beat' stories, *Adrift in Soho* (1961), to speculative projections into the future and psychological thrillers. Published in 1963, *Man Without a Shadow* (American title, *The Sex Diary of Gerard Sorme*) purports to be the intimate confession of the central character from *Ritual in the Dark*. The work was attacked as pornographic, but as the author claims, it 'owes more to Gabriel Marcel's *Metaphysical Journal* than to Frank Harris.' In the fictitious diary Gerard defends the mad Austin more precisely than he did in the earlier novel, where he had finally decided Austin was not justified.

Now, however, he has decided that 'Austin was dimly, vaguely trying to follow his own deepest nature to some unheard-of form of self-expression.' Identifying the 'sexual force' as 'the nearest thing to magic — to the supernatural — that human beings ever experience,' the diarist justifies the intensity of his own sex drive. He then proceeds to illustrate his sexuality so vividly that the book had to be cleared in court before it could be sold in England — after which, of course, it sold fairly well.

Critical reception of *Man Without a Shadow* followed the usual pattern of ambivalence, vituperation and adulation. One critic, Stanley Kauffmann in the *New Republic*, hazarded a guess that 'Colin Wilson is a spoof and that Kingsley Amis, Malcolm Muggeridge and Peter Ustinov go away together on occasional weekends and compose a Colin Wilson book.' A few years later Wilson himself, perhaps rationalizing, admitted that he viewed the work as 'a volume of tongue-in-cheek pronography and diabolism . . . which embodies, in fictional form, the ideas expounded in my phenomenological study, *Origins of the Sexual Impulse*.' *Origins of the Sexual Impulse* is the fifth volume, published in 1963, in the so-called Outsider cycle. In it Wilson draws heavily upon Edmund Husserl and Gestalt psychologists for his 'facts'.

Another work of fiction also published in 1963 testifies to Wilson's excitement at that time about his own intuitions. *The World of Violence* (American title, *The Violent World of Hugh Greene*) is a slow-paced story told in the first person by a narrator who often stops to philosophize about the significance of his education and other experiences. In the tradition of the *Bildungsroman*, the work is concerned with identifying the most significant variables in the hero's growth and in fixing the sources of his mature convictions and strange habits. Like his creator, Hugh Greene is a prodigy, self-taught and eager for knowledge. As a child he begins to question the value of ordinary experience as an index to knowledge. As he moves from 'The Outer Dark' to 'The Inner Dark' (subtitles for the two parts of the novel), Hugh relates to various kinds of violence and experiments personally with brutality. After a series of 'vastations' he attacks the meaning of existence and his own Outsider-ism, much as Wilson himself had done by studying in the British Museum Reading Room. There he reads 'straight through' Berkeley, Hume, Kant, Hegel, William James, Husserl and others — all in three months!

Critical opinion of this novel tended to follow the usual pattern: Bad but also good, or passionate but illiterate, or well-meaning but hopeless. Indeed, the violent world that Hugh was trying to understand resembles the novel itself — not easy to solve. In the last sentence of the novel the searcher concludes that 'the contradictions of the bundle of responses

called a human being can never be resolved as simply as the contradictions of philosophy.'

Nevertheless, Wilson goes on trying, sometimes introducing the very
contradictions he loves to wrestle with—often unsuccessfully. Wilson's
fifth novel, *Necessary Doubt* (1964), takes its title from Paul Tillich's
theology. The main character, Professor Zweig, is an 'existential theologian,' so there are plenty of problems to deal with, including the
nature of God as well as of man. The plot revolves about a manhunt for
the son of a famous surgeon. The surgeon's recent suicide has aroused
suspicions. Zweig knows the family and undertakes the responsibility.
He can identify emotionally with the hunted, and paradoxically the
hunter in this novel feels more guilt than the hunted. Eventually
Zweig is joined in the hunt by two friends, an eccentric mystic and
a detective. When they find the surgeon's son they also encounter
moral complexities, for the man is not clearly and unequivocally 'guilty'.
The killer believes sincerely that he has benefited his victims by encouraging them, with the help of pills, to kill themselves. So Zweig finally
arranges for the killer's escape, defending his decision, explaining that
the man is a visionary rather than a criminal—a typical Wilson distinction,
and one that is all too familiar among supporters of supermen theories:
special people with special powers should be given special privileges.

Within the covers of the novel the doubts work well, however, for
they are the proper stuff of fiction. As one reviewer concluded: 'the
whole odd mixture of miscellaneous erudition and casual flim-flam does
somehow add up. Partly this is because of the audacity of it all, the sheer
cheek. Partly it is because of Mr Wilson's persistence in search of
significance, even here. But basically it is because he continues to try to
find out what is really important in life.'

Encouraged by such half-understanding at least, Wilson continued
to write fiction while pondering and reworking his philosophy in non-
fiction. The novels that follow *Necessary Doubt* include an 'unconventional detective story', *The Glass Cage* (1966); a Lovecraft imitation,
The Mind Parasites (1967); another parable *qua* novel, *The Philosopher's
Stone* (1969); another 'crime novel', *The Killer* (1970); another
adventure of Gerard Sorme in *The God of the Labyrinth* (1970); an
advanced piece of speculative fiction called *The Black Room* (1971); a
novel which was planned as the first of a series and is exactly what the
title promises, *The Schoolgirl Murder Case* (1974); and another science-
speculative piece of fiction, *The Space Vampires* (1976).

Wilson's novels are not ordinary story books. They are sometimes
repetitious, even naively plotted. Their *ideas* are worth some attention,

although once one grasps the concept of 'mind parasites' and 'black rooms', there is little difficulty in perceiving what each work is trying to say. Wilson's admiration of the 'Lovecraft tradition' has been an important aspect of his speculative fiction. Lovecraft's 1926 essay, 'Supernatural Horror in Literature', claims that his kind of fiction encourages extending the narrow boundaries of ordinary science by exploiting the fear of the unknown. Wilson's novel *The Mind Parasites* projects a conflict many years from now with the Tsathogguans, wily microscopic parasites that menace civilization by infecting the best minds of the age. It is meant to frighten the reader, and perhaps it does frighten some; yet Wilson admits that at least the opening pages of 'flaccid prose' did not 'come off', adding: 'but what the hell. I'd rather get on with another book than tinker about with it.'

In 'another book', *The Philosopher's Stone*, Wilson speculates about breaking barriers in human consciousness by inserting a bit of special metal in the frontal lobe of the brain to stimulate the imagination. The conclusion is pretentious: 'Man should possess an infinite appetite for life. It should be self-evident to him, all the time, that life is superb, glorious, endlessly rich, infinitely desirable.' Yet both novels are enthusiastically humanistic and optimistic in their messages.

The Black Room is perhaps Wilson's most intense projection of his conviction that human consciousness is still slumbering and that it needs real awakening. Wilson's quest is not for the noble primitive who got lost in the past but for a new self which must be radically discovered and then perfected. A 'black room' is a device for cutting off information from the outside. In a lightproof and soundproof room an individual is outside the outside by being truly inside. In such a room — metaphor for cutoff state — a person either survives because he is strong enough to keep his awareness alive by himself or eventually capitulates to the blackness and the silence and 'loses his mind'. The idea of a black room begins as a metaphor, develops into a device for brainwashing, and ends up in Wilson's novel as a crisis experience in which 'danger and difficulty unite the whole being'.

The Space Vampires refines the mind-parasite metaphor and adds humanoids and various trappings of outer space. It builds into an exciting and more nearly conventional thriller as plot dominates didacticism without sacrificing philosophical intent. Wilson has always seen an affinity between crime and creativity, and between detecting crime and saving souls. Psychic visions and occult phenomena are facts to him as they are for many readers, who may, however, ultimately confuse their facts with fantasies once useful as escape mechanisms. (What happens to reality when it becomes more fantastic than fiction has been the concern of many contemporary storytellers, some of whom have given up on inventing new stories.)

In *The Schoolgirl Murder Case*, for example, a novel meant to be popular and readable, Wilson throws away chances at suspense in the interests of his kind of truth. The suspect has been under suspicion all along and no one is surprised at the ending. One may be surprised, however, at the combining of magic and brothel and the fact that the detective is more of a clergyman, finally, than one could have predicted. After he has solved the crime, which revealed, in passing, that this is a bad world, he still insists it is a good one.

To sum up Wilson's significance is not easy, for his urgency to communicate can quickly change any *genre* into a vehicle for his ideas, and the critic often evaluates *genre* rather than ideas, according to Wilson's most often voiced complaint. He is not a *great* novelist, not a *great* dramatist, not a *great* literary critic, music critic or philosopher – as he has hoped. He is, however, remarkably earnest, versatile and informed, and nearest greatness when he speaks as a 'new existentialist'. In 1966 he published a readable volume modestly called *Introduction to the New Existentialism* with the emphasis on the *newness* of his ideas. In this work he outlines the case for his claim of having broken with the dead-end, old and pessimistic existentialism of Sartre and others. Again and again Wilson objects to accepting an empty and meaningless universe. Stressing the evidence that consciousness is intentional, he rejects Sartre's gloomy conclusion that such intentionality is only apparent and thus bad faith. In a 1967 essay, 'Existential Psychology: A Novelist's Approach', Wilson explores the metaphor of a debilitating robot in human beings that cuts off creativity. And finally his interest in Abraham Maslow's ideas motivated him to write a book called, less modestly, *New Pathways in Psychology* (1972), in which he exhorts mankind to increase and intensify awareness until all who are able to see the 'third world' as a *real* place. Wilson insists that this higher reality is 'there all the time, like China or the moon. . . . It is fundamentally a world of pure *meaning*'.

The thirst for more and more knowledge must perforce always outrun research. Wilson has sought the byways as well as the highways to satisfy his hydrophytic thirst, evaluating and re-evaluating the special powers of others, such as mystics, occultists, and assorted dreamers and visionaries. As a self-styled existential critic he digs for the effect on him of the work of others, rejecting as inadequate many sacred works of the orthodox canons. His own canon is long and complicated, and this essay neglects necessarily many nuances. Colin Wilson, however, has earned his place in history—whether literary history or the history of ideas is still moot only because at this time historians in general disagree with him that there is no difference. Literature is the handmaiden of ideas for Wilson. To misunderstand that point is to try him in the wrong court for crimes he never intended to commit.

Introduction to
The Philosopher's Stone

JOYCE CAROL OATES

'The unconscious mind may include all man's past; but it also
includes all his future.'—Colin Wilson

Of the many excellent writers in England today, four strike me as
especially exciting because they are struggling to express, in widely differing bodies of work, our crucial contemporary problem: how to get
into the future, how to emerge from a condition of confusion, despair,
nihilism, how to create values that will allow man to evolve into a higher
form of man. While their contemporaries in England and, sadly, all too
frequently in America, are content to joke about the past or the future,
in works of art that are often technically brilliant but morally quite
played-out, John Fowles, Doris Lessing, Margaret Drabble and Colin
Wilson are consciously attempting to imagine a new image for man, a
new Self-Image freed from ambiguity, irony and the self-conscious
narrowness of the imagination we have inherited from nineteenth-
century Romanticism.

Colin Wilson has given a name to this strange, tantalizing, deathly
inheritance of ours which, like all neuroses, we half-love and will defend:
he calls it 'original sin', the capacity for man's self-destruction, which
grows out of his self-loathing, which grows inevitably out of the very
psychological and philosophical revolutions that once freed him from
even more stifling bonds. The Darwinian, Freudian and behaviourist
assumptions about man's slavery to his 'lower nature', his helplessness
in the hands of natural forces, merge, tragically enough, with the science
of economics developed by Adam Smith, Ricardo and Malthus . . . and
against this sense of oppression, of a total denial of 'freedom', the poet
must rebel. He must rebel, if he is to live. And, rebelling, he must hate;
he finds himself *hating*. And, in the words of that arch-ironist and hater,
Robert Musil, 'One can't be angry with one's own time without damage
to oneself'.

Colin Wilson's imagination is essentially one which draws together,
unifies, makes brilliantly clear what might remain obscure or fragmented.
In a sense, there are no new 'ideas', but only new relationships, new
emphases, surprising new combinations of what was already known or

half-known. He is a teacher, fundamentally; yet he recognizes the limitations of the form of direct statement or argument, the need for us to reimagine even our ideas in terms of fiction. He has written a number of works of fiction, some of which are novels and some of which are, in my opinion, parables, most of them dramatic reconstructions of his central dilemma: how to bring the Outsider into civilization, how to overcome the 'original sin' that is our wound, or perhaps, in a perverse way, our 'gift'. Like Nietzsche, Wilson believes that if man were only capable of realizing his own potential—the full use of his brain—there would be no need for gods, no need to transcend the human level at all. As the young protagonist of *The Philosopher's Stone* says, after having submitted to a brain operation which allows him extraordinary powers of concentration, he is really freed now to experience *ordinary* consciousness. If we could be 'ordinary'—'normal'—this to us would be godliness. 'It's everyday consciousness that's sub-normal,' the hero says.

Since the first publication of *The Philosopher's Stone*, a number of works have appeared in America that deal with this very theme, and quite exciting, revolutionary works they are, indeed—Roszak's *The Making of a Counter-Culture*, Leonard's *The Transformation* and Castaneda's several books about the Yaqui sorcerer Don Juan. *The Philosopher's Stone* is a peculiar, quirky, exasperating and ingenious variation on a theme by Lovecraft, one of the rare works of science fiction that uses horror not as an emotion so much as an *idea*, the stimulus for forcing the reader to think. Wilson has said that he will leave to other writers the challenge to make people feel emotions; he believes they feel too often and think too little. It is the intention of *The Philosopher's Stone* to make us *think*.

Yet there is always something mysterious about a parable, for it is an art form that is not simply allegorical—in the sense that it can be figured out, added up like a column of numbers, its separate parts constituting a rigid and highly explicable system; the best parables resist any ultimate interpretation. The unresolved conclusion of *The Philosopher's Stone* invites speculation, absorbing, as it seems to, the reader's personality into the protagonist's. (Another science-fiction novel of Wilson's, *The Mind Parasites*, 'explains' *The Philosopher's Stone*; but each novel stands alone.) It is a personality that may have begun with an aggressive faith in existential subjectivity, but which ends with the vigorous synthesis of the 'scientific' and the 'artistic' visions: 'Man is a creature of life and the daylight; his destiny lies in total objectivity.'

If the evolutionary development of man is about to become conscious, in fact if it is a part of man's process of becoming human, then the life force must be acknowledged as something quite separate from, or at least quantitatively superior to, any emotional or fragmented vision of it. We seem to be moving toward a rejection of the traditional Western philosophical inquiry, 'Who am I?' to the traditional Eastern inquiry, 'What am I?' Such a movement is, of course, a tremendous leap – the substitution of the word *what* for the ego-centred word *who* really constitutes a near-miraculous transformation.

Though he uses the arguments and many of the rhetorical devices of rationalism, Wilson is really a man of faith – that is, a 'man of faith' who believes in the meaningfulness of the universe, though he cannot quite yet decipher these meanings. In his excellent introduction to the encyclopaedic *The Occult*, surely one of the finest books on that subject, Wilson states that 'there are "meanings" floating around us from which we are normally cut off by habit, ignorance and the dullness of the senses. . . . The higher the form of life, the deeper its capacity for registering meaning, and *the more powerful its hold on life.*' Liberation consists in our being able to accept the otherness of the universe and, having faith in its order, our assuming the responsibility for developing our species in the direction of comprehending this order – the realizing of dormant, long-neglected powers of reason and intuition. Wilson has been greatly influenced by Nietzsche and Shaw, and, like them, he is rigorously individualistic, set in opposition to easy, familiar, conventional modes of thought. He is often too blunt and too outrageous for his own good, preferring at times to simply state his prejudices rather than explain them, or to put forth startling conclusions without the gentle, step-by-step development we are accustomed to in literary criticism. His belief that H.G. Wells may be the greatest of twentieth-century novelists may or may not be entirely serious, but it provokes passionate opposition, it does at least cause us to think. And is Shakespeare a 'second-rate mind'? Lawrence thought so also, as did Tolstoy; and Wilson does cause us to rethink the prejudices that automatically assign to any Shakespearean work an aura of the near-divine. Without exactly agreeing with Wilson that Shakespeare, like Bacon, is 'second-rate', I suspect that the personalities Shakespeare considered worth the scrutiny of his poetic imagination are no longer representative of typical or probable or even possible modes of behaviour for his audiences – in short, that his tragic heroes are to some extent victims of the passage of time, products of a consciousness that took much more seriously than we the danger of emotional turmoil in ostensibly 'superior' human beings. Wilson's sweeping rejection of Shakespeare, however, is part of his recognition that a belief in evolutionary humanism *as a progressive phenomenon* in history necessitates a systematic, remorseless examination and rejection of much of the past, not because it is the 'past', but because its models of human behaviour are not really models any longer. There is a pragmatic, rather harsh, and perhaps dramatically political side to Wilson's imagination which he has not yet developed.

Similarly, one of the concepts of Wilson's own form of existential psychology is that of the 'Self-Image', in opposition to the fixed and deterministic Id-psychology of Freud; the 'Self-Image' is primarily an *image*, a fantasizing of the ego in the service of the transcendental ego, and cannot be traced back to the simple desire for the cessation of hunger, or 'relief', that Freud generally believed must characterize fantasies. Wilson would agree with the humanist psychologists that it is necessary to acknowledge all of man's physical limitations, but, once the subnormal is transformed into the normal, once man is healthy, his life will be a process of a continual revitalization of the will: it is a climbing 'towards high states of self-awareness by means of a series of self-images,' as he says in his book on the American psychologist Abraham Maslow (*New Pathways in Psychology: Maslow and the Post-Freudian Revolution*). Man cannot drift upward; he must will himself upward, through the transformation of personality into ever new and ever more complex states of consciousness. Maslow acknowledged that, in *The Philosopher's Stone*, Wilson had explored areas of intentionality that humanist or 'third-force' psychology had yet to investigate, though since Maslow's death in 1970 much has been done along these lines, notably through bio-feedback experiments. Wilson's prophetic qualities, which at times make him seem like a historian writing from some future time, may be best illustrated by *The Philosopher's Stone* and its companion-parable, *The Mind Parasites*. In any case, one accepts his basic premise—that man must come into active, conscious control of his own brain, or the species will become extinct. It is an either/or proposition that lends itself to dramatic treatment, indeed.

Colin Wilson became famous, as American readers know, with the publication of *The Outsider*. This was in 1956; he was twenty-five years old. He had left school at the age of sixteen, was almost entirely self-taught, and had, from the age of twelve, 'been preoccupied with the question of the meaning of human existence, and whether all human values are not pure self-delusion. . . .' (Afterword to the 1963 edition of *The Outsider*). He became obsessed with the idea that there must be a scientific method for investigating the question of human existence, and while in

his early 'teens he read Shaw, Eliot, Goethe and Dostoevsky, at the same
time pursuing scientific studies. Like the hero of *The Philosopher's Stone*,
he sensed himself divided between the 'poetic' and the 'objective', but,
unlike his fortunate hero, he had not a magical godfather like Sir Lyell
to give him direction. For many years he worked mainly as an unskilled
labourer, enduring frustrations and hardships that would have driven
most people to despair. Wilson's sense of being 'alienated' from society
is, then, no literary affectation—hardly the Romantic or existential disenchantment with life that characterizes most of the literature of alienation of our time. It is difficult for Americans to realize the class distinct-
ions that still exist in England, and the 'curious state of apathy' in which
young working-class people grow up; to read Wilson's rather precocious
autobiography, *Voyage to a Beginning*, is an instructive experience.
Wilson's habitual energy, his habitual optimism, are all the more extraordinary in the light of his social background. In many ways he seems
more 'American' than 'English', and he acknowledges in an essay on
culture in the Soviet Union (included in *Beyond the Outsider*) that
Americans possess a tremendous intellectual vitality he finds admirable
and, if they could conquer their strange sense of 'insignificance', their
uniting with the Soviet Union could produce 'the greatest civilization
ever known to man'.

As an Englishman, however, he is an Outsider. He understands deeply
and intuitively the tragedy of isolation, the 'fallacy of insignificance'
that can come to deaden not only a class of society but an entire society.
Yet his ability to designate this impotence of the soul as a 'fallacy', and to
somehow set himself apart from it, is an unfashionable act. It goes against
the dominating Western belief in the necessary 'tragedy' of human existence, the belief in an essential 'absurdity' at the heart of man's relationship with the universe. It is not at all a popular stand, though *The Outsider* became both a critical and popular success. Misunderstood by many
readers, *The Outsider* was neither a glorification of despair nor a rejection
of it, but an attempt to formulate what Wilson saw as the crucial problem
for civilization: 'the adoption of a religious attitude that can be assimilated as *objectively* as the headlines of last Sunday's newspapers'. The individual begins this effort as an Outsider; he may finish it 'as a saint'.

Not since Lord Byron's overnight fame had any English writer found
himself so praised—unfortunately for Wilson. We know from Byron's
letters how he came to loathe his early 'exaggerated nonsense' and to
feel guilt, even, for having contributed to the corruption of public taste.
Byron became a true Outsider, and the kind of disgust with life-as-lived
he tried to express is one of the challenges Colin Wilson has had to face,

both as a philosophical principle and as an experience. Raised to premature heights of fame, Wilson was of course denounced almost at once by many of the critics who had initially praised him. It is amazing, the hysterical venom that has been directed against Colin Wilson, especially by reviewers for the prestigious English journals. His remark in the introduction to *Beyond the Outsider*, that criticism of his works contained a 'note of violence, as if my publishing a book were somehow a calculated affront', is no exaggeration. It is unimaginable that any American writer, producing book after book dedicated to exploring the 'neurosis' of modern civilization, and informed above all by an optimistic and prophetic vision, would be subjected to such gratuitous violence. Part of the difficulty lies in the reluctance of many educated Englishmen to take seriously, even to accept as intelligent, anyone who has not attended a university. Again, the differences between America and England are enormous.

With very little critical encouragement, and nearly as little financial security, Wilson has continued his investigation of modern civilization steadily since 1956, and has at this time published thirty books on a great variety of subjects. Though the books are dissimilar in content— ranging from the pornography of violence of *Lingard*, to speculative historical analysis in *Rasputin and the Fall of the Romanovs*, to Wilson's own theory of the sexual impulse in *Origins of the Sexual Impulse*—they overlap in theme. As Wilson states in the Preface to *The Occult*, 'A single obsessional idea runs through all my work—the paradoxical nature of freedom.' *The Philosopher's Stone* is a succinct statement of that theme, shaped into a teasing parable that is, among other things, a parody of science fiction, and a masterful interweaving of fact and outlandish fiction in the manner of Borges (to whom the novel is dedicated). Like Borges, Wilson believes that the mind of man must confront labyrinths; but unlike Borges, Wilson is willing to take on the challenge of the labyrinth, confident that the mind of man can illuminate—or has the capacity to illuminate—this riddle that the 'Ancient Old Ones' have presented us. The problem is not really freedom, but man's narrow, self-absorbed relationship to 'original sin', his acting as a willing host for the 'mind parasites' of chronic drowsiness.

How to wake from our sleep, how to achieve a pure, perfect, uncorrupted mind? *The Philosopher's Stone* analyzes and rejects, through the case of the brain-injured mystic, Dick, the Romantic assumption of an essential   passivity in the experience of ecstasy. Dick is subject to flashes of beauty that all but annihilate him, but he does not control them and cannot even understand them. He is passive, and passivity is only half the process of being human; therefore he must die. His 'existence' is not truly human, and the life force cannot grow through him. Yet it will have to be through an evocation of the 'underground', the suppressed 'occult' that the higher consciousness is ultimately attained. Powers long phased out of civilization by the conscious mind must be realized once more, in the form of a recognizable young hero who emerges, as Wilson himself did, from an all-but-undifferentiated mass ego of 'dirt and boredom' in a working-class village in England.

In spite of his emphasis upon the individual, Wilson ultimately believes that man must act by co-operating with others; so there is not a single hero in the novel but a dual-hero, 'Lester-Littleway'. In both men there is 'some obscure force struggling' to emerge, and the temptations to withdraw from the cerebral battle are made attractive — why continue 'living in our absurd, dehydrated, sterilized world of ideas and aesthetic emotions?' Yet to fall back into simplicity, into passivity, is not possible; this would be suicide. (In *The Mind Parasites* many of the hero's colleagues do commit suicide.) One cannot turn off his energies, as Blake knew well; the frustration of the creative urge always results in destruction — either the death of others or of the self. There is no choice but to go forward.

'Aaron Marks' of this novel is, of course, Abraham Maslow; Marks's 'value experiences' are Maslow's 'peak experiences', the instances of epiphany or ecstasy Maslow studied. (See Maslow's *Toward a Psychology of Being* and *The Farther Reaches of Human Nature*.) Since I am no admirer of Lovecraft, I cannot trace the maniacal ways by which Lovecraft's obsessions are utilized for Wilson's own ends, though there is, near the end of *The Philosopher's Stone*, a plethora of fanciful detail that would do justice to a genuine madman's vision. Perhaps there is something of David Lindsay here too, though Wilson is quite contrary to both Lindsay and Lovecraft in his essential affirmation of our civilization. Though he may believe — seriously or not — that 999,999 out of a million people are all but hopeless, he also believes that Mankind as a whole is destined to realize immortality.

As Wilson states in his book on Maslow: 'The age of ambiguity is over. It may not be obvious yet, but it is.'*

---

*This article first appeared as an Introduction to *The Philosopher's Stone* (Warner Books, 1973).

25

The Sage of Tetherdown*

H. D. PURCELL

When I first read about the 'Suggestopaedia' of Georgi Lozanov[1] (in *Superlearning* by Sheila and Nancy Ostrender and Lynn Schroeder, London, Souvenir Press, 1979), I immediately thought of Colin Wilson. For forty years I had learnt poetry just before going to sleep, when the Alpha rhythms (7-14 cycles per second) are dominant in the brain, repeating what I had learnt immediately on waking in the early morning. On the basis of these thousands of lines learnt by heart, plus a thorough external English honours degree from London University, I constructed the two-year course entitled 'Four Hundred Years of English Poetry' which I teach at the University of Vienna. Suggestopaedia promised the same tranquil, trancelike, receptive state of mind at other times of day, as well as before and after sleep.

Reduced to its essentials, Suggestopaedia is a synchronisation of slow music, slow breathing, a slow pulse-rate and information read out in fixed cycles of eight, ten or twelve seconds—say, holding the breath for four seconds while the piece of information is read out, breathing out for two seconds to the musical background and breathing in for another two seconds (perhaps while a translation of the following piece of information in another language is quickly read out).

The only slow music to work up to now has been baroque *largos* and *larghettos* (Bach, Albinoni, Vivaldi, Corelli, Handel, Telemann), though Ravi Shankar's sitar music (helpful in Raja-yoga) may perhaps work as well. A quick piece by, say, Boccherini or Mozart (e.g. a minuet) is useful in reawakening the subject to the rhythm of every day. Other kinds of music are out, and a book by Dorothy Retallack, entitle-entitled *The Sound of Music and Plants* (Marina del Rey, DeVorss & Co., 1973) explains why. She played different kinds of music to her plants. When they heard the baroque kind, they put down healthy roots, grew stronger and taller, and leaned forward to embrace the microphone. When they heard rock music, they leaned away, shrivelled up and died! Dorothy Retallack is fond of Debussy—not so the plants, which just leaned away a little. It all goes to show that the Greeks were right to associate different kinds of music with different psychic effects. The point is of special interest to me in connexion with my campaign against

*'Tetherdown' is the name of Colin Wilson's house in Cornwall.—Ed.

acoustic pollution in public places. Last Saturday, as I punted up
river, throwing up the pole with a long, easy stroke, I wondered how
best to bring my displeasure vividly to the attention of the pop music
purveyors. Perhaps a campaign against cruelty to plants offers a promising line of action? But I digress.

Anyone can breathe or read slowly, and synchronisation with the
music only involves the problem that different parts of the same movement may be played at different speeds—especially by trendy conduct-
ors anxious to improve on the composers. This problem can be solved
with the aid of a metronome, a microphone and a tape-recorder. But
there remains the problem of how to bring about a drop in the pulse
rate. As the body slows down, the mind speeds up—up to a certain point.
Finding a solution to this difficulty is much less easy. We live very much
under stress nowadays, and pulse rates of over seventy per minute are
regarded as 'normal'. They also induce headaches and block the learning
process with Beta rhythms (+14 cycles per second). Self-hypnotism is
not the answer, as this induces Theta and Delta rhythms, which also
block learning. The recitation of *mantras*, for example, leads to a slight
but definite increase in Theta rhythms. As Colin might have put it, the
trouble is that complete relaxation precludes concentration, and concentration raises stress.

The optimum rate for awareness in most people is around sixty heart-
beats per minute (so that the coincidence with the actual number of
seconds in a minute may not be coincidental), and this rate lies exactly
between those of *largos* (40-60 beats per minute) and *larghettos* (60-66
beats per minute), though I personally find that much slower *largo*
rhythms are suitable in my case—probably because the pulse rate seldom
or never falls as far as that of the music. In fact, I think that the music—
synchronised with the breathing and information—may usefully be
played much slower than the pulse rate, thus helping to bring it down.
The Goldberg variations on Bach, especially the *arias* at the beginning
and end, which were successfully designed to defeat the insomnia of
Count Keyserlinck, are a famous example of the influence of slow
music.

Lozanov and his disciples have also devised a whole range of preliminary exercises to bring down the pulse rate. Physical relaxation is
induced by tensing and relaxing every set of muscles in the body, from
the toes to the scalp and back again. Sensation of heat and weight are
induced in the extremities, and imagined light is made to flow through
the body in both directions. The mind is induced to concentrate on the
different colours of the spectrum in natural progression associated with

downward movement (e.g. from the top to the bottom storey of a big building), which simulates descent into the subconscious. A vision of natural perfection is intensely visualised—as in *Kubla Khan* or the bowery island in a lake so often visualised by Shelley. (I can actually *see* the choppy waves and the snowy mountains beyond. I can actually *feel* the breeze and *sense* the movement of the branches on either side of me.) A feeling of complete affirmation is also induced, emphasising a positive attitude towards the learning process and life in general. No wonder pupils of Lozanov regard their sessions with him as among the happiest experiences of their lives.

The elements of Lozanov's systems are not new. They certainly owe something to the 'Autogenic Training' developed by J.H. Schulz[2] in the 1930s and have a lot in common with Dr Raymond Abrezol's 'Sophrology' (see *Superlearning*, pp. 138ff.) and Dr A.G. Odessky's 'Psychological Gymnastics' (see *Superlearning*, chapter 2). Lozanov also drew upon native Bulgarian tradition (perhaps Catharist in its ultimate origins?). His great personal contribution was to synchronise the four elements of his system, as was discovered by Dr Jane Bancroft, (see *Superlearning*, bibliography section I, pp. 305-6), Professor of French at Toronto University. She visited Sofia and was fobbed off with the usual generalised course devised for Westerners; but she managed to smuggle herself into a course devised for Russians, where she found that information was being delivered in eight-second sequences synchronised with both deep breathing and slow music.

To get some idea of what all this signifies in practice, consider that the Berlitz teaching method,[3] in which only the target language is used and which has been going strong since the last century, induces the average student to learn about two hundred words in thirty teaching hours, and even these will be quickly forgotten if not soon rehearsed. Lozanov, who is also mainly concerned with language teaching claims up to 1,800 words per day imprinted in the consciousness of his pupils! Nor need the method be confined to languages. I have tried it successfully with facts of physics and geography, as also complicated street directions, always with success. No wonder the Soviet military showed special interest in Suggestopaedia. It was this interest which finally resulted in the Party ideologists getting off Lozanov's back. Nor is it surprising to hear that the Pentagon showed special interest in Dr Bancroft's revelations.

Yes, yes, I can hear someone say—this is all very well, but what has it to do with Colin Wilson? The answer is everything, as Colin himself will have seen in my opening paragraph. As he states in the preface to

his book, *The Occult*: 'A single obsessional idea runs through all my
work: the paradoxical nature of freedom. . . . Man's consciousness is
as powerful as a microscope . . . But microscopic vision is narrow vision.
We need to develop another kind of consciousness that is the equivalent
of the telescope' (pp. 9-10). This is the Faculty X of his book, *The
Philosopher's Stone*.

Colin's simile of the microscope is a summing up of Western philosophy from Descartes down to Logical Positivism. Like a crab with
one claw huge and the other atrophied, Western man has seen an absurd
over-development of the left side of the brain at the expense of the
right, of analysis as against synthesis—taking butterflies to pieces in
order to understand them, or else pinning them to a board, as opposed
to observing them living in relation to their environment. But the
remedy does not lie merely in emphasising the activities of the right-
hand side of the brain—the seat of creativity arising out of the subconscious—though it was this creativity which produced the superlative art
of Magdalenian man and, I would add, all genuine art ever since.
(Besides, Magdalenian man also produced a flint technology with the
left side of his brain which was superior to anything seen up to that
time.) No, what Colin is saying is that we must combine both left and
right sides of the brain, intensifying thought by narrowing it to a laser
beam, but combining it with an awareness which enables us to reach
telescopically far into the recesses of the imagination—and perhaps
eventually far into the recesses of the Universe. Certainly, Charles Lind-
bergh thought that was the only way we should ever penetrate beyond
the solar system.

Colin quotes from an astonishingly wide range of authors as regards
methods whereby a state of creative awareness combined with analytical detachment may be induced. Lozanov's methods will merely add to
the long list, though I believe that the element of synchronisation will
interest Colin. What is more, Colin has shown himself capable of apply-
ing his own lessons. His gift of concentration is phenomenal. Take his
The Craft of the Novel, which is one of the best works of criticism I
have ever read—certainly the best written in the twentieth century. It
does not indulge in the usual 'lit. crit.', but tells us what the books are
about and what the author is aiming at, while putting whole periods in
perspective. When I started it, I assumed that new ideas would naturally
occur first in peotry, which I conceive of as a higher form than the novel.
But Colin demonstrated that this is by no means necessarily so. Since
then I have come to recognise that poetry is not so much what the
poets says as the way he says it. He also demonstrated how the modern

psychological novel took its origins from Samuel Richardson's obsession with the mind of a maidservant, summing up *Pamela* (half a million words in its complete form) and *Clarissa* (three-quarters of a million) so succinctly and well. Of how many works summed up by Colin might that be said! And how grateful we should be for his indefatigable industry and synthesising mind.

Colin is the great autodidact—necessarily, because his main concern is with matters which lie outside the normal educational field. Going to university would merely have stultified his mind, unless perhaps he had studied some wholly new science like radioastronomy. He is the sort of man who takes nothing on trust, but investigates for himself. For example, he had little or no opportunity to sample fine wines in his youth, and when he decided to find out more his method was character-istic. He wrote a book about wine and a good one (*A Book of Booze*, Gollancz, 1974). He also learnt to appreciate music, literature and the whole range of the arts: a feat made possible by his secret talisman, the realisation that works of art are not just to be judged by the pleasure they give but by the ability of their creators to perceive. That is what life is all about: perception. And the great enemy with which there can never be any truce is not suffering, but boredom. In *The Outsider*, at the very beginning of his literary career, he attracted attention by describ-ing how remarkable minds had been faced with this menace. Later, in a cycle of six books, culminating in *Beyond the Outsider*, he wrote about methods of inducing perception, but attracted little attention in the media. It was predictable. The talking classes which manipulate modern societies love to worry about problems but hate people with practical solutions. After all, if people are no longer in need of help, what function do the opinion-formers and experts have? (I find, for instance, that medical doctors dislike herbal remedies precisely because they work.) So it's all right to agonise over the human condition, but seek-ing solutions to the problem of existential *ennui* is quite another matter. Besides, the talking classes had switched off their hearing aids when the charge of elitism was brought against him. Colin's psychology is founded on the undoubted existence of a dominant five per cent., who alone, it would seem, have the power to make the great perceptual breakthrough (though others may well benefit from their perceptions, rather as termin-als are linked to a computer).

Colin studies the methods of other autodidacts so that he may explain the essentials of their achievements to those with the capacity to under-stand. He is the great teacher trying to make his pupils independent of him, so that they may find their own solutions—not the petty teacher trying to make his pupils dependent by saying only part of what he means. The petty teacher treats his material rather as though it were a drug, and the pupil is only given enough to get him hooked.

What is more, Colin is a moralist of a kind—not in the sense of imparting a whole list of coercive injunctions based on unexamined propositions, but in the sense of seeking out what is valid in the *mores*, or traditional customs, of the tribe. Thus when he explains that homosexuality is rare or non-existent in primitive tribes, but is found in cities as it is among crowded rats (*The Occult*, p. 193), I can sense a *frisson* passing through the London literary coteries. He also shows how drugs, while they may have an initially beneficial effect in putting a person in touch with his suppressed subconscious, are really a dead end because they inhibit the concentrating power of the left side of the brain, the co-operation of which is essential in order to attain true perception: 'Drugs, then, are the worst possible way of attempting to achieve "contemplative objectivity". They increase the mind's tendency to accept its own passivity instead of fighting against it' (ibid., p. 178). It is the same with murder. Colin's crime novels are psychologically interesting because he sees that the murderer is trying to express himself in such a way as to break free of his boredom and frustration. But the method he chooses is like a drug—it must be repeated if he is to renew even the temporary satisfaction it brings. Only the great path to perception is eternally valid. As a seer of the way (Persian *Rahbin*) Colin deserves to be called a sage, without any reservations.

But 'Sage of Tetherdown'? Doesn't that imply a certain provinciality? I am an unsympathetic commentator when it comes to discussing the provincial. I can see, for example, that Colin's appreciation of poetry must be limited by his provincial lack of foreign languages (I mean, beyond a smattering of French and German). This does not prevent him from showing excellent critical taste in his quotations from the English poets, but he has taken the ideas of the whole world within his purview, and no doubt long ago decided that he could hardly learn all the languages in which those ideas are expressed. So he concentrates on the ideas and sticks almost entirely to translations. For me, the way the poet expresses himself is quite as important as what he has to say. I think of poetry in relation to Richard Dawkins's theory of memes, enunciated in his book, *The Selfish Gene* (OUP., 1976). His memes are the smallest recognisable constituents of cultural phenomena, which resemble genes in that they cannot exist separately, and so must devise strategies for survival in combination with other, balancing, memes. Remove some of these (e.g. in translating or modernising a text) and the rest are at risk.

Occasionally, in his books on the paranormal, Colin himself expresses reservations about some of the evidence which he adduces. Why adduce it, then? Because he is determined to ensure that so much which has been rejected out of hand in the past should at least be considered on its merits. He is no more to be held responsible for every detail of what he quotes than was Robert Burton in *The Anatomy of Melancholy* (first published in 1621), that great work of the Jacobean period which was so often enlarged and reprinted up to 1676. In fact, Colin's works on the paranormal amount to a great modern version of *The Anatomy*. He anatomises melancholy in order to dispel it and provides us with a thousand serendipitous facts and allegations to titillate the jaded palate and awaken the reader to the fascination of life.

But it is dangerous to dismiss Colin's evidence out of hand when he does not query it himself. Some years ago he personally showed me that I was a dowser. That is the kind of practical demonstration which makes one think. I am therefore willing to try out the experiments he describes, whether with a pendulum, with megaliths, or with dreams. Even when I disagree with his conclusions, I find that he forces me to think. For instance, I do not believe that man first became aware of colours within the last couple of thousand years (*The Occult*, p. 30). Homer's wine-dark sea is a direct reflection of the rosy-fingered dawn, as I discovered when I came up on deck at five o'clock in the morning in the Aegean (and the red sunset is reflected as a darker wine). The palaeolithic cave-painters could certainly distinguish between the red, yellow and black oxides they used for colouring their drawings, and even Neanderthal man understood the decorative value of flowers, to judge by their use in the ceremonial burial of his own kind and of bears. The eye has always had the capacity to perceive what it is formed to perceive, and the new colours which Colin expects men to recognise in the future are doubtless already to be found in the unnamed hues of the great painters. (Memling, for instance, has a greeny-blue which is not quite turquoise but is quite unforgettable.) On the other hand, I recognise that there are language difficulties associated with colours. The Welsh word *glas* appears to mean blue or green, or grey even — any colour that water can be, or light eyes. But I am open to correction by someone who knows Welsh better than I. *Scarpe gialle* (yellow shoes) in Italian are brown shoes to us, and the Italians had to borrow the word *blu* from French to describe dark blue as opposed to cerulean (*azzuro*). So my awareness of colour has been heightened. Similarly, I think I have convinced Colin that cruelty was not invented in settled societies.[4] It already existed in the Palaeolithic era, as some cave drawings in Italy show, but I am very ready to believe that the incidence of cruelty greatly increased with the advent of settled societies. Again, I regard the evidence in favour of extraterrestial influences as very weak, but I have also come to see that there must be some explanation for the extraordinary number of UFO sightings which are made yearly, even if it is only psychological.

On occasion, I find myself disagreeing with Colin about more important problems, notably where Lamarck and Cuvier are concerned. Cuvier was evidently wrong to reject evolution as the explanation for changes in the flora and fauna of the earth, but his doubts about Lamarck's theory were fully justified scientifically, and his catastrophism also appears to have been justified, in the light of modern research, not only where the disappearance of the dinosaurs is concerned but also with regard to the effects of planets approaching the earth in more recent times. Colin's predilection for Lamarck is a spill-over from his basically Shavian notion of self-willed evolution, and his sympathy even extends so far as to embrace Lysenko, whose experiments have never been reproduced under laboratory conditions. In any case, I think the doctrine of Lysenko conflicts radically with Colin's own theory of the dominant five per cent. Why only five per cent. if this is not part of a genetic survival strategy? The fundamental difference between us is that I think man has built-in limitations, whereas Colin thinks that the sky is the limit. Not that this prevents me from believing that evolution may be speeded up—and suffering enormously reduced—through a policy of humanely administered genetic selection. Nor does it stop me from agreeing with Colin that many people realise only a part of their potential.

A subjective assessment is all that I can attempt in an article. Any objective assessment would fill many books, and no doubt will. Meanwhile, I am content to recall some highlights from my reading of his varied works: the murderer Sundheim in *The Glass Cage*, for instance, who has all the elemental force of Bill Hopkins's anti-hero in *The Leap*; the extraordinary immediacy of Lindsay's or Lovecraft's work brought first to my attention; the realisation that Hesse's Siddhartha, for all his wonderful oneness with nature, is essentially a passive being; the realisation that Whitehead is probably the greatest philosopher of the twentieth century. I could go on and on—so could many other readers. Suffice it to affirm that Colin is not just a remarkable mind but one of the major writers of our century, and that he is alive now.

NOTES

1. Author of *Suggestology and Outlines of Suggestopedy* (New York, Gordon

and Breach, 1980) and numerous papers on the subject.

2. Johannes H. Schultz, joint author with W. Luthe, of *Autogenic Training: A Psychophysiologic Approach in Psychotherapy* (New York, Grune and Stratton, 1959.

3. Language teaching courses published in the UK by Cassell & Co. and in the US by Macmillan.

4. See *A Criminal History of Mankind*, pp. 108 ff.

26

An Interview with Colin Wilson

PETE BARRACLOUGH

Question: Why did you start writing?

Answer: I had always been an obsessive collector of knowledge and I turned to literature simply because it was an emotional outlet for my frustrations. I was just sick of being in a dead-end job, of being stuck in an awful dirty area. *The Outsider* really came out of the terrific emotional strain of my 'teens, of working in jobs I really hated. There was just no opportunity for me in Leicester. No one cared for my particular thinking or what I wanted to be. My uncle suggested that I wrote plays about someone who won the football pools or something like that. What I hated about Leicester was the pervading lack of seriousness. I hated the mediocrity, the second-rateness. There was one friend of my mother's who made me want to vomit every time she came into the room because she epitomised mediocrity of the stupidest kind. Thus I was forced to stand on my own feet intellectually at an early age.

Question: How did you come to write *The Outsider*?

Answer: I had written several short stories and plays and had them refused. But then I started throwing my ideas down on paper about this character called 'The Outsider', simply because I felt that modern society is full of people who are just too intelligent for the system they get ground up in. It was purely autobiographical, although of course it was also about other 'outsiders'. It wasn't just a matter of being a social misfit. There was the problem of being stranded in a universe you don't understand. And that's why I became so interested in the great men like Shaw, Hemingway, Nijinsky, van Gogh and so on. I saw the relationship between them, and what they had in common.

The Outsider was all in my head and I got books out of the British Museum as I needed them. In fact I wrote the whole book in the Museum Reading Room. And as it turned out, I was lucky. The publishers accepted it after it was only a quarter-finished. And to everyone's amazement it was a huge success, however like most writers with their first books I expected it to be successful so it didn't surprise me.

It had been something that had been bursting to come out for many years. I knew I had something important to say. I read the writers of the time, W.H. Auden and Graham Greene and I thought 'what a bunch of second raters'. None of them seemed to understand anything and modern literature seemed so superficial.

Question: During the hoo-hah which followed publication of *The Outsider* you were quoted as saying that you were a genius. Do you still consider this to be true?

Answer: From a very early age I was aware that I was far more intelligent than the other kids in school. And during my 'teens I stopped myself from sinking into complete gloom by comparing myself with others who had been in the same position. I identified with Keats, Shelley and Shaw. Yes, I do feel that I have genius, although that's something that only the future will decide. However, I assume that's what will happen.

Question: You said in *The Outsider* that Western civilisation was heading for break-up and that was fifteen years or so ago. Do you still believe this, and how would you like to see society evolving as an alternative?

Answer: Yes, I do. Human beings never really get any wiser. They just go from generation to generation being stupid. We improve in the technical sense, yes, but it's the question of man's evolvement on a mental level that interests me.

Question: You really think that this is possible?

Answer: Yes, but only by a small number of people. But I'm certain that mankind is on the brink of a big evolutionary change. So much so that in another hundred years' time, there will be a completely different type of man in existence. We are greater than our Stone Age ancestors because we have more powers of one kind or another, mainly mental. But nevertheless we are still so many emotional cripples at the mercy of boredom, a sense of futility, lack of direction and so on. We claim to have a mental capacity which distinguishes us from animals, yet if you place a man in a blackened room, he becomes an idiot in a few days. Obviously we have no real mental capacity or the room wouldn't worry us. In other words we have no real inner life. It shouldn't be so but it is. Now is it possible for us to develop the mental powers we possess in embryo to something much bigger?

Question: In your book, *The Mind Parasites*, the human mind is held back by parasitic aliens inside. Obviously this is just fanciful science fiction. But does it have any basis of truth as far as you are concerned?

Answer: I do feel that something is holding us back but I don't believe it's a positive thing like parasites.

Question: Aldous Huxley believed that LSD was the secret doorway to hidden perception. Do you agree with this and have you tried hallucinatory drugs?

Answer: Actually I describe the effects of mescalin in the appendix to *Beyond the Outsider*. I found I hated it. It made me vomit, but I experienced no visual effects like Huxley. However, it did plunge me into a wonderfully benevolent universe — a feeling of happiness and warmth. On the other hand it completely destroyed my powers of concentration. I felt rather like a mother sow with about fifty baby pigs sucking at my teats all at the same time. Something was being taken out of me in terrific quantities and I was really glad when the experience was all over. I told Joy that I would never take the filthy stuff again.

Question: You don't believe then that drugs are the answer to mental development?

Answer: No, not at all. It's got to be a natural evolvement because you're not going to save man from his own stupidity by drugs. They just make him stupider.

The thing is that we all experience certain mystical moments of insight and intensity when we feel curiously in control. By reading poetry, listening to music or looking at a beautiful view we get a definite glimpse of power we possess, our mental potentiality. It's a feeling of strength. But with mescalin everything is very beautiful but you feel curiously weak. Drugs just intensify certain faculties at the expense of others.

Question: What then is the secret of perception?

Answer: The interesting thing is that often we do it involuntarily. For example if some enormous crisis suddenly disappears, you get an intense feeling of happiness, of freedom. Obviously we have this all the time but habit cuts it off from us. We're free yet in some strange way we're stuck in boredom and narrowness.

Question: In *The Philosopher's Stone*, the heroes learn the secret of immortality as an extension of achieving full mental perception. Does this also tie in with your philosophy?

Answer: I certainly do believe that if man could escape this tendency towards boredom and recognise his freedom, this automatically would remove a large part of the drift towards death. It's largely a matter of willpower and creative drive.

Question: How long do you think it will take before we learn this power and reach the 'Golden Age'?

Answer: That's impossible to answer. I'm not thinking in terms of how soon the revolution will come. I'm concerned how long it will be before two or three people can break through this net which covers humans mentally. I can see it so clearly.

Question: Presumably you want to be one of the first to do it?

Answer: Precisely. The course of human evolution has been that man has pushed himself away from the animals. Instead he's created this capacity to grasp science. But I think it's time we re-established contact with our animal powers but on a much higher level. We all possess occult powers. Certainly poets do to an unusual degree. They have the power of sinking gently into an inner world: the subconscious mind which is connected to the deep forces that animals are close to. And we should all be able to do this.

Question: Do you still feel generally the same about life as you did in your youth and early manhood when you wrote *The Outsider*?

Answer: Yes, indeed. In fact I'm one of the few people who hardly change at all. There's been no essential change in me from the age of fifteen until now. I feel the same, my ideas are the same, although my insights have deepened. It's almost as if from the beginning I was programmed to do a certain thing and I've carried it out in a curiously narrow way.

Question: What are your politics at the moment and have you any sympathies with the New Left?

Answer: Actually I never cared much for this sort of thing, although I always labelled myself a socialist. I'm not now incidentally, not because of the government, purely for philosophical reasons. I just feel that as soon as you get state control, you immediately get a universal damn-you-jack attitude rather than the enthusiasm when people are working for themselves. I don't think I'd vote Conservative, because I've been against the Tories all my life. In fact I don't think I'll vote at all.

Question: You did write *An Encyclopaedia of Murder*. Why were you interested in such a macabre subject?

Answer: It was partly a childhood influence. My mother used to read me detective stories when I was young and after a period of revulsion against them in my 'teens during my scientific period, I just went back to them for nostalgic reasons. Also murder underlines the sheer futility of humans who just drift along, devaluing their lives. The murderer clearly wastes his own life and that of his victim.

Question: Do you consider that your writing has matured in any way?

Answer: Yes of course. But don't forget that *The Outsider* anyway was a fairly mature work because it had been cooking for so long. It took me three months to write, but my lifetime, until then, to research. However, there's none of my books that I'm ashamed of, or regret writing. The significance of what I'm saying and doing is not yet fully grasped. Not at all in fact. However, the climate of opinion is changing slowly towards me. Things have loosened up in many ways!

Question: I believe you were an atheist when you first achieved literary success. Is this true?

Answer: No, not exactly. I certainly wasn't a Christian, but I had been interested in mysticism and states of consciousness which go beyond the ordinary, so obviously I wasn't an atheist.

Question: Do you believe that some force governs the universe?

Answer: Yes, but not in the religious sense. In the 1950s they discovered that the genes in our bodies appear to work through cybernetic programming, through a substance called DNA. But the question is 'what does the programming?' Obviously this can only be done by some higher intelligence. We live in a meaningful universe.

Question: Recently you've been writing science fiction, although I believe you were fairly derisory of the medium. Why then did you start writing it?

Answer: It's just that I've always tried to impose some kind of form and order on the modern novel by parodying other forms.

It's not only science fiction I've written but novels parodying detective stories, spy stories, etc., and I've even just written one imitating a pornographic novel.

Question: In your autobiography you claimed that it was virtually impossible for an author to make a good living. How in fact have you fared?

Answer: We're nearly always broke you know. I made about £16,000 from *The Outsider*. But normally an author only gets about £2,000 per book. I just about make a living but I've never broken through financially in that I've had money to spare. Being permanently broke has been a good thing because as a result I've done a number of fairly good novels quickly for the money, without worrying too much about the artistic side. Both *Necessary Doubt* and *The Mind Parasites* were reasonably good books written in quite a short time.

Question: Is writing then a way for you to make enough cash to live and think?

Answer: It's part of the reason I've written so much certainly. I've never had much luck with having my books turned into films, although *Ritual in the Dark*, the book about Jack the Ripper, was almost accepted.[1] This would have brought enough to allow me five years just concentrating on my ideas and nothing else. As it was I had to go to America on lecture tours and similar things.

Question: Which of your books do you consider have been the most important?

Answer: I've written thirty of course and I suppose the most important was *The Outsider*. However some of my books since then have said very basic things. My third book, *Age of Defeat*, was a very important one and now in America it's on certain psychological syllabuses in colleges which obviously pleases me.

You see, I did six books in the Outsider cycle, all attacking the problem from a different point of view. Probably the most readable was *Origins of the Sexual Impulse*, although it was panned by the critics. I've also written books on Rasputin, Shaw, music, literary essays and of course ten novels.

Question: What about the last three years?

Answer: Actually I've written an enormous amount. I wrote the book on Shaw which is now out, one of my best. And the next two to be published are shockers. One called *The God of the Labyrinth* ends in a wild sex orgy. And the other, *The Killer*, is a really brutal novel. It's about a pantie-fetishist sex-killer and I just put everything into it. The English edition has been hacked to pieces but the American one is complete.

Question: Your first play was turned down by the Royal Court Theatre; have you had any success with playwriting since then?

Answer: Funnily enough my first published play will be out in a couple of weeks' time and it's called *Strindberg*. It should be presented some time at The Mermaid. I've written several plays but none of them have ever been put on.

Question: Do you think this is because it's particularly difficult presenting philosophy on stage?

Answer: No, it's not that. I'm just not basically a theatre type. Obviously someone like David Campton, the Leicester playwright, is theatre obsessed but I never was.

Question: At one time you were an international celebrity, continually interviewed by the world's press. You even acquired an image of the polo-necked working-class son made good. Are you glad that it's now all over?

Answer: In fact I moved down here to get away from all that, because it was partly the publicity that completely prevented what I was saying from getting over. I came down just after *The Outsider* was written and I've been here ever since.

As it is I get a lot of people writing to me asking me about my books. That's why I've got a notice on the garden gate saying 'no visitors without appointment'. They come banging on the door in the summer wanting to talk with me about my books. The amount of time I waste doing this sort of thing is incredible. The trouble is that the more well-known you are, the more it happens. And this aspect of fame, I hate.

Question: Looking back on your life as an author have you enjoyed it and what are your plans for the future?

Answer: Yes, of course I have. And I suppose I'll go on writing for the rest of my life. I love reading and as an author I'm given the time to do just that. It's a nice place here and I enjoy the quiet. I'd hate to have to go back and live in a city.

Question: At the height of your early success you were quoted as saying that you wished to be an atomic bomb on the minds of our time. Do you think you've achieved this ambition or are you still working on it?

Answer: I haven't achieved it certainly because what I'm saying isn't yet understood. However, the first book about my work is appearing later this year written by a Professor of the University of Miami.[2] He also wrote a book on Lawrence Durrell, and of course this is a definite sign of something happening, but here the terrific backwash of opinion against me which followed *The Outsider* has never recovered.

Question: Do you think then that your success will come in America?

Answer: No, not necessarily. I'm still far from a successful author in that I've not completed what I set out to achieve in the way of impact.

Question: Surely it's not the success of your writing that concerns you, but the success of your particular message, your philosophy?

Answer: Exactly, but this is still totally unknown. As far as my ideas go I've had absolutely no influence on the present time; people like Freud and Shaw achieved this in later life. But my period is still to come.

Question: When exactly?

Answer: Oh, I don't know, it may sound conceited but I've never doubted for a minute that I'm the most significant writer of the twentieth century. I've always taken this totally for granted. And obviously I assume that sooner or later the world will take it for granted too . . . *

NOTES

1. The first of Colin Wilson's books to be filmed was *The Space Vampires*, released as 'Lifeforce' in 1985. – Ed.

2. John A. Weigel's book (see bibliography). – Ed.

*This interview was first published in *The Leicester Chronicle*, 29 May 1970.

Five Reviews of *The Outsider*
1956~57

27

Loser Take All

CYRIL CONNOLLY

I feel a quickening of interest in this extraordinary book because I suggested 'The Outsider' as the English title of M. Camus's *L'Etranger*, on which Mr Wilson extensively draws. He is a young man of twenty-four who has produced one of the most remarkable first books I have read for a long time, a blending of the philosophic approach with literary criticism reminiscent of Mario Praz (*The Romantic Agony*) or Mr Aldous Huxley's didactic anthologies. He himself acknowledges his chief debt to Niebuhr's *Nature and Destiny and Man* and to some doctrinaire essays by Mr Eliot.

Nevertheless the effect is original, and Mr Wilson avoids the likely pitfalls: his book is far from being an anthology or a collection of appreciations of favourite authors wired clumsily together round an uncertain theme, like an ill-made bouquet. He has a quick, dry intelligence, a power of logical analysis which he applies to those states of consciousness which generally defy it. He has read prodigiously and digested what he has read, and he loves what is best. His faults are due, I imagine, to his skill in typing (the only autobiographical fact he supplies); a succession of minor inaccuracies in quotations and titles, a general gracelessness and a hurried pontificating manner inclined to repetitions.

But enough! What I admire most is that Mr Wilson has found an intelligent yard-stick; he sees the Outsiders as the seekers after truth—whether through the mind, the emotions or the spirit—who are unable to adapt themselves to the 'insiders', the ordinary members of society. The Outsiders suffer from fluctuations in their awareness of themselves and their apprehensions of reality; they cannot accept the world. They doubt and question, they do not know who they are, they are 'looking for a way back to themselves' or trying to re-experience some momentary illumination; they see the normal world as an illusion; for some the illusion serves but to conceal a ghastly horror and absurdity, of which they have petrifying glimpses; for others it screens off a universe of total ecstasy, where 'everything that lives is holy'. Some, like van Gogh, experience both sensations, painting light in motion and the dance of matter while they proclaim with their last breath that 'misery will never end'.

What makes this book so interesting is the unconventional selection of material and the orderly marshalling of the Outsiders according to the different fences on the course to self-realisation (or abnegation or annihilation) at which they fall. Thus we begin with some very earthy types who have had a moment of vision in battle or who suffer from a general sense of not belonging; such are the narrator of Camus's *The Outsider* or one or two Hemingway heroes, or M. Roquentin of Sartre's *La Nausée*, or the anonymous *voyeur* of Barbusse's *L'Enfer*; we move on to 'the Romantic Outsider' (the usual crop) and then to van Gogh, T.E. Lawrence and Nijinsky, who sought escape from their isolation through various disciplines. We then come to Nietzsche, Tolstoy and Dostoevsky and the theme deepens until we reach the Outsider as visionary and find Blake, George Fox, Ramakrishna and Gurdjieff as examples of spiritual emancipation.

Mr Wilson does not write as one who believes in a particular religion but rather as an intellectual who is being forced more and more into accepting religion as the only solution to the problem of the Outsider. In other words the anxiety and uneasiness, the sheer horror of being oneself in the modern world is not to be cured by reason or even by a study of philosophies which set out to explain them, like Existentialism; the unpleasant symptoms have to be lived through, leading to worse, in order that the final mystical experience may be attained. The Outsider has it within him to become a saint. Yet though Mr Wilson is drawn to religion, and all his arrows point that way, he never departs from his standard of intellectual analysis. Shaw, Wells and Granville Barker interest him as much as Axel or the Karamazovs or Herman Hesse.

I think it is clear that, despite the wars and politics and materialism of the twentieth century, certain precursors, prophets, mystics and artists who made no compromise of any kind with the bourgeois notion of reality are coming into their own; those who could write, like van Gogh, 'Well, as to my work, I've risked my life for it, and my reason has half foundered', are directing those who have little life and less reason; Mr Wilson's Outsiders are like prisoners who have sawn through a bar or two, started a tunnel, or even, like Blake and Ramakrishna, escaped for long periods from their cells. The nihilistic Outsider, tortured by the meaninglessness of the universe when he glimpses it as if banking in an aeroplane, has a bad time of it; the disillusioned Outsider, who returns to the fold, his vision faded, fares little better. The mystic alone is rewarded — but the incidence of madness, the obsession with suicide, in Mr Wilson's anti-humanist Outsiders is disquieting. Is Outsidership a schizophrenic preserve?

If you are living a very ordinary dull life at low pressure, you can safely regard the Outsider as a crank who does not deserve serious consideration, but if you are interested in man in extreme states or in man abnormally preoccupied by questions about the nature of life . . .

Then you should keep an eye on Mr Wilson, and hope his sanity, vitality and typewriter are spared.*

*This review of *The Outsider* was first published in *The Sunday Times*, 27 May 1956.

28

Unlucky Jims

PHILIP TOYNBEE

It is by no accident that this book has been given the same title as the
English translation of Camus's *L'Etranger*. Mr Wilson has taken Camus
as one of his starting points and has explored the literary theme of the
Outsider through Camus and Sartre, Barbusse and Hemingway, Herman
Hesse, T.E. Lawrence, Nijinsky and van Gogh, Kafka, Rilke, Blake and
Dostoevsky.

It is an exhaustive and luminously intelligent study of a representative theme of our time—and what makes the book truly astounding is
that its alarmingly well-read author is only twenty-four years old. I know
that such extraneous information ought not to affect one's judgement,
but the publisher has thought fit to include it in his blurb and it is point-
less to deny that this fact has coloured all my reading of this remarkable
book. Who is Colin Wilson? How did he have *the time*? Is he an outsider
himself?

From the age of the writer one would expect him to be defiantly on
the side of the fictional heroes whom he discusses. Certainly he *is* on
their side, but the note of defiance is subdued and the predominating
tone is one of passionate but intelligent sympathy. Sometimes Mr Wilson
is over-didactic, and he is given to the provocative aside which, because
it is neither explored nor explained, can leave the reader in a state of
frustrated irritation. It is surely not true, for example, that Aldous
Huxley offers no solution to the outsider's problem. It is surely not true
that Kafka's attitude is that of a healthy man rebuking his sick neighbours;
or that Sartre favours commitment to any cause provided that it is altruist-
ic; or that Kierkegaard would have been amused by Tolstoy's preoccupation with sexual impurity; or that Dostoevsky was a half-atheist. And if
it is true, as Mr Wilson strenuously insists, that Shaw is to be placed with
Pascal and St Augustine as a religious thinker, then so odd an assertion
must be made good or not made at all.

There are many hasty and even superficial judgements in this book,
and Mr Wilson's desire to discover his theme in as many places as possible leads him to burst its seams by stuffing in a multitude of incom-
patibles. If Camus's Mersault is an outsider, then it is difficult to see how
Ramakrishna can be one too.

But when all this is said *The Outsider* remains a most impressive study,
of a kind which is too rare in England. French books of this kind are

more familiar, but the fact that Mr Wilson is English gives him certain advantages over like-minded Frenchmen. He does not share their prevalent love of the elliptical and the paradoxical, and when he is making a point he usually makes it fully and carefully:

> Freedom posits free-will: that is self-evident. But Will can only operate when there is first a motive. No motive, no willing. But motive is a matter of *belief*; you would not want to do anything unless you believed it possible and meaningful. And belief must be belief in the *existence* of something; that is to say, it concerns what is *real*. So ultimately, freedom depends upon the real. The Outsider's sense of unreality cuts off freedom at the root. It is as impossible to exercise freedom in an unreal world as it is to jump while you are falling.

In Sartre these careful sentences would probably appear as '*La realité, c'est la liberté*' —and for my part I prefer Mr Wilson's more explanatory treatment.

It is in his general conviction that all the men and women of our time who have truly felt and thought have become outsiders as a result of their study of the world and of themselves. They are outsiders because they become convinced that ordinary 'bourgeois' values are worthless and that 'bourgeois' behaviour is meaningless. Searching for a higher purpose in life, they have usually failed to find one and yet have refused to compromise with the valueless world around them. Exiles from hearth and home, embittered nomads, suicides and murderers, what they all have in common is an absolute refusal to abandon their high but thwarted standards.

It is a romantic view, but not, for that reason, a false one. Whatever may be said for or against our society it clearly lacks that spiritual and social integration which existed, for example, in the France of Louis the Fourteenth and which alone provides the bed in which classical thought and literature can sprout. Nor does Mr Wilson make the romantic error of glorying in this unhappy and destructive state of things. He is concerned with finding a solution for his outsiders, and he suggests one at the end in the only area where it can seriously be sought.

Here, in a tentative plea for 'a new religious age', he is necessarily and quite properly vague. He is not a Christian, and those in our time who are non-Christian seekers for a new religious truth are condemned to vagueness. But clarity of analysis is certainly still needed, whatever may follow at last from that, and Mr Wilson's book is a real contribution to our understanding of our deepest predicament.*

* This review of *The Outsider* was first published in *The Observer*, 27 May 1956.

29

Thoughts on *The Outsider*

J. B. PRIESTLEY

Two clever young men, newcomers on the scene, have done very well this summer out of what one of them calls *The Outsider*. This newcomer is, of course, Mr Colin Wilson, whose dashing study of *The Outsider* has had such a well-deserved success. The other is Mr John Osborne, whose first play, *Look Back in Anger*, itself a full-length portrait of a *lumpen* Outsider, pulled so many persons of distinction into the Royal Court Theatre, after having had some dismal notices from the daily Press, like many another first play trying to say something. The gossip writers have told us that both these clever young men have been on the telephone all day and half the night refusing, accepting, or agreeing to consider wonderful offers from publishers, editors, play and film producers. And if this is true, then I for one am delighted, all the more so because after thirty-five years as a professional writer, years during which many of my friends and I have done pretty well in various departments, I have never succeeded in penetrating into, never have had any first-hand experience of, this world the gossip writers know in which the telephone fairly blazes with dazzling offers.

So it looks as if these young Outsiders are after one bound further *In* than most of us have ever been, living as we do in some modest suburb of the spirit, neither quite Out nor In. Now they will have to be very careful, dined and wined as they will be by some of our most artful Insiders. For example, Mr Osborne has in him a streak of Barriesque gooey sentimentality, which already can see husbands as bears and wives as teeny-weeny squirrels, that he will have to restrain when the Insider boys go after it. Edwardian though I may be, I should like to see him harder, not softer. I say Edwardian, because his chief character, the *lumpen* Outsider, is caught reading one of my pieces in this paper, and dismisses it and me as so much Edwardian nostalgia. A bit much, as people like to complain, seeing that most of my contributions to this paper have been attempts to take a genuine look at our present time — discovering, for example, political apathy about two years before the politicians and leader-writers found it out.

There are some strange goings-on in this play — for childless young women rarely start ironing about six o'clock on Sunday evening, and by that time most young men with a passion for the Sunday papers have read them hours before — and too many essential points are not made and other points made too often; but it held my attention (even if I did not roar my approval as often as the *lumpen-intelligentsia* that night in the audience seemed to do) just because it is a reasonably honest portrait of a young man of our time. This young man was rotten with self-pity — his girls were worth ten of him — but that does not make him less representative of this age. (Many successful American novels, like the reviewers who praise them, are also loaded with self-pity.) His tragedy is that, while he has enough zest and energy to keep his loud complaining talk going night and day, he has not sufficient to make more of his own life and to help other people to make more of theirs. As he sees himself, he is a revolutionary without a cause. He arrived just after the revolution that never happened. Our politicians can do nothing for him, because they cannot inspire him — and he needs to be inspired — and they cannot successfully nag him, if only because he never stops nagging himself. He ought to emigrate to a country where he can either man the barricades or make some quick easy money and spend it riotously. Low-level security, perfect for people who are anxious not to die rather than to live, is not what this type needs. He is, in his own way, one of Mr Colin Wilson's Outsiders.

Mr Wilson's book, as so many people have already pointed out, is a remarkable production for a young man of twenty-four, although, as nobody seems to have pointed out, it is also the kind of book you want to write when you are twenty-four and, if you develop (as Mr Wilson shows every promise of doing), when you are forty-four wish you had not written. Part of its success — and this takes nothing away from Mr Wilson's achievement — is due to the fact that our more mature critics ought to be writing books with this breadth and attack, and are either too timid or too lazy to do it. So Mr Wilson, piling up his notes in reading rooms and then desperately tearing into the big job, well deserves to succeed. He is all over the place, bringing in every name he can remember, but it is fun lumbering after him. There is some rough going on the way. He seems to me to lump together, simply as Outsiders, too many people who are sharply and often profoundly different. And the dichotomy of Outsider and Bourgeois is altogether too simple. Like most clever young men, hurrying home with a pile of books and glowering at the passers-by, he magnifies the gulf between men of genius and ordinary stupid people, and is too certain all the latter are what they appear to be at a first impatient glance. He cannot believe that stockbrokers may have strange dreams, that butchers cutting off chops may be touched with intimations of immortality, that the grocer, even as he hesitates over the sugar, may yet see the world in a grain of sand.

This brings us to Blake, who is included among Mr Wilson's Outsiders. But a category into which can be shovelled Blake and Sartre, van Gogh and Bernard Shaw, George Fox and Nijinsky, is becoming altogether too broad. Mr Wilson even accepts the last published work of H.G. Wells, *Mind at the End of its Tether*, as proof that Wells, just before he died, changed from Insider to Outsider. But Wells was always less of an Insider than Mr Wilson imagines—he could be described as an Outsider at heart always vainly and impatiently trying to find an Insider's cure and solution—and that strange psychological document, *Mind at the End of its Tether*, seems to me a projection on to the universe of his own dis-solution already accepted by his unconscious. Again, while it may be true that all Outsiders cannot complacently accept this world and this life, feel that all is strange and unreal, and must tell the truth at all costs, their personalities are so widely various, they represent so many differ-ent psychological types, that any discussion of them based on their common likeness does not take us very far. And clearly a man might be an Outsider and not be a genius nor yet have any recognisible talent, but just be an endlessly tiresome talker, like the young man in Mr Osborne's play. There are more of these Outsiders than there are of men with genius or talent, but Mr Wilson keeps clear of them in his book, just as the rest of us try to avoid them in life.

Even Outsiders with genius or great talent are often seen to be lop-sided, too introverted, unhappily egoistical. If they are artists—and serious contemporary art, in almost all forms, is now often held to be the product of this temperament and of no other—their work may have a strange fascinating intensity, almost a hypnotic power, and yet leave us feeling dissatisfied and uneasy. Nor does this mean that it is disturb-ing our bourgeois complacency, for we may not have any to disturb. (The really complacent bourgeois do not bother about serious contem-porary art.) We may feel dissatisfied and uneasy because this art is not giving us what we want from art. Sometimes it is as if we went hungry into a restaurant and were served with broken glass. I remember a few years ago, when somebody close to me was desperately ill, wandering round the West End one afternoon, just for a brief break, and coming upon a shop that had just opened, to offer us all that was most signif-icant and searching in the art and letters of our time. I knew there would be no soothing syrup in that shop, did not expect it, but did think there might be something that would give a lift to the spirit. But no such luck. The massed Outsiders glared at me out of ruin and horror.

But who, Mr Wilson will ask, are responsible for this ruin and horror? The Insiders, he will triumphantly reply. But if the Outsiders have all

the genius and great talent, could they not occasionally cast about for
something that might possibly inspire Insiders with a little courage, faith,
hope? Insiders change too, and now are hardly the complacent bourgeois
of Mr Wilson's text. After all, this is 1956, not 1856; people are reading
Bertrand Russell and Arnold Toynbee, not Macaulay. I write as one not
entirely committed by temperament to either party, being an Inside
Outsider or an Outside Insider, for I have it on the highest authority
that I am balanced between extreme introversion and extraversion. But
while I have a natural sympathy with most rebels, while I understand
more or less what the serious Outsider artist is up to, I can never help
feeling uneasy and vaguely depressed when I run into the whole proces-
sion of Twentieth Century arts, for example in such a book as William
Gaunt's *The March of the Moderns*. What a weird gang it is! What a hell
broth and Bedlam of appalling handicaps—like a doctor's museum and
a psychiatrist's casebook—that have to find compensation through this
wealth of talent! And how far gone our society must be if all its most
representative art must be fetched from the misfits! Where now are all
the glorious old Insider Artists, who were the ordinary men of their
time writ large, who created out of an abundance of energy and joy, who
praised God for all their fellows? We are trapped now, it seems, in a
most vicious circle, for we work to produce ruin and horror, our artists
are those on the Outside who have a blazing vision of this ruin and
horror, we turn from life to the arts to encounter more ruin and horror,
and in our despair, finding neither the courage and hope to do better
nor even the will to endure, we pile up the ruin, heighten and deepen
the horror. Mr Wilson declares—and I agree with him—that the Outsider
demands a religious solution. But if the Outsider is poisoned by an embittered egoism, if he wants to hurt and not to heal, if there is more
hate than love in him, if he uses his gifts to deny the essential goodness
in life, always adds ruin to our ruin, horror to our horror, can he bring
us nearer to that solution? We are waiting for God, not for Godot.*

*This review of *The Outsider* was first published in *The New Statesman*, 7 July 1956.

30

The Outsider

KENNETH WALKER

The subtitle of this outstanding book by a man of only twenty-four is 'An enquiry into the nature of the sickness of mankind in this mid-twentieth century'. That mankind is gravely ill the author has not the slightest doubt and his book is both a catalogue of symptoms and a search for a cure. The Outsider is a man who has seen too much and too deeply to be able to fit himself into the insulated world of the bourgeois, 'or to accept what the bourgeois sees and touches as reality'. He has nothing in common with Eliot's hollow and stuffed men who lean together and make-do. 'He has found an "I" but it is not his true "I"', and his sole business has become 'to find his way back to himself'.

Taking Camus' work *L'Etranger* as his starting point and as a title, Mr Colin Wilson conducts us on a long literary tour and shows us how other outsider writers have attempted to find a cure for mankind's sickness, rarely with any success. He surveys the various remedies suggested by Barbusse, Sartre, Hemingway, Herman Hesse, T.E. Lawrence, Nijinsky, Kafka, Rilke, Blake, H.G. Wells, and Dostoevsky, and pronounces them either useless or else worse than the disease they are supposed to cure. If Mr Wilson's book contained nothing beyond this masterly survey of literature it would be well worth reading, but it is a book of far wider scope. It represents the search of a young man of great integrity and discernment for some higher purpose in life than mere living. What makes his work still more unusual is that, unlike Sartre, Samuel Beckett, and other hypochondriac outsiders of the St Germain school, he avoids glorying in his own ill-health and actually wants to get well. He sees his sickness for what it is, a miserable and destructive form of spiritual paralysis.

What is the remedy for it? Mr Wilson realises the need for some form of spiritual revival but of a much broader kind than that with which the Church would be able to provide us. Necessarily he becomes less precise when outlining the form this return to religion might take, but two writers of very different temperament are of particular interest to him in this connection, Ramakrishna, the Hindu saint, who proclaimed the unity of all the great world faiths, and 'that strange man of genius George Gurdjieff'. Again this young man has shown astonishing insight. *The Outsider* is the most remarkable book upon which the reviewer has ever had to pass judgement. It is true that like many other young men, the author

is occasionally guilty of making snap judgements such as that the late
Bernard Shaw should be grouped with St Augustine and Pascal amongst
the religious thinkers, but such errors seem so trivial against the general
background of this book that they are scarcely worthy of mention.*

*This review was first published in *The Listener*, vol. 55, p. 767, 7 June 1956.

31

Colin Wilson's *The Outsider*

SIR OSWALD MOSLEY[1]

It is always reassuring when men and things run true to form. It was, therefore, satisfactory that the silliest thing said in the literary year — the most frivolous and superficial in judgement — should emerge with the usual slick facility from the particular background of experience and achievement which has made Mr Koestler the middle-brow prophet. He wrote of Mr Colin Wilson's remarkable book in *The Sunday Times*: 'Bubble of the year: *The Outsider* (Gollancz), in which an earnest young man imparts his discovery to the world that genius is prone to *Weltschmerz*'.

Otherwise Mr Wilson's book had a very great success, and well deserved it. In fact, it was received with such a chorus of universal praise that it became almost suspect to those who believe that a majority in the first instance is almost always wrong, particularly when at this stage of a crumbling but still static society the opinion of the majority is so effectively controlled by the instruments of a shaken but yet dominant establishment. Why has a book so exceptional, and so serious, been applauded rather than accorded the 'preposterous' treatment which English literary criticism reserved for such as Spengler? The first answer is that Mr Wilson's mind is very attractive, and his lucid style makes easy reading; the suggestion that this book is so difficult that everyone buys it but no one reads it, would brand the reading public as moronic if it had any vestige of truth. The second answer is that Mr Wilson has as yet said nothing, and consequently cannot be attacked for the great crime of trying to get somewhere; somewhere new in thought, or worse still, somewhere in deed and achievement. What he has so far published is a fine work of clarification. A strangely mature and subtle mind has produced a brilliant synopsis of the modern mind and spirit. He does not claim to advance any solution, though he points in various directions where solutions may be found; 'it is not my aim to produce a complete and infallible solution of the Outsider's problem, but only to point out that traditional solutions, or different solutions, do exist'. No one could possibly yet guess where he is going, or what he may ultimately mean. He probably does not know himself; and, at his age, it is not a bad thing to be a vivid illustration of the old saying: 'no man goes very far, who knows exactly where he is going'. What makes this book important is that it is a symptom and a symbol; a symptom of the present division between those who think and those who do; a symbol of the search in a world of confusion and menace by both those who think and those who do for some fresh religious impulse which can give meaning and direction to life. To achieve this, those who only do need sensitivity to receive a vision of purpose without which they are finally lost, while those who only think and feel require, in order to face life, the robustness and resolution which in the end again can only be given by purpose.

Mr Wilson begins his 'inquiry into the nature of the sickness of mankind in the twentieth century' at the effective point of the writers who have most influence in the present intellectual world. They are mostly good writers; they are not among the writers catering for those intellectuals who have every qualification except an intellect. They are good, some are very good: but at the end of it all what emerges? One of the best of these writers predicted that at the end of it all comes 'the Russian man' described by Mr Wilson as 'a creature of nightmare who is no longer the *homo sapiens*, but an existentialist monster who rejects all thought'. As Hesse, the prophet of this coming, put it: 'he is primeval matter, monstrous soul stuff. He cannot live in this form; he can only pass on'. The words 'he can only pass on' seem the essence of the matter; this thinking is a chaos between two orders. At some point, if we are ever to regain sanity, we must regard again the first order before we can hope to win the second. It was a long way from Hellas to 'the Russian man'; it may not be so far from the turmoil of these birth pangs to fresh creation. It is indeed well worth taking a look at the intellectual situation; where Europeans were, and where we are.

> But who'er can know, as the long days go
> That to live is happy, hath found his heaven.

wrote Euripides in the *Bacchae* (Professor Gilbert Murray's translation), which to some minds is the most sinister and immoral of all Greek tragedies. For others these dark mysteries which were once held to be impenetrable contain the simple message that men do themselves great hurt if they reject the beauty which nature offers, a hurt which can lead to the worst horrors of madness. *'Il lui suffit d'éclairer et de développer le conflict entre les forces naturelles et l'âme qui prétend se soustraire à leur empire'* —wrote Gide in his Journal— *'Je recontrai les* Bacchantes, *au temps où je me débattais encore contre l'enserrement d'une morale puritaine'*. To anyone familiar with such thinking it is not surprising to find the dreary manias of neo-existentialism succeeding the puritan tradition.

Man denies at his risk the simple affirmation: 'Shall not loveliness be loved for ever?' The Greeks, as Goethe saw them, felt themselves at home within 'the delightful boundaries of a lovely world. Here they had been set; this was their appropriate place; here they found room for their energy, material and nourishment for their essential life'. And again he wrote: 'feeling and thought were not yet split in pieces, that scarce remediable cleavage in the healthy nature of man had not yet taken place'. Goethe was here concerned with the early stages of the disease to whose conclusion Mr Wilson's book is addressed.

This union of mind and will, of intellect and emotion in the classic Greek, this essential harmony of man and nature, this at-one-ness of the human with the eternal spirit evoke the contrast of the living and the dying when set against the prevailing tendencies of modern literature. For, as Mr Wilson puts it very acutely: when 'misery will never end' is combined with 'nothing is worth doing', 'the result is a kind of spiritual syphillis that can hardly stop short of death or insanity'. Yet such writers are not all 'pre-occupied with sex, crime and disease', treating of heroes who live in one room because, apparently, they dare not enter the world outside, and derive their little satisfaction of the universe from looking through a hole in the wall at a woman undressing in the next room. They are not all concerned like Dostoevsky's 'beetle man' with life 'under the floor boards' (a study which should put none of us off reading him as far as the philosophy of the Grand Inquisitor and a certain very interesting conversation with the devil in the *Brothers Karamazof*, which Mr Wilson rightly places very high in the world's literature). Many of these writers of pessimism, of destruction and death have a considerable sense of beauty. Hesse's remarkable *Steppenwolf* found his 'life had become weariness' and he 'wandered in a maze of unhappiness that led to the renunciation of nothingness'; but then 'for months together my heart stood still between delight and stark sorrow to find how rich was the gallery of my life, and how thronged was the soul of wretched Steppenwolf with high eternal stars and constellations . . . this life of mine was noble. It came of high descent, and turned, not on trifles, but on the stars.' Mr Wilson well comments that 'stripped of its overblown language', 'this experience can be called the ultimately valid core of romanticism – a type of religious affirmation'. And in such writing we can still see a reflection of the romantic movement of the northern gothic world which Goethe strove to unite with the sunlit classic movement in the great synthesis of his Helena. But it ends generally in this literature with a retreat from life, a monastic detachment or suicide rather than advance into such a wider life fulfilment. The essence is that these people feel themselves inadequate to life; they feel even that to live at all is instantly to destroy whatever flickering light of beauty they hold within them. For instance De Lisle Adam's hero Axel had a lady friend who shot at him 'with two pistols at a distance of five yards, but missed him both times'. Yet even after this dramatic and perfect illustration of the modern sex relationship, they could not face life: 'we have destroyed in our strange hearts the love of life . . . to live would only be a sacrilege against ourselves . . . ' 'They drink the goblet of poison together and die in ecstasy'. All of which is a pity for promising people, but, in any case, is preferable to the 'beetle man', 'under the floor boards', wall-peepers, *et hoc genus omne*, of burrowing fugitives; 'Samson you cannot be too quick', is a natural first reaction to them. Yet Mr Wilson teaches us well not to laugh too easily, or too lightly to dismiss them; it is a serious matter. This is serious if it is the death of a civilisation; it is still more serious if it is not death but the pangs of a new birth. And, in any case, even the worst of them possess in some way the essential sensitivity which the philistine lacks. So we will not laugh at even the extremes of this system, or rather way of thinking; something may come out of it all, because at least they feel. But Mr Wilson in turn should not smile too easily at the last 'period of intense and healthy optimism that did not mind hard work and pedestrian logic'. He seems to regard the nineteenth century as a 'childish world' which presaged 'endless changes in human life' so that 'man would go forward indefinitely on "stepping stones of his dead self" to higher things'. He thinks that before we 'condemn it for short-sightedness', 'we survivors of two world wars and the atomic bomb' (at this point surely he outdoes the Victorians in easy optimism, for it is far from over yet) 'would do well to remember that we are in the position of adults condemning children'. Why? – is optimism necessarily childish and pessimism necessarily adult? Sometimes this paralysed pessimism seems more like the condition of a shell-shocked child. Health can be the state of an adult and disease the condition of a child. Of course, if serious Victorians really believed in 'the establishment of Utopia before the end of the century', they were childish; reformist thinking of that degree is always childish in comparison with organic thinking. But there are explanations of the difference between the nineteenth and the twentieth century attitude, other than this distinction between childhood and manhood. Spengler said somewhere that the nineteenth century stood in relation to the twentieth century as the Athens of Pericles stood in relation to the Rome of Caesar. In his thesis this is not a distinction between youth and age – a young society does not reach senescence in so short a period – but the difference between an epoch which is dedicated to thought and an epoch which has temporarily discarded thought in favour of action, in the almost rhythmic alternation between the two states which his method of history observes. It may be that in this most decisive of all great periods of action the intellectual is really not thinking at all; he is just despairing. When he wakes up from his bad dream he may find a world created by action in which he can live, and can even think. Mr Wilson will not quarrel with the able summary of his researches printed on the cover of his book: 'it is the will that matters'. And he would therefore scarcely dispute the view just expressed; perhaps the paradox of Mr Wilson in this period is that he is thinking. That thought might lead him through and far beyond the healthy 'cowboy rodeo' of the Victorian philosophers in their sweating sunshine, on (not back) to the glittering light and shade of the Hellenic world—*das Land der Griechen mit der Seele suchend*—and even beyond it to the radiance of the *zweite Hellas*. Mr Wilson does not seem yet to be fully seized of Hellenism, and seems still less aware of the more conscious way of European thinking that passes beyond Hellas to a clearer account of world purpose. He has evidently read a good deal of Goethe with whom such modern thinking effectively begins, and he is the first of the new generation to feel that admiration for Shaw which was bound to develop when thought returned. But he does not seem to be aware of any slowly emerging system of European thinking which has journeyed from Heraclitus to Goethe and on to Shaw, Ibsen and other moderns, until with the aid of modern science and the new interpretation of history it begins to attain consciousness.

He is acute at one point in observing the contrasts between the life joy of the Greeks and the moments when their art is 'full of the consciousness of death and its inevitability'. But he still apparently regards them as 'healthy, once born, optimists', not far removed from the modern bourgeois who also realises that life is precarious. He apparently thinks they did not share with the Outsider the knowledge that an 'exceptional sense of life's precariousness' can be 'a hopeful means to increase his toughness'. The Greeks, of course, had not the advantage of reading Mr Toynbee's *Study of History*, which does not appear on a reasonably careful reading to be mentioned in Mr Wilson's book.

However, as Trevelyan[2] puts it, Goethe followed them when he 'firmly seized and plucked the nettle of Greek inhumanity, and treated it as the Greeks themselves had done, making new life and beauty out of a tale of death and terror'. Yet, in the continual contrast from which the Greeks derive their fulness of life: 'healthy and natural was their attitude to death. To them he was no dreadful skeleton but a beautiful boy, the brother of sleep'. It is an attitude very different to Dostoevsky's

shivering mouse on the ledge, which Mr Wilson quotes: 'someone condemned to death says or thinks an hour before his death, that if he
had to live on a high rock, on such a narrow ledge that he'd only
have room to stand, and the ocean, everlasting darkness, everlasting
solitude, everlasting tempest around him, he yet remains standing in a
square yard of space all his life, a thousand years, eternity, it were better
to live so than die at once'. But is the attitude of the 'once born Greek'
so inferior to the possibly many times born ledge clinger? On the contrary, is not the former attitude a matter of common observation among
brave men and the latter attitude a matter of equally common observation among frightened animals whose fear of death is not only pathetic
but irrational in its exaggeration. Mr Wilson's view of the Greeks seems
to rest in the Wincklemann Wieland stage of an enchanted pastoral
simplicity. He has not yet reached Goethe's point of horror when he
realised the full complexities of the Greek nature and only emerged to
a new serenity when, again in Trevelyan's words, he realised: 'they had
felt the cruelty of life with souls sensitive by nature to pain no less than
to joy. They had not tried to shut their eyes to suffering. They had
used it, as all great artists must, as material for their art; but they had
created out of it, not something that made the world more horrible to
live in, but something that enriched man's life and strengthened him to
endure and to enjoy, by showing that new life, new beauty, new greatness, could grow even out of pain and death.'

Jaeger[3] quotes Pythagoras to express something of the same thought;
'that which opposes, fits; different elements make the finest harmony
ever'.

Were these 'once born' people really much less adult than the Outsider in his understanding that 'if you subject a man to extremes of heat
and cold, he develops resistance to both'? Perhaps they even understood
that if we subject ourselves to more interesting extremes we may learn
to achieve Mr Wilson's desire (and how right he is in this) 'to live more
abundantly'. And Mr Wilson certainly does not desire to rest in the Outsider's dilemma; he is looking for solutions. In Hellas he may find something of a solution, and much more than that; the rediscovery of a
direction which can lead far beyond even the Greeks.

As a sensitive and perceptive student of Nietzsche he is aware of
Dionysus, but is not so fully conscious of the harmony achieved between
the opposing tensions of Apollo and Dionysus. 'Challenge and response'
too, was more attractive in the Greek version; Artemis and Aphrodite
had a charming habit of alternating as good and evil in a completely
natural anticipation of Goethe's *Prologue in Heaven*, which we shall later

regard as the possible starting point of a new way of thinking, and of
that modern writing of history which supports it with a wealth of detail.
But we should first briefly consider Mr Wilson's view of Nietzsche and
others who are rather strangely classified with him; it is a surprise at
first to find him described as an existentialist, though in one sense it is
quite comprehensible. For instance, Thierry Maulnier's play *Le Profan-*
ateur recently presented essentially Nietzschian thought in an existialist
form. But to confine Nietzsche to existentialism is to limit him unduly,
even if we recognise, as the author points out, that definitions of
existentialism have greatly varied in recent times, and also, as all can
observe, that Nietzsche may be quoted in contradictory senses almost
as effectively as the dominant faith of our time. The finer aspects of
Nietzsche seem beyond this definition; for instance the passage in
Zarathustra which culminates in the great phrase: *seinen Willen will nun*
der Geist, seine Welt gewinnt sich der Weltverlorene, or again the
harmony of mind and will in the lovely passage of *Menschliches,*
Allzumenschliches which seems a direct antithesis of the currently
accepted view of Existentialism: 'The works of such poets—poets, that
is, whose vision of man is exemplary—would be distinguished by the
fact that they appear immune from the glow and blast of the *passions*.
The fatal touch of the wrong note, the pleasure taken in smashing the
whole instrument on which the music of humanity has been played, the
scornful laughter and the gnashing of teeth, and all that is tragic and
comic in the old conventional sense, would be felt in the vicinity of
this new art as an awkward archaic crudeness and a distortion of the
image of man. Strength, goodness, gentleness, purity, and that innate
and spontaneous sense of measure and balance shown in persons and
their actions . . . a clear sky reflected on faces and events, knowledge and
art at one: the mind, without arrogance and jealousy dwelling together
with the soul, drawing from the opposites of life the grace of seriousness, not the impatience of conflict: all this would make the background
of gold against which to set up the real portrait of man, the picture of
his increasing nobleness'.[4] But far more than a whole essay of this length
would be needed to do justice to Mr Wilson's interpretation of Nietzsche
and in particular, perhaps, to examine his possible over-simplification
of the infinite complexities of the eternal recurrence. There is little
enough space to cover the essential thinking of this remarkable book,
and we must omit altogether a few of the more trivial little fellows who
sometimes detain the author. Why, for instance, does he lose so much
time with Lenin's 'dreadful little bourgeois', who crowned the career
of a super egoist with the damp surmise that the world could not long

survive the pending departure of Mr H.G. Wells? Here again Mr Wilson is acute in linking Wells with greater figures like Kierkegaard in the opinion that 'philosophic discussion was completely meaningless'. Kierkegaard was a 'deeply religious soul' who found Hegel 'unutterably shallow'. So he founded modern Existentialism with the remark: 'put me in a system and you negate me – I am not a mathematical symbol – I am'. Is such an assertion of the individual against the infinite 'unutterably shallow', or is it relieved from this suggestion by the depths of its egotism? Such a statement can really only be answered by the unwonted flippancy of Lord Russell's reply to Descarte's *'cogito ergo sum'*; 'but how do you know it is you thinking'? Kierkegaard concluded that you cannot live a philosophy but you 'can live a religion'; but the attempt of this pious pastor to live his religion did not restrain him from 'violently attacking the Christian Church on the grounds that it had solved the problem of living its religion by cutting off its arms and legs to make it fit life'. All these tendencies in Kierkegaard seem to indicate a certain confusion of Existentialism with Perfectionism – from which exhypothesi it should surely be very remote – but certainly qualify him as father of the inherent dissidence of modern Existentialism, and, perhaps, inspired M. Sartre to confer on the Communist Party the same benefits which the founder's assistance had granted to the Church. All this derives surely from that initial impulse of sheer anarchy with which he assailed the Hegelian attempt at order. 'There is discipline in heaven', as one of Mr Wilson's favourite remarks (also more competence to exercise it, we may add) and we are left in the end with a choice between Kierkegaard's great 'I am' and Hegel's majestic symbol in his *Philosophy of History* concerning the conflicting forces of the elements finally blending in a divine harmony of order. Yes, it is good that it is so plain where it all began; such pious and respectable origin. After the initial revolt against all sense of order it is not a long journey from 'I am' to Sartre's *'l'homme est une passion inutile'*, and to his hero, Roquentin, who finds that 'it is the rational element that pushes into nihilism' and that his 'only glimpse of salvation' comes from a negro woman singing 'Some of these days'; yes, they certainly got rid of Hegel, but 'these days' scarcely belong to Kierkegaard. Yet when they have reached 'the rock bottom of self contempt' they need again 'something rhythmic, purposive'; so man cannot live, after all, by 'I am' alone. Sartre wanted freedom from all this and found that 'freedom is terror', during one of his all too brief experiences of action. Mr Wilson comments with rare insight: 'freedom is not simply being allowed to do what you like'; 'it is intensity of will, and it appears under any circumstances that limit man and arouse man to more life'. If you do not 'claim this freedom' you 'slip to a lower

form of life'; at this point the author seems to reach the opposite pole
to the original premise of the existentialist theory. He states his position
in this matter in a particularly fine passage: 'Freedom posits free will;
that is self-evident. But will can only operate when there is first a motive.
No motive, no willing. But motive is a matter of belief; you would not
want to do anything unless you believed it possible and meaningful. And
belief must be belief in the existence of something; that is to say, it concerns what is real. So ultimately freedom depends on the real. The Outsider's sense of unreality cuts off his freedom at the roots. It is as impossible to exercise freedom in an unreal world as it is to jump while you
are falling'. How much nearer to clarity, sanity and effective purpose is
this thinking than Sartre's 'philosophy of commitment', which is only to
say that, 'since all roads lead nowhere, it is as well to choose any of
them and throw all the energy into it . . .' It was at this point no doubt
that the Communist Party became the fortunate receptacle of the great
'I am' in its flight from the nightmare of the 'useless passion', and a few
existential exercises in 'freedom' from self were provided for Mr Sartre
until a change of weather rendered such exercises temporarily too uncomfortable. But again, yet again, we must seek freedom from our own
besetting sin of laughing too easily and lightly at serious searchers after
truth, when they on occasion fall into ridiculous situations; as Aristotle
remarked to Alexander when the King caught him in an embarrassing
position: 'Sire, you will observe the straits to which the passions can
reduce even the most eminent minds'. Despite all the nonsense, there is
much to be said for Sartre. He is a great artist, one of the greatest masters
of the theatre in all time. It is to be hoped that Mr Wilson will one day
extend his study of him to include *Le Diable et le Bon Dieu*. It is not
merely a narrow professional interest which makes us regard this play as
his greatest work — the incidental fact that in the first act he presents
some of us as others see us, and in the last act as we see ourselves — but
the manner in which he reviews nearly the whole gamut of human
experiences in the body of the play. It is when he ceases to think and as
a sensitive artist simply records his diverse impressions of this great age in
an almost entirely unconscious fashion, that Sartre becomes great; so in
the end, he is the true Existentialist.

But Mr Wilson moves far beyond Sartre in regarding the thinkers of
an earlier period; notably Blake. At this point he recovers direction. The
reader will find pages 225 to 250 among the most important of this book,
but he must read the whole work for himself; this review is a commentary and an addendum, not a précis for the idle, nor a primer for those
who find anything serious too difficult. The author advances a long way

when he considers Blake's 'skeleton key' to a solution for those who
'mistake their own stagnation for the world's'. Here we reach realisation
that the 'crises of living demand the active co-operation of intellect,
emotions, body on equal terms'; contact is made here with Goethe's
Ganzheit, although it is not mentioned. 'Energy is eternal delight' takes
us a long way clear of the damp caverns of neo-existentialism and

> When thought is closed in caves
> Then love shall show its root in deepest hell

brings us nearer to the thought of Euripides with which this essay began.
To Blake the greatest crime was to 'nurse unfulfilled desire'; he was not
only an enemy of the repressive puritanism and of all nature-denying
creeds, but realised their disastrous effect upon the human psyche. He
sought consciously the harmony of mind and nature, the blessed state
the Greeks found somewhere between Apollo and Dionysus.

> The law that abides and changes not, ages long
> The eternal and nature born — these things be strong

declare the chorus in the *Bacchae* in warning to those who deny nature
in the name of morality or reason.

> A strait pitiless mind
> Is death unto godliness.

Yet the great nature urge is not the enemy of the intellect but its equi-
poise and inspiration, declares the Bacchanal.

> Knowledge, we are not foes
> I seek thee diligently;
> But the world with a great wind blows,
> Shining, and not from thee;
> Blowing to beautiful things . . .

It is when intellect becomes separate from nature and combats nature
that the madness, 'the vastation' descends; the mind seeks flight from
life in the womb-darkness whence it came; the end is under the floor
boards, and worse, far worse. When intellect fails in a frenzy of self
denial and self destruction, life must begin again at the base. Then the
Euripidean chorus declares

> The simple nameless herd of humanity
> Has deeds and faith that are truth enough for me.

When mind fails, life is still there; and begins again, always begins again.
Did these 'once born' Greeks really see less than some of the wall-
peepers, less even than the more advanced types considered in this
fascinating book? Wretched 'Steppenwolf', you had only to look over
your shoulder to see more constellations than you had ever dreamt. And
it was no junketing cowboy in a hearty's rodeo who wrote

> Not to be born is past all prizing
> But when a man has seen the light
> This is next best by far, that with all speed
> He shall go thither, whence he came.

No men ever had a deeper sense of the human tragedy than the Greeks;
none ever faced it with such brilliant bravery or understood so well not
only the art of grasping the fleeting, ecstatic moment, but of turning
even despair to the enhancement of beauty. Living was yet great; they
understood *dennoch preisen*; they did not 'leave living to their servants'.
Mr Wilson in quoting Aristotle in the same sense as the above lines of
Sophocles—'not to be born is the best thing, and death is better than
life'—holds that 'this view' lies at one extreme of religion, and that 'the
other extreme is vitalism'. He does not seem at this point fully to understand that the extremes in the Hellenic nature can be not contradictory
but complementary, or interacting. The polarity of Greek thought was
closely observed and finely interpreted by Nietzsche in diverse ways.
But it was left to Goethe to express the more conscious thought beyond
polarity in his *Faust: the Prologue in Heaven*:

The Lord Speaks to Mephistopheles:

> *Des Menschen Thätigkeit kann allzuleicht erschlaffen*
> *Er liebt sich bald die unbedingte Ruh;*
> *Drum geb' ich gern ihm den Gesellen zu*
> *Der reizt und wirkt, und muss, als Teufel, schaffen.*

What is this but the definite statement that evil is the instrument of good?
It is not only a better key to *Faust* than most of the tomes which have
been written in analysis of this world masterpiece, but it is also the
effective beginning of a new way of thinking. It was very obliging of Mr

Toynbee to collect so many facts in support of the thesis which becomes visible to any sentient mind in reading the first few pages of *Faust*, and his final intrusion of a personal opinion supported by belief rather than by fact detracts only slightly from his painstaking support for creative thought. 'Challenge and Response' was born in *Faust*; and more, much more. Mr Wilson moves towards this way of thinking on page 239 in the course of his study of Blake, and to us it is his most interesting moment. He writes 'the whole was necessary' . . . 'evolution towards God is impossible without a fall'. This passage follows the penetrating observation: 'Yet it is the Outsider's belief that life aims at more life, and *higher forms of life*' (our italics). At this point this interesting thinker and gifted writer reaches towards that decisive movement of European thought which began, perhaps, originally with Heraclitus and evolved through philosophers, prophets and poets, such as Goethe combined in his own genius, until it touched thinkers like Shaw and Ibsen in the modern age. This remarkable young man may end as the saint whom he suggests in his last line may be the Outsider's goal, or worse, much worse, as just a success; yet the fact will remain that at this point he touched reality.

May we end with a few questions based on that doctrine of higher forms which has found some expression in this Journal and in previous writings? Is it not now possible to observe with reason and as something approaching a clearly defined whole, what has hitherto only been revealed in fitful glimpses to the visionary? What are the means of observation available to those who are not blessed with the revelation of vision? Are they not the thoughts of great minds which have observed the working of the divine in nature and the researches of modern science which appear largely to confirm them?

Is it not possible by following such thinking and such observation of science to arrive at a new religious impulse? Can we not now see the wholeness, the harmony and the purpose of life by a process of normal thought, even more surely than the sensitive artist in the ecstasy of vision and at least as surely as the revealed faiths which have been accorded to some? Has modern man not reached the point where he requires neither prophets nor priests to show him truth? Can he not now open his eyes and see sufficient truth to guide him, in the thought and discovery of the human intellect during nearly 3,000 years of striving by the human will toward the light? Is it not at least clear that life began in a very low form and has reached a relative height by a process which it is easier to believe is inspired than the subject of an almost incredible series of chances? Is it not clear that a persistent and in the end consist-

ent movement from lower to higher forms is the process and purpose
of life? It is at least what has so far happened, if we regard the process
over an appreciable period of time. And if this be the purpose it solves
the problem of the individual; he has no duty and should have no
purpose but to place himself at the disposal and to the service of that
higher purpose. It is true that the divine work in nature during the
movement from lower to higher forms is apparently subject to restriction
and almost to paradox. The reckless, brutal waste of nature in experiment
with types which fail, the agony and useless extinction of a suffering
child without trace of purpose and with still less trace of kindness or of
goodness, etc., all indicate some failure of power, or lack of direction,
which are not easily explained by any process of thought limited to the
confines of this world. Even these phenomena of fitful horror are, of
course, explicable if men be more than once born, and various degrees
of solipsistic explanation could also exist. But in the light of this world
and its observed events they are admittedly not easily explained in
terms of coherent, and certainly not of beneficent purpose. Yet is it
really necessary to be able to explain every method of the process in
order to observe the result of the process as a whole? Aristotle helps us
again to some extent: 'the process of evolution is for the sake of the
thing finally evolved and not for the sake of the process'. While, too, we
cannot explain all the apparent freaks of nature—freaks of seemingly
gratuitous horror—we can now in considerable degree explain the
method of nature which to a large extent contains a purpose for suffering. Primitive types simply do not move except under the impulse of
necessity. There can in the beginning be no movement from lower to
higher forms except under the stress of pain. But there can and should
come a point in evolution when man moves forward by motive power
of the fire within and not by pressure of the agony without. At some
point the spirit, the soul—call it what you will—is ignited by some spark
of the divine and moves without necessity; yet, again it is a matter of
common observation that this only occurs in very advanced types. In
general it is only the 'challenge' of adverse circumstance which evokes
the 'response' of movement to a higher state. Goethe expressed this
thought very clearly in *Faust* by his concept of evil's relationship to
good; he also indicated the type where the conscious striving of the
aspiring spirit replaces the urge of suffering in the final attainment of
salvation: *wer immer strebend sich bemüht, den können wir erlösen*. In
the early stages of the great striving all suffering, and later all beauty
must be experienced and sensed; but to no moment of ecstasy can man
say, *verweile doch, du bist so schön*, until the final passing to an infinity

of beauty at present beyond man's ken. Complacency, at any point, is
certainly excluded. So must it be always in a creed which begins effectively with Heraclitus and now pervades modern vitalism. The philosophy
of the 'ever living fire', of the *ewig werdende* could never be associated
with complacency. Still less can the more conscious doctrine of higher
forms co-exist with the static, or with the illusory perfections of a
facile reformism. Man began very small, and has become not so small;
he must end very great, or cease to be. That is the essence of the matter.
Is it true? This is a question which everyone must answer for himself,
after studying European literature which stretches from the Greeks to
the vital thought of modern times and, also, the world thinking of many
different climes and ages which in many ways and at most diverse points
is strangely related. He should study, too, either directly or through the
agency of those most competent to judge, the evolutionary processes
revealed so relatively recently by modern biology, and the apparently
ever increasing concept of ordered complexity in modern physics. He
must then answer two questions: the first is whether it is more likely
than not that a purpose exists in life?—the second is whether despite all
failures and obscurities the only discernable purpose is a movement from
lower to higher forms? If he comes at length to a conclusion which
answers both these questions with a considered affirmative, he has reached the point of the great affirmation. The new religious impulse which
so many seek is really already here. We need neither prophets nor priests
to find it for ourselves, although we are not the enemies but the friends
of those who do. For ourselves we can find in the thought of the world
the faith and the service of the conscious and sentient man.*

NOTES

1. Published originally under the pseudonym of 'European'.
2. Humphrey Trevelyan, *Goethe and the Greeks* (Cambridge University Press).
3. Werner Jaeger, *Paideia*, 3 vols.
4. Professor Heller's translation in his book *The Disinherited Mind* (Bowes and
Bowes).

*This review-article was first published in *The European*, February 1957.

32

Postscript

URI GELLER

[*There were not many who declined my invitation to contribute to this volume. This was indeed remarkable as I was a complete stranger to all but three of the writers, scholars and friends of Colin Wilson whom I contacted. Those who were obliged to refuse, due to pressure of work and/or my strict deadline, did so reluctantly, asking me to pass on their best wishes and congratulations to Colin. I have to admit, however, to being initially disappointed when, instead of a three-thousand-word essay, I received just one paragraph from Uri Geller. But upon reading that paragraph it seemed to me that he had summed up the feelings of all who know Colin Wilson well. It is for that reason that I include Mr Geller's contribution in its entirety. – Editor.*]

Dear Mr Stanley,

This one paragraph will sum up what I have to say about Colin Wilson.

Colin Wilson is one of the most wonderful people that I had the pleasure to work with; he is comfortable to be with, witty, pleasant and happens to be a brilliant writer. His deep belief in the paranormal field and the solid information he has distributed to millions of his readers through his books has no doubt contributed important knowledge that will stay in the minds of people for ever and beyond.

My best wishes,

Sincerely,

Uri Geller

Bibliography

For a detailed listing of Colin Wilson's work see Colin Stanley's *The Work of Colin Wilson*, to be published shortly by Borgo Press, USA.

BOOKS AND PAMPHLETS BY COLIN WILSON IN CHRONOLOGICAL ORDER*

1956

The Outsider. Victor Gollancz, London; Houghton Mifflin, Boston

1957

Religion and the Rebel. Victor Gollancz, London; Houghton Mifflin, Boston.

1959

The Age of Defeat. Victor Gollancz, London; published in the USA as *The Stature of Man* by Houghton Mifflin, Boston.

1960

Ritual in the Dark. Victor Gollancz, London; Houghton Mifflin, Boston.

1961

Adrift in Soho. Victor Gollancz, London; Houghton Mifflin, Boston.
Encyclopaedia of Murder (with Pat Pitman). Arthur Barker, London; Putnam, New York (published 1962).

1962

The Strength to Dream. Victor Gollancz, London; Houghton Mifflin, Boston

1963

Man without a Shadow. Arthur Barker, London.

*U.S. and U.K. original hardback editions only, except when published exclusively in paperback.

1963 cont.

Origins of the Sexual Impulse. Arthur Barker, London; Putnam, New
    York.
Sex Diary of Gerard Sorme (US edition of *Man without a Shadow*), Dial
    Press, New York.
The Violent World of Hugh Greene. Houghton Mifflin, Boston.
Voyage to a Beginning. (Limited edition of 700 copies) C. & A. Woolf,
    London.
The World of Violence (U.K. edition of *The Violent World of Hugh
    Greene*). Victor Gollancz, London.

1964

Brandy of the Damned. John Baker, London.
Necessary Doubt. Arthur Barker, London; Trident Press, New York.
Rasputin and the Fall of the Romanovs. Arthur Barker, London; Farrar,
    Straus, New York.

1965

Beyond the Outsider. Arthur Barker, London; Houghton Mifflin, Boston.
Eagle and Earwig. John Baker, London.

1966

Chords and Discords (U.S. edition of *Brandy of the Damned*). Crown
    Publishers, New York.
Glass Cage. Arthur Barker, London; Random House, New York (publish-
    ed 1967).
Introduction to the New Existentialism. Hutchinson, London; Houghton
    Mifflin, Boston (published 1967).
Sex and the Intelligent Teenager. Arrow Books, London; Pyramid
    Pubs, New York (published 1968).

1967

Colin Wilson on Music (previously published as *Chords and Discords* and
    Brandy of the Damned). Pan Books, London.
The Mind Parasites. Arthur Barker, London; Arkham House, Sauk City.
Ritual in the Dark (screenplay). Pequod Productions, New York.

1969

Bernard Shaw: a Reassessment. Hutchinson, London; Atheneum New
York.
A Casebook of Murder. Leslie Frewin, London; Cowles Book Co., New
York (published 1970).
The Philosopher's Stone. Arthur Barker, London; Crown, New York
(published 1971).
Poetry and Mysticism. City Lights Books, San Francisco.
Voyage to a Beginning (Commercial edition). C. & A. Woolf, London;
Crown Pubs., New York (extended edition).

1970

God of the Labyrinth. Hart-Davis, London.
The Killer. New English Library, London.
Lingard (U.S. edition of *The Killer*). Crown Pubs., New York.
Poetry and Mysticism (Extended English edition). Hutchinson, London.
Strindberg. Calder and Boyars, London; Random House, New York.

1971

The Black Room. Weidenfeld and Nicolson, London.
The Hedonists (U.S. edition of *God of the Labyrinth*). New American
Library, New York.
The Occult. Hodder and Stoughton, London; Random House, New
York.

1972

L'Amour: the Ways of Love. Crown Pubs, New York.
*New Pathways in Psychology: Maslow and the Post-Freudian Revol-
ution*. Victor Gollancz, London; Taplinger, New York.
Order of Assassins. Hart-Davis, London.

1973

Strange Powers. Latimer New Directions, London; Random House,
New York (published 1975).
Tree by Tolkien. Covent Garden Press, Inca Books, London; Capra
Press, Santa Barbara (published 1974).

1974

A Book of Booze. Victor Gollancz, London.
Herman Hesse. Village Press, London.
Hesse — Reich — Borges (U.S. edition of Village Press booklets). Leaves
  of Grass, Philadelphia.
Jorge Luis Borges. Village Press, London.
Ken Russell: a Director in Search of a Hero. Intergroup Pub., London.
Return of the Lloigor. Village Press, London.
The Schoolgirl Murder Case. Hart-Davis, MacGibbon, London; Crown
  Pubs, New York.
Wilhelm Reich. Village Press, London.

1975

The Craft of the Novel. Victor Gollancz, London.
Mysterious Powers. Aldus Books/Jupiter Books, London; Danbury
  Press, Danbury, Conn.
They Had Strange Powers (another U.S. edition of *Mysterious Powers*).
  Doubleday, New York.
The Unexplained. Lost Pleiade Press, Lake Oswego.

1976

Enigmas and Mysteries. Aldus Books, London; Doubleday, New York.
The Geller Phenomenon. Aldus Books, London; Danbury Press,
  Danbury, Conn.
The Space Vampires. Hart-Davis, MacGibbon, London; Random House,
  New York.

1977

Colin Wilson's Men of Mystery. W.H. Allen, London.
Dark Dimensions — a Celebration of the Occult (U.S. edition of
  Colin Wilson's Men of Mystery). Everest House, New York.

1978

Mysteries. Hodder and Stoughton, London; Putnam, New York.
Mysteries of the Mind (originally published as *Mysterious Powers*)
  Aldus Books, London.

1978 cont.

Science Fiction as Existentialism. Bran's Head Books, Hayes, Middx.

1979

The Haunted Man: the Strange Genius of David Lindsay. Borgo Press,
    San Bernardino.

1980

The Book of Time. Westbridge Books, Newton Abbot; David and
    Charles, Vermont.
Frankenstein's Castle: the Double Brain: Door to Wisdom. Ashgrove
    Press, Sevenoaks; Salem House Ltd, Salem, N.H.
The New Existentialism (new edition of *Introduction to the New
    Existentialism*). Wildwood House, London.
Starseekers. Hodder and Stoughton, London; Doubleday, New
    York.
The War Against Sleep. Aquarian Press, Wellingborough, Northants.

1981

Anti-Sartre (with an Essay on Camus). Borgo Press, San Bernardino.
The Directory of Possibilities (with John Grant). Webb and Bower,
    Exeter; Rutledge Press, New York; State Mutual Books, New York.
Poltergeist! New English Library, Sevenoaks, Kent; Putnam, New York.
The Quest for Wilhelm Reich. Granada, St Albans; Doubleday, New
    York.
Witches. Dragon's World Ltd, Limpsfield, Surrey; A. & W. Pubs, New
    York (published 1982).

1983

Access to Inner Worlds: the Story of Brad Absetz. Rider, London.
Encyclopaedia of Modern Murder, 1962-82 (with Donald Seaman).
    Arthur Barker, London; Putnam, New York (published 1985).
*A Novelization of the Events in the Life and Death of Grigori Efimovich
    Rasputin* (contained in an anthology entitled *Tales of the Uncanny*)
    Reader's Digest, New York.

1984

A Criminal History of Mankind. Granada, London; Putnam, New York.
The Janus Murder Case. Granada, London.
Lord of the Underworld: Jung and the Twentieth Century. Aquarian
Press, Wellingborough, Northants.
*The Psychic Detectives: the Story of Psychometry and Paranormal Crime
Detection*. Pan Books, London; Mercury House, San Francisco
(published 1985).

1985

Afterlife. Harrap, London.
The Bicameral Critic (edited by Howard F. Dossor). Ashgrove Press, Bath;
Salem House, Salem, N.H.
The Essential Colin Wilson. Harrap, London; Celestial Arts, Berkeley
(published 1986).
Lifeforce (reissue of *The Space Vampires*). Warner, New York.
Personality Surgeon. New English Library, Sevenoaks, Kent; Mercury
House, San Francisco (published 1986).
Rudolf Steiner. Aquarian Press, Wellingborough, Northants.

1986

The Book of Great Mysteries (with Dr Christopher Evans). Robinson
Publishing, London.
An Essay on the 'New' Existentialism. Paupers' Press, Nottingham.
G. I. Gurdjieff: the War Against Sleep. Aquarian Press, Wellingborough;
Borgo Press, San Bernardino.
The Laurel and Hardy Theory of Consciousness. Robert Briggs Assoc-
iates, San Francisco.
Scandal!: an Encyclopaedia (with Donald Seaman). Weidenfeld &
Nicolson, London; Stein & Day, New York.

1987

Aleister Crowley: the Nature of the Beast. Aquarian Press,
Wellingborough.
The Encyclopedia of Unsolved Mysteries (with Damon Wilson). Harrap,
London.
Jack the Ripper: Summing Up and Verdict (with Robin Odell). Bantam

1987 cont.

Press, London.
Marx Refuted (with Ronald Duncan). Ashgrove Press, Bath.
The Musician as 'Outsider'. Paupers' Press, Nottingham.
Spider World: the Tower. Grafton, London.
Spider World: the Delta. Grafton, London.

1988

Autobiographical Reflections. Paupers' Press, Nottingham.
Existentially Speaking: Essays on Philosophy and Literature. Borgo
  Press, San Bernardino.
The Misfits: a Study of Sexual Outsiders. Grafton, London.
The Sex Diary of a Tantric Magician (proposed title only; reprint of
  Man Without a Shadow). Ronin Publishing, Berkeley, California.

Forthcoming:

Beyond the Occult. Bantam Press, London.
True Crime (Introduction by Howard F. Dossor). Robinson Publishing,
  London.
Untethered Mind (Edited by Howard F. Dossor). Ashgrove Press, Bath.
Written in Blood [Study of crime. Publication details not finalised.
  Book likely to appear Spring 1989.]

SELECTIVE LIST OF ARTICLES PUBLISHED BY COLIN WILSON*
(arranged chronologically)
CHOSEN BY HOWARD F. DOSSOR

1. 'On Margate Sands . . .', *Encounter*, 1957, pp. 25-33.
2. 'Alexis Kivi', *The Aylesford Review*, Winter 1960-61, pp. 15-20.
3. 'A Manifesto for the Young', *Birmingham Bulletin*, No. 2, Autumn
   1963.

*The criterion for selection is that they should not have appeared in any book
published under Colin Wilson's name. Reference should also be made to: *The
Bicameral Critic*, edited by Howard F. Dossor, 1985; *The Essential Colin Wilson*,
1985; *Eagle and Earwig*, 1965; *The Strength to Dream*, 1962. For a comprehensive
list of over 400 essays, see my Bibliography and Guide. – Ed.

4. 'The Problem of Life-Devaluation', *Transition* (Kampala, Uganda), vol. IV, no. 17, 1964, pp. 24-27.

5. 'Towards a New Criminology', *Crime and Detection*, November 1966, pp. 11-27.

6. 'The New Trend in Murder', *Edgar Wallace Mystery Magazine*, vol. 3, no. 29, 1966, pp. 47-54.

7. 'Homage to E.H. Visiak', *Aylesford Review*, vol. 8, no. 4, Summer 1967, pp. 221-236.

8. 'The Thinkers', *Daily Telegraph Magazine* 1 November 1968, pp. 62 *et seq*.

9. 'An Introduction to James Drought', *Sunday Los Angeles Times Calendar Magazine*, 15 January 1967, cover story.

10. 'The Poetry of A.L. Rowse, *Poetry Review*, vol. 61, 1970, pp. 140-160.

11. 'The Man Without Qualities', *Books and Bookmen*, March 1971, pp. 4-6.

12. 'The Dominant Five per Cent', *The Criminologist*, May-August 1970, pp. 72-84.

13. 'The Dominant Killer', *Men Only*, vol. 38, no. 5, 1973, pp. 19 *et seq*.

14. 'A Doomed Society', *Journal of Human Relations*, vol. 21, no. 4, 1973, pp. 395-410.

15. 'Dominance and Sex' *in* Gross, L. (ed.), *Sexual Behaviour: Current Issues* (Spectrum Publications, Flushing, NY, 1974), pp. 127-135.

16. 'The Fuehrer in Perspective', *Books and Bookmen*, September, October, November 1974.

17. 'The Flawed Superman' *in* Harrison, M. (ed.), *Beyond Baker Street* (Bobbs Merrill, NY, 1976), pp. 311-333.

18. 'Standing Stones of Cornwall', *South West Review*, no. 2, October 1977, pp. 56-61.

19. 'Royalty and the Ripper' *in* Alexander, M., *Royal Murder* (Frederick Muller, London, 1978), pp. 203-221.

20. 'A New Look at the Paranormal' *in* Schuckburg, T. (ed.), *The Bedside Book* (Windward, London, 1979), pp. 176-193.

21. 'The Search for the Real Arthur' *in* Duxbury, B. & Williams, M., *King Arthur Country in Cornwall* (Bossiney Books, St Teaths, 1979), pp. 91-100.

22. 'The Real Charlotte', *Encounter*, Sept.-Oct. 1982, pp. 9-18.

23. 'A.E. van Vogt' *in* Blieler, E.F. (ed.), *Science Fiction Writers* (Charles Scribners Sons, NY, 1982), pp. 209-217.

24. 'Literature and Pornography' *in* Bold, A. (ed.), *The Sexual Dimension*

in Literature (Vision & Barnes and Noble, 1982), pp. 202-219.

25. 'James Webb and the Occult', *Light* (London), Summer 1982, pp. 69-83.

PUBLISHED BOOKS ABOUT AND PARTIALLY ABOUT
COLIN WILSON AND HIS WORK
(arranged alphabetically by author)

Allsop, Kenneth. *The Angry Decade*. Peter Owen, London, 1958. Reprinted, J. Goodchild, 1985.

Bendau, Clifford P. *Colin Wilson: the Outsider and Beyond*. Borgo Press, San Bernardino, 1979.

Bergström, K. Gunnar. *An Odyssey to Freedom: Four Themes in Colin Wilson's Novels*. Acta Universitatis Upsaliensis, Studia Anglistica Upsaliensia, no. 47: Uppsala, Sweden, 1983.

Campion, Sidney. *The World of Colin Wilson*. Frederick Muller, London, 1962.

Farson, Daniel. *Out of Step*. Michael Joseph, London, 1974.

Hewison, Robert. *In Anger: Culture in the Cold War, 1945-60*. Weidenfeld and Nicolson, London, 1981.

Holroyd, Stuart. *Contraries: a Personal Progression*. Bodley Head, London, 1975.

Stanley, Colin. *The Work of Colin Wilson: an Annotated Bibliography and Guide*. Borgo Press, San Bernardino, 1989.

Tredell, Nicolas. *The Novels of Colin Wilson*. Vision Press, London, 1982.

Weigel, John A. *Colin Wilson*. Twayne, Boston, 1975 (Twayne's English Authors Series, no. 181).

Wilson, Colin. *Voyage to a Beginning*. C. & A. Woolf, 1969. (Extended version: Crown, New York, 1969). Reprinted, Cecil Woolf, 1987.

Notes on the Contributors

Pete Barraclough, born 1946 in Sleaford, Lincs, was Features writer on the *Leicester Chronicle*, 1969-75, and is now Head of Sports at Television South-West in Plymouth. Pete interviewed Colin Wilson for the *Leicester Chronicle* in the early 1970s at a time when Wilson was shunning publicity in an attempt to shake off his angry-young-man image. He agreed to be interviewed by the *Chronicle* because he had read the paper as a boy in Leicester.

K. GUNNAR BERGSTRÖM

Born 1932 at Stjärnsund, Sweden. Studied for one year at Uppsala University in 1952 before doing military service. Worked in a bank and then studied philosophy, Finnish, German and English at the University of Stockholm. In 1983 he took his doctor's degree. Published *An Odyssey to Freedom: Four Themes in Colin Wilson's Novels* in the same year. During the 1970s contributed to the Swedish leftist magazine *Frihetlig Socialistisk Tidskrift*. Now lives in Handen and works as a postman.

SIDNEY CAMPION

Born in Coalville, Leicestershire. Author, journalist, barrister, lecturer, schoolmaster, sculptor. From 1940 until retirement in 1957, Head of Press and Broadcast Division, GPO Headquarters. Publications included: *Sunlight on the Foothills* (1941), *Towards the Mountains* (1943) and *The World of Colin Wilson* (1962). A further study of Colin Wilson's work, *The Sound Barrier*, was completed but never published. Died in 1978.

CYRIL CONNOLLY

Born 1903. Author and literary journalist. Educated at Eton and Balliol College, Oxford. Founded and edited *Horizon* in 1939. Literary editor of *The Observer*, 1942-43. Contributed weekly to *The Sunday*

Times. Publications include: *The Rock Pool* (1935), *Previous Convictions* (1963) and *Evening Colonnade* (1973). Died in 1974.

R.H.W. DILLARD

Born 1937. Became professor of English and chair of the Creative Writing Program at Hollins College, Virginia, in 1974. Editor and regular contributor to the *Hollins Critic*. Publications include: *The Day I Stopped Dreaming About Barbara Steele* (1966), *After Borges* (1972) and *First Man on the Sun* (1983).

HOWARD F. DOSSOR

Howard Dossor is a senior administrator at La Trobe University, Melbourne, Australia, having entered administration through the teaching profession at both secondary and tertiary levels. He has a theological background which led him to an interest in *The Outsider* in 1956. His continuing interest in Colin Wilson came to fruition with the publication of *The Bicameral Critic* which he edited and introduced.

DANIEL FARSON

Son of the American writer, the late Negley Farson, who formed a close relationship with Colin Wilson in spite of the difference in their ages. After Daniel's varied career as a Parliamentary Correspondent, G.I., Cambridge undergraduate, photographer for *Picture Post* and merchant seaman, he joined Independent Television and his first interview was for 'This Week' with Colin Wilson. Later he resigned from television in order to write and his autobiography, *Out of Step*, described his encounters with Colin in the first, giddy days following the fame of *The Outsider*. His other publications include a study of Jack the Ripper and a biography of Henry Williamson.

MARILYN FERGUSON

Marilyn Ferguson was born and educated in Colorado. She is the author of *The Aquarian Conspiracy: Personal and Social Transformation in the 1980s* and *The Brain Revolution*. Co-author, with her husband Ray Gottlieb, of the forthcoming *The Visionary Factor: a Guide to Remembering the Future*. Since 1975 she has published *Brain/Mind Bulletin*. She has lectured widely in the U.S., Canada and Europe.

ALLEN GINSBERG

Born in 1926. Author of numerous volumes of poetry including *Howl and Other Poems*, *Empty Mirror*, *Reality Sandwiches*, *Poems All Over the Place*. Won the National Book Award in 1974 for *The Fall of America: Poems of these States*. Has featured in several films including *Wholly Communion* (1965), *Chappaqua* (1966) and *Renaldo and Clara* (1978). Director of Kerouac School of Poetics, Naropa Institute, Boulder, Colorado.

TOM GREENWELL

Born in 1923. Chief Leader Writer of *The Yorkshire Post* from 1961 until his retirement in 1988. Awarded the OBE in 1983. Served in World War II with the Royal Navy. Joined Foreign Office Signals Intelligence (GCHQ) in 1945, leaving in 1953 to make a career in literary and newspaper journalism. Contributed verse and reviews to a number of magazines and was a regular reviewer of books on Shakespeare and his period for *John O'London's Weekly*. In the late 1950s was a gossip-writer with the London *Evening Standard* and *The Daily Sketch*. He is married and lives in Leeds.

JONATHAN GUINNESS

Jonathan Guinness is a former chairman of the Monday Club, a director of several companies and author of *The House of Mitford* (1984).

STUART HOLROYD

Born 1933 in Bradford, Yorkshire, Stuart Holroyd published his first book, *Emergence from Chaos*, in 1957, and since then has written 19 books ranging over a variety of subjects, from literature to the paranormal, as well as an autobiographical memoir of the 1950s, *Contraries*, from which some of the text of the essay in this volume has been extracted. He now lives in London and in France, and has recently completed *The New Perspectives Dictionary*, which will be published in 1989 by Routledge & Kegal Paul.

BILL HOPKINS

Born in Cardiff, 1928. In 1944 joined the British United Press as sub-editor at the Ministry of Information. 1946 – shipped to Germany for the Occupation. Demobbed 1949. Joined the Crusade for World Government for eighteen months, then spent two years travelling on the Continent, writing poetry and articles. Tried, unsuccessfully, to launch a weekly journal, *The Saturday Critic*, then joined the staff of *The New York Times* London bureau for three years. His novel *The Divine and the Decay* was published in 1957. This has recently been reprinted as *The Leap!* (1984). He is also the author of an extended essay in the symposium *Declaration* edited by Tom Maschler (1957). He lives in London and is currently working on a playscript.

OSWALD MOSLEY

Born 1896. Educated at Winchester and Sandhurst. Served in France during World War I. Was elected as a Member of Parliament during the 1920s. Formed his own 'New Party' in 1931. Founded the British Union of Fascists in 1932. Publications included: *The Greater Britain* (1932), *My Answer* (1946), *My Life* (1968). Author of numerous pamphlets, articles and editor of *The European*. He died in 1980.

JOYCE CAROL OATES

Born 1938. American novelist and short-story writer with an international reputation. Educated at the universities of Syracuse and Wisconsin. She is now a professor of English at Princeton. A string of novels include: *Do with Me what You Will* (1973), *Belle Fleur* (1980) and *Marya: a Life* (1987). Her latest, *You Must Remember This*, has just been published.

JUNE O'SHEA

Owned a general secondhand bookstore in Los Angeles for some years, then decided to specialize in criminology, psychology and psychiatry. Her contribution to this volume describes her unique relationship with Colin Wilson who dedicated his *Space Vampires* to her. Her fine collection of his books, letters and manuscripts is now held by the University of California, Riverside.

J.B. PRIESTLEY

Born in 1894. Prolific novelist, short story writer, playwright, essayist and broadcaster. His novels include: *The Good Companions* (1929), *Angel Pavement* (1930) and *Lost Empires* (1965). But he will probably be best remembered as author of the 'time' plays: *I Have Been Here Before* (1937), *Dangerous Corner* (1932), *Time and the Conways* (1937) and *An Inspector Calls* (1945). He died in 1984.

H.D. PURCELL

Professor Purcell works mainly at the Vienna University of Economics and Business Administration, and holds degrees from Oxford, London and Cambridge. He has also worked in a number of other countries, including Canada, Italy, Turkey, Persia, Northern Ireland, Libya, Nepal and Qatar. He wrote a history of *Cyprus* (1970), reviews of a large number of books on the Middle East for *International Affairs* and articles on literary and political subjects for other journals.

RENATE RASP

German novelist. Daughter of the actor Fritz Rasp. Has published volumes of poems and several novels. Renate Rasp is a summer resident of Newquay in Cornwall, returning to Munich for the winter months.

JOHN RETY

Was the editor in the 1950s of the coffee-house journal *Intimate Review*, which printed many now famous writers (such as Colin Wilson and Michael Hastings) for the first time. His own book *Supersozzled Nights or Htuoy's Backward Youth* was 'a resounding failure which has effectively stopped me writing for the past thirty years'. The contribution to this book marks his return to the literary arena and he is now at work on two books simultaneously, *Confessions of an Hungarian D.P.* and the bi-lingual *Conversations with a Dead Grandmaster*. He believes that 'human history suffers from bad script writers and that the whole thing should be rewritten and that people should be paid for living, the only job that cannot be palmed off to anybody else'.

DONALD SEAMAN

Born 1922. Spent twenty-five years on the staff of *The Daily Express* before moving to Cornwall where he is a near neighbour of Colin Wilson. Apart from writing a number of spy thrillers, including *The Defector* (1975) and *The Duel* (1979), he has collaborated with Colin Wilson on *The Encyclopaedia of Modern Murder* (1983) and *Scandal! an Encyclopaedia* (1986). His new novel *Rogue Bear* has just been published.

BROCARD SEWELL

Born 1912. Educated at Weymouth College, London University, St Edmund's College, Ware, Collegio Sant' Alberto, Rome, etc. Pre-war: on staff of *G.K.'s Weekly*, then Saint Dominic's Press, Ditchling. 1941-45, served in R.A.F. 1945-54, ecclesiastical studies in England, Belgium and Rome. 1952 entered the Carmelite Order. Ordained priest in 1954. 1955-68 edited *The Aylesford Review*. 1969-72 lectured in Eighteen-Nineties Studies, Dept. of English, St Francis Xavier University, Antigonish, NS. Publications: biographies of Montague Summers, Cecil Chesterton and John Gray. Shorter memoirs of Cardinal Philip Howard, Baron Corvo, Father Vincent McNabb, Olive Custance, Henry Williamson and others. Also, *The Vatican Oracle* (on the Papacy and birth-control) and *My Dear Time's Waste* (autobiography).

COLIN STANLEY

Born Topsham, Devon, 1952. Educated at the Exmouth School, Devon. Left school in 1970 and worked for several years for Devon Library Services before moving north and taking up his present position of library assistant at the University of Nottingham. Author of several booklets of poetry and prose; compiler and publisher of an index to *The Aylesford Review* (1984). His *The Work of Colin Wilson: an Annotated Bibliography and Guide* was published recently in the US. Runs the Paupers' Press from his home in Nottingham. He is married with two children.

PHILIP TOYNBEE

Born in 1916. Novelist, critic and journalist. Son of the historian Arnold Toynbee. Educated at Rugby and Christ Church, Oxford. During World War II served in the Intelligence Corps and Ministry of Economic Warfare. Joined *The Observer* in 1950 as a foreign correspondent and subsequently became a highly influential book reviewer. Author of a number of experimental novels, including *Tea with Mrs Gordon* (1947), *Pantaloon* (1961), *Two Brothers* (1964) and *Views from a Lake* (1968). He died in 1981.

NICOLAS TREDELL

Born Leicester, 1950. MA in Modern Literature, University of Kent. Published *The Novels of Colin Wilson*. Contributing editor *PN Review* since 1983. Writes regularly on literary and cultural matters for *PN Review*. Teaches for the University of Sussex Centre for Continuing Education, the WEA and Eastbourne College of Arts and Technology. Currently working on a novel.

A.E. van VOGT

Born 1912. Author of numerous short stories and novels including: *The War Against the Rull*, *The Voyage of the Space Beagle*, *The Mind Cage*, *Away and Beyond*, *The Book of Ptath* and *Moonbeast*. Recipient of the Anne Radcliffe Literary award, 1968. Guest of Honour at the

European Science Fiction Convention, Brussels, 1978. He is married and lives in Hollywood.

KENNETH WALKER

Born 1882. Emeritus Surgeon, Royal Northern Hospital. A leading specialist in genito-urinary diseases. Educated at the Leys School and Caius College, Cambridge; then entered St Bartholomew's Hospital, qualifying in 1906. Author of a number of books and articles on his specialist subject and others on sex, philosophy, mystical experience and religion. Met Gurdjieff on several occasions and became a member of P.D. Ouspensky's Study Society. This led to the publication of *Venture with Ideas* (1951), *A Study of Gurdjieff's Teaching* (1957) and *The Making of Man* (1963). He died in 1966.

ALAN HULL WALTON

Author, journalist, scholar and translator. Publications include translations of *Selections from Baudelaire* (1943), *The Technique of Eroticism* by Lo Duca (1962), *L'Art et L'Amour* by Florent Fels (1952), *Justine, or the Misfortunes of Virtue* by De Sade (1964). He also edited *My Life* by Havelock Ellis (1967) and Sir Richard Burton's translation of *The Perfumed Garden of the Shaykh Nefzawi* (1963). Author of *Ballet Shoes* (poems; 1943), *New Vistas* (a sexo-sociological study; 1943) and *Aphrodisiacs: from Legend to Prescription* (1958). Contributed regularly to *Books and Bookmen*.

JOHN A. WEIGEL

Born 1912. Achieved advanced degrees in literature at Western Reserve University and in psychology at Columbia University. Became professor of English at Miami University, Ohio, in 1956. Has published numerous articles, verses and reviews. Publications include full-length studies of the work of *Lawrence Durrell* (1965) and *Colin Wilson* (1975).

ANGUS WILSON

Born 1913. Educated at Westminster and Merton College, Oxford.

1942-46 on the staff of the Foreign Office. Deputy Superintendent of British Museum Reading Room, 1949-55. Began to write in 1946. Has lectured at various colleges and universities in the U.S., U.K. and on the Continent since the late 1950s. Author of numerous novels and non-fiction including: *Hemlock and After*, *Anglo-Saxon Attitudes*, *A Bit Off the Map*, *The World of Charles Dickens*. His novels *Late Call* and *The Old Men at the Zoo* have both recently been adapted for television. Awarded the CBE in 1968 and Knighted in 1980. He now lives in France.

Index

compiled by Colin and Gail Stanley

600/ 20/1/93 .